应用型本科院校"十三五"规划教材/经济管理类

Accounting English

会计英语

（第3版）

主　编　刘莹莹　李丽娜
副主编　徐菡博　张艳芳

哈尔滨工业大学出版社
HARBIN INSTITUTE OF TECHNOLOGY PRESS

内容提要

本书根据国际企业会计准则体系及我国的会计改革的最新成果编写,共分为10个单元,主要内容包括会计概述、企业组织形式、财务报表、会计循环、流动资产、非流动资产、流动负债、非流动负债、所有者权益和财务报表分析。每个单元都结合应用型财会专业本科生及本课程的特点对重点内容进行讲解,可培养学生的分析能力和综合运用知识能力。

本书适合应用型本科院校财会专业学生、教师及爱好者学习使用。

图书在版编目(CIP)数据

会计英语/刘莹莹,李丽娜主编. —3版—哈尔滨:哈尔滨工业大学出版社,2020.7

ISBN 978-7-5603-8916-5

Ⅰ.①会… Ⅱ.①刘…②李… Ⅲ.①会计-英语-高等学校-教材 Ⅳ.①F23

中国版本图书馆 CIP 数据核字(2020)第 124344 号

策划编辑	杜 燕
责任编辑	李广鑫
出版发行	哈尔滨工业大学出版社
社 址	哈尔滨市南岗区复华四道街10号 邮编150006
传 真	0451-86414749
网 址	http://hitpress.hit.edu.cn
印 刷	哈尔滨市颉升高印刷有限公司
开 本	787mm×960mm 1/16 印张17.5 字数375千字
版 次	2013年6月第1版 2020年7月第3版 2020年7月第1次印刷
书 号	ISBN 978-7-5603-8916-5
定 价	38.00元

(如因印装质量问题影响阅读,我社负责调换)

《应用型本科院校"十三五"规划教材》编委会

主　　任　修朋月　竺培国

副主任　王玉文　吕其诚　线恒录　李敬来

委　　员　（按姓氏笔画排序）

丁福庆　于长福　马志民　王庄严　王建华

王德章　刘金祺　刘宝华　刘通学　刘福荣

关晓冬　李云波　杨玉顺　吴知丰　张幸刚

陈江波　林　艳　林文华　周方圆　姜思政

庹　莉　韩毓洁　蔡柏岩　臧玉英　霍　琳

杜　燕

序

哈尔滨工业大学出版社策划的《应用型本科院校"十三五"规划教材》即将付梓，诚可贺也。

该系列教材卷帙浩繁，凡百余种，涉及众多学科门类，定位准确，内容新颖，体系完整，实用性强，突出实践能力培养。不仅便于教师教学和学生学习，而且满足就业市场对应用型人才的迫切需求。

应用型本科院校的人才培养目标是面对现代社会生产、建设、管理、服务等一线岗位，培养能直接从事实际工作、解决具体问题、维持工作有效运行的高等应用型人才。应用型本科与研究型本科和高职高专院校在人才培养上有着明显的区别，其培养的人才特征是：①就业导向与社会需求高度吻合；②扎实的理论基础和过硬的实践能力紧密结合；③具备良好的人文素质和科学技术素质；④富于面对职业应用的创新精神。因此，应用型本科院校只有着力培养"进入角色快、业务水平高、动手能力强、综合素质好"的人才，才能在激烈的就业市场竞争中站稳脚跟。

目前国内应用型本科院校所采用的教材往往只是对理论性较强的本科院校教材的简单删减，针对性、应用性不够突出，因材施教的目的难以达到。因此亟须既有一定的理论深度又注重实践能力培养的系列教材，以满足应用型本科院校教学目标、培养方向和办学特色的需要。

哈尔滨工业大学出版社出版的《应用型本科院校"十三五"规划教材》，在选题设计思路上认真贯彻教育部关于培养适应地方、区域经济和社会发展需要的"本科应用型高级专门人才"精神，根据前黑龙江省委书记吉炳轩同志提出的关于加强应用型本科院校建设的意见，在应用型本科试点院校成功经验总结的基础上，特邀请黑龙江省9所知名的应用型本科院校的专家、学者联合编写。

本系列教材突出与办学定位、教学目标的一致性和适应性，既严格遵照学科体系的知识构成和教材编写的一般规律，又针对应用型本科人才培养目标及与之相适应的教学特点，精心设计写作体例，科学安排知识内容，围绕应用讲授理论，做到"基础知识够用、实践技能实用、专业理论管用"。同时注意适当融入新理论、新技术、新工艺、新成果，并且制作了与本书配套的PPT多媒体教学课件，形成立体化教材，供教师参考使用。

《应用型本科院校"十三五"规划教材》的编辑出版，是适应"科教兴国"战略对复合型、应用型人才的需求，是推动相对滞后的应用型本科院校教材建设的一种有益尝试，在应用型创新人才培养方面是一件具有开创意义的工作，为应用型人才的培养提供了及时、可靠、坚实的保证。

希望本系列教材在使用过程中，通过编者、作者和读者的共同努力，厚积薄发、推陈出新、细上加细、精益求精，不断丰富、不断完善、不断创新，力争成为同类教材中的精品。

第 3 版前言

随着国际贸易范围的不断扩大,我国越来越多地参与国际竞争。整个中国的经济和社会发展既面临着千载难逢的发展机遇,又面临着史无前例的严峻挑战。随着贸易和融资壁垒的逐步解除,外国企业落户中国,中国企业走向世界,这是世界经济一体化发展的必然趋势。会计作为一门世界通用的商业语言,其国际化的发展方向已成定局。美国会计学会(AAA)下属的会计教育改革委员会(AECC)要求,会计教育要加强对会计思想的培育,进一步强化学生的交流性技巧,重视会计教育的国际化。我国的会计工作已经处在一个全新的国际经济环境之中,所以,AECC 的要求对我国会计专业的教改工作也是适用的。

本书每个单元都有配套的自测题和练习题,这样编排是为了使读者通过练习,更好地掌握所学内容。本书最后附录部分为比较国际会计,主要目的是使读者能够了解国际会计核算惯例,了解不同国家会计核算体系。

本书由哈尔滨剑桥学院刘莹莹、黑龙江科技大学李丽娜任主编,哈尔滨剑桥学院徐菡博、哈尔滨剑桥学院张艳芳任副主编。主编负责全书框架结构、制订编写大纲并总纂定稿。本书正文主要分两部分,第一部分为英文,第二部分为中文译文。各部分分工如下:第一部分 Unit One、Unit Two 以及第一单元、第二单元参考译文由张艳芳编写,共计 5.0 万字;Unit Three、Unit Four 以及第三单元、第四单元参考译文由徐菡博编写,共计 6.2 万字;Unit Five、Unit Six、Unit Seven 以及第五单元、第六单元、第七单元参考译文、Appendix 由刘莹莹编写,共计 14.5 万字;Unit Eight、Unit Nine、Unit Ten 以及第八单元、第九单元、第十单元参考译文由李丽娜编写,共计 8.5 万字。

本书在编写过程中,我们参考了大量的英文原版书籍和资料,在此,谨向这些文献的作者表示衷心的感谢。

由于编者水平和时间有限,书中难免有疏漏和不足,恳请读者批评指正,以利于本书的改进与完善。

编 者
2020 年 5 月

目 录

Part I English Text ········· 1

Unit One Introduction to Accounting ········· 3
  1.1 Definition of Accounting ········· 5
  1.2 Users and Classifications of Accounting ········· 5
  1.3 Accounting Assumptions and Principles ········· 6
  1.4 Accounting Elements & Accounting Equation ········· 8
  1.5 Recording Business Transactions: Double-Entry System ········· 12
  Exercises ········· 14

Unit Two Forms of Business Ownership ········· 17
  2.1 Sole Proprietorships ········· 18
  2.2 Partnerships ········· 19
  2.3 Corporations ········· 20
  2.4 Sole Proprietorship and Partnership Accounting ········· 21
  2.5 Accounting for Stock Transactions and Dividends ········· 22
  Exercises ········· 25

Unit Three Financial Statements ········· 28
  3.1 Definition ········· 30
  3.2 Purpose of Financial Statements by Business Entities ········· 30
  3.3 Balance Sheet ········· 31
  3.4 Income Statement ········· 32
  3.5 Retained Earnings Statement ········· 34
  3.6 Cash Flow Statement ········· 34
  3.7 Relationship of Financial Statements ········· 36
  Exercises ········· 37

Unit Four Accounting Cycle ········· 41
  4.1 Journals & Ledgers ········· 42
  4.2 Trial Balance ········· 45
  4.3 Adjusting Entries ········· 46
  4.4 Closing Entries ········· 52
  4.5 Adjusted Trial Balance ········· 53

  Exercises ··· 54
Unit Five Current Assets ·· 58
  5.1 Cash and Cash Equivalents ·· 60
  5.2 Accounts Receivable ··· 62
  5.3 Inventory ··· 67
  Exercises ··· 74
Unit Six Non-Current Assets ··· 78
  6.1 Long-term Investment ·· 80
  6.2 Fixed Assets ·· 84
  6.3 Intangible Assets ·· 92
  Exercises ··· 94
Unit Seven Current Liabilities ··· 98
  7.1 Definition of Current Liabilities ·· 101
  7.2 Accounts Payable ··· 102
  7.3 Short-term Borrowings ·· 104
  7.4 Short-term Notes Payable ··· 105
  7.5 Unearned Revenue ··· 107
  7.6 Dividends Payable ·· 109
  7.7 Accrued Liabilities ·· 110
  7.8 Contingent Liabilities ·· 112
  Exercises ·· 114
Unit Eight Non-Current Liabilities ·· 119
  8.1 Definition of Non-Current Liabilities ·· 120
  8.2 Time Value of Money ·· 120
  8.3 Bonds Payable ·· 126
  Exercises ·· 129
Unit Nine Owners' Equity ·· 130
  9.1 Shareholders' Rights and Privileges ··· 131
  9.2 Accounting for Stock Issues ··· 133
  9.3 Accounting for Treasury Stock ·· 134
  9.4 Retained Earnings ·· 135
  Exercises ·· 136
Unit Ten Financial Statement Analysis ·· 138
  10.1 Horizontal Analysis ·· 139
  10.2 Vertical Analysis ·· 143

  10.3 Ratio Analysis ……………………………………………………… 147
  Exercises …………………………………………………………………… 155
Part II 参考译文 ………………………………………………………… 159
第一单元 会计概述 ………………………………………………………… 161
第二单元 企业组织形式 …………………………………………………… 167
第三单元 财务报表 ………………………………………………………… 171
第四单元 会计循环 ………………………………………………………… 177
第五单元 流动资产 ………………………………………………………… 185
第六单元 非流动资产 ……………………………………………………… 193
第七单元 流动负债 ………………………………………………………… 201
第八单元 非流动负债 ……………………………………………………… 210
第九单元 所有者权益 ……………………………………………………… 215
第十单元 财务报表分析 …………………………………………………… 218
Part III **Key to Exercises** ………………………………………………… 231
Appendix **Causes of International Differences** ……………………… 246
References ………………………………………………………………………… 267

Part I   English Text

Unit One

Introduction to Accounting

Teaching Objectives

Upon completion of this chapter, you will:
1. Understand the meaning of accounting and each accounting principle.
2. Understand the meaning of the accounting elements and the accounting equation.
3. Know the structure of T-account and understand how to make correct entries based on double-entry system.

Vocabulary

accounting	会计,会计学
profit-seeking	营利性的
not-for-profit	非营利性的
budget	预算
forecast	预测
classification	分类
creditor	债权人
accounting principle	会计原则
Generally Accepted Accounting Principles (GAAP)	一般公认会计准则
accounting period	会计期间
depreciation	折旧
accrual basis	权责发生制
full disclosure principle	充分披露原则
operating results	经营成果

maturity	（款项的）到期
investment	投资
profit distribution	利润分配
terminology	术语
consumption	消耗
recovery	（款项的）收回
liquidity	流动性
property, plant, and equipment	土地,厂房和设备
fixed assets	固定资产
intangible assets	无形资产
receivable	应收款项
short-term investment	短期投资
patents	专利权
copyright	版权
trademark	商标
goodwill	商誉
outflow	（资金等的）外流,流出
International Accounting Standards Committee(IASC)	国际会计准则委员会
settlement	解决,（债务的）清算
current liabilities	流动负债
long-term liabilities	长期负债
equilibrium	平衡关系
on account/credit	赊账
general expense	一般费用,总务费用
collection	（账款的）收取,收回
withdraw	提取,提款
debit	借记,借方
credit	贷记,贷方
balance	余额
debit balance	借方余额
credit balance	贷方余额

TEXT

Accounting is known as the language of business. It is used by every profit-seeking business organization that has economic resources such as money, machinery, and buildings to provide relevant financial information on their resources and the effects of the use of these resources. Not-for-profit organizations also utilize accounting in order to measure their activities.

1.1 Definition of Accounting

Accounting can be defined as the information system that identifies, records and communicates economic events to the interested users for the purpose of decision-making. Another definition is the recording, reporting, and analysis of financial transactions of a business. Early accounting tended to focus on the traditional record-keeping functions of the accountant. Modern accounting, in contrast, involves more planning, controlling and budgeting and forecasting.

1.2 Users and Classifications of Accounting

Accounting information is used to satisfy the needs of two main groups of users: external users who are outside a business but have direct financial interest in the business, such as owners, investors, creditors, and brokers; internal users like managers, employees and unions that have direct concerns in a business.

Accordingly, accounting is split into two types: financial accounting and managerial accounting. Financial accounting is related to the preparations of financial reports and statements for users mainly outside the business, and is also called external accounting. While managerial accounting mainly provides information to internal management of a firm for decision-making, it's also called internal accounting since it's used basically inside the business.

1.3　Accounting Assumptions and Principles

To develop accounting standards, there are a series of assumptions and principles that serve as basic guidelines in accounting activities called Generally Accepted Accounting Principles (GAAP). These assumptions and principles form a foundation for financial reporting internationally.

1. Assumptions

(1) **Monetary Unit Assumption**

The monetary unit assumption requires that only those things that can be expressed in money are included in the accounting records. This assumption has important implications for financial reporting. Because the exchange of money is fundamental to business transactions, it makes sense that a business is measured in terms of money. However, it also means that certain important information needed by investors, creditors, and managers is not reported in the financial reports as they can't be measured in terms of money. For example, customer satisfaction is important to every business, but it is not easily quantified in dollar terms, thus it is not reported in the financial statements.

(2) **Economic Entity Assumption**

Economic entity assumption is also called accounting entity assumption. The economic entity assumptions states that every economic entity must be separately identified and accounted for. In light of this, an economic entity's accounting must be independent of other entities and the owner of the enterprises. That means a company is a separate entity from its owners and its accounting reflects only the financial activities of the company, not the owner. It must be ensured that all the transactions of the company, and only those transactions are reported in the company's financial reports. In particular, it is necessary to ensure that transactions of the owners are excluded. For example, if you are a stock holder in Dove, the amount of cash you have in your personal bank account is not reported in the Dove's financial report.

(3) **Time Period Assumption**

The time period assumption states that enterprises shall account for their transactions and prepare financial statements for distinct time periods. In other words, the life of business is artificially split into equal short time periods to make it easier to calculate profits and reflect the financial situation of business. This is called an accounting period, typically one month, one quarter or one year. This principle is an important supplement to the previous assumption.

(4) **Going Concern Assumption**

The going concern assumption states that the business will remain in operation in the foreseeable future unless sufficient and negative proofs are provided to stop it. This assumption makes sure asset evaluation, depreciation calculation and accounting report are prepared in a continuous mode.

2. Principles

(1) **Historical Cost Principle**

It requires that assets are recorded at cost when they're obtained or the expenses incurred on acquisition rather than fair market value. This also applies to liabilities. For example, if Wal-Mart purchases a piece of land for $300 000, the cost of the land is reported at this amount in the financial reports, regardless of how much its market value increased. This principle provides information that is reliable, which removes the opportunity to provide subjective and potentially biased market values, but it's not very relevant.

(2) **Revenue Recognition Principle**

This principle requires revenues or expenses to be recorded when revenues are actually realized and when expenses are incurred, rather than when cash is received. This way of accounting is called accrual basis accounting.

(3) **Full Disclosure Principle**

This principle requires that all circumstances and events that would make a difference to financial statement be disclosed. If an important item can not be reasonably reported directly in the financial statements, notes should be made about it.

(4) **Matching Principle**

This principle requires that revenues have to be matched with related expenses or costs in accounting. Expenses are recognized not when the work is performed, or when a product is produced, but when the work or the product actually makes its contribution to revenue. This principle helps to calculate the net income or loss in a certain accounting period.

1.4 Accounting Elements & Accounting Equation

Accounting is meant to reflect the movement of operating funds of a business. To accomplish this objective, accounts are set up to provide useful information about these fund movements. An account is an element in the accounting system that is used to classify and summarize measurements of business activity.

1. Accounting Elements

(1) **Definition of Accounting Elements**

Accounting elements refer to the basic classification for accounting objects, and the specification of accounting calculation objects. They are used for the purpose of reflecting and determining the operating results of a business.

(2) **Classifications of Accounting Elements**

In static terms, all forms of economic resources a business owns (called assets in accounting) have a specific source. They do not just appear. There are normally two usually a business can attain funds: first is loans from outsiders (called creditors) that can be used only for a limited period of time and need to be repaid at the time of maturity; the other is the owner's investments in the business that can be used for the long term. It participates in profit distribution and will either increase or decrease the assets of the business. The former source is in accounting terminology called liabilities, the latter is called owner's equity. Assets, liabilities and owner's equity are the three basic accounting elements that are contained in the balance sheet.

Dynamically, the operating activities of a business will inevitably cause changes in the capital value of a business. The consumption and recovery of the capital are called expenses and revenues respectively. These two are presented in the income statement.

Based on their economic content, accounting elements can be divided into assets, liabilities, owner's equity, revenues, expenses. Economic contents of accounts refer to specific contents of accounting objects. Such classification helps understand the content of calculation and supervision of each account, and helps analyzing the financial statements.

◆**Assets**

A more complete definition of assets are: any economic resources of monetary value owned or controlled by a business that are expected to benefit future operations, such as cash, land, buildings, etc. As to their liquidity, assets can be divided into three main groups: current assets; property, plant and equipment (fixed assets); and intangible assets.

Current assets are those that are expected to be converted to cash or used up by the business within one year or an operating cycle longer than one year. It can be subcategorized into cash, receivables (money owed to the company), prepayment, inventories (goods held for sale), short-term investments, etc.

Current assets are like blood to the business without which the measurement of all economic activities of the business, such as purchases, sales, etc., will be impossible, just as the inflow and outflow of the current assets forms the normal business activities.

Property, plant and equipment, also known as fixed assets, refer to long-term or relatively permanent assets owned by a company. They usually have relatively long lives and include land, buildings, machinery, furniture and equipment, etc. They are also considered material, tangible assets.

Intangible assets are those assets owned by a company such as patents, copyrights, trademarks or goodwill, etc. They do not have physical substance, yet they for the most part, are very valuable to the company.

◆ **Liabilities**

According to the International Accounting Standards Committee (IASC), a liability is recognized in the balance sheet when it is probable that an outflow of resource indicating economic benefits will result from the settlement of a present obligation. A much simpler understanding is liabilities are debts owed to outsiders (creditors). Liabilities are often easy to identify, because most of them carry the titles with the word "payable". For instance, accounts payable, notes payable, etc. Liabilities fall into two categories: current liabilities and long-term liabilities.

Current liabilities are debts or obligations that must be repaid within one year or within the accounting period longer than one year. Common forms of current liabilities are accounts payable, notes payable, interest payable, tax payable, etc. The purpose of borrowing current liabilities is to meet the short-term demands of the business operation.

Long-term liabilities involve a pay back period longer than a year. Compared with current liabilities, long-term liabilities are normally of substantial amount.

◆ **Owner's Equity**

Owner's equity refers to the resources invested in the business by the owner or accumulated during the course of operations. If it's an incorporated company, it's called stockholder's equity. According to the accounting equation, owner's equity in a business is the difference between the assets and the liabilities.

It stands for the owner's claim against the business assets which mainly falls in two parts: paid-in capital (owner's investment), and retained earnings (earnings accumulated during the business operation).

◆ **Revenues**

Revenues are cash inflows or other enhancements of assets of an entity or settlement of its liabilities or a combination of both in the normal operation of business activities. Revenues cause increase in owner's equity.

◆ **Expenses**

Expenses are outflows or other using up of assets or incurrence of liabilities or a combination of both in the normal operation of business activities. Expenses result in a decrease in owner's equity.

2. Accounting Equation

Assets, liabilities and owner's equity and the relationship among them portray the financial position of a business. This equilibrium is called the accounting equation with assets on the left side, liabilities and owner's equity on the right side. Accounting equation lays the theoretical foundation for accounting practice and extremely important for both the double-entry system and the preparation of financial statements.

Transaction ① Invested $3 000 cash in the business.

```
              Assets   =  Liabilities  +  Owner's Equity
①Cash       + $3 000                     Capital   + $3 000
 Balance      $3 000                                 $3 000
```

Transaction ② Purchased office equipment for $2 000 on credit.

```
              Assets   =  Liabilities  +  Owner's Equity
①Cash       + $3 000                     Capital   + $3 000
②Office                  Accounts        Payable
 Equipment  + $2 000     + $2 000
 Balance      $5 000       $2 000          $3 000
```

1.5 Recording Business Transactions: Double-Entry System

Transactions are economic events that affect the financial position of a business entity. A company may have hundreds or even thousands of transactions every day. But the accounting equation remains in balance regardless.

We have seen how assets equal the aggregate of liabilities and owner's equity. It's because of the principle of duality, which means that all economic events have double effects, either increase or decrease or both, that will offset and balance each other. This concept is called double-entry system. In order to get a further understanding of this, we need to start from the basic concept-account.

1. Setup of Account

We have introduced the basic accounting elements. Included in them are accounts that fall into categories of assets, liabilities and owner's equity, revenues and expenses. Each account includes different specific content because business transactions are complex. For example, both cash and inventory are assets but they have a different nature. That is why we further classify the accounting elements into different accounts, the basic device of accounting. Accounts are the foundation of recording accounting entries and preparing financial statement. The table below is a list of a company's accounts called chart of accounts. The accounts listed are numbered in order to facilitate accounting identification and transaction entry.

2. T-account

Title of Account

Left or debit side	Right or credit side
Debit balance	Credit balance

The simplest and most popular form of the account in practice is T-account. It is so called because it looks like the English letter T.

A T-account is made up with 3 parts: the account title, debit side and credit side. The left side of the T-account is called Debit, and the right side is called Credit. Pay attention to the fact that the words debit and credit mean only "left" and "right", not "increase" or "decrease". Very often these two terms are abbreviated as Dr. and Cr.

When an amount is entered to the left side of an account, regardless of the account title, it's called a debit to the account or the account has been debited; when an amount is placed on the right side of an account, it's called a credit to the account or the account has been credited. The difference between the debit and the credit side of an account is called the account balance.

3. The Rule of Debit and Credit

From the above discussion, we know that we have to keep the accounting equation balanced and at the same time the amount debited must equal the credit.

These rules can be illustrated graphically as follows:

	Assets	=	Liabilities	+	Owner's Equity
	Dr. | Cr.		Dr. | Cr.		Dr. | Cr.
① Always True					
② Increase	+		+		+
③ Decrease	-		-		-
④ Normal Balance	×		×		×

	Revenues	Expenses
	Dr. | Cr.	Dr. | Cr.
① Always True		
② Increase	+	+
③ Decrease	-	-
④ Normal Balance	×	×

Exercises

Exercises 1.1 Multiple Choice

1. Which of these is (are) an example of an asset account?　　　　　(　　)
   A. Service Revenue.　　　　　　　　B. Withdrawals.
   C. Supplies.　　　　　　　　　　　　D. All of the above.

2. Wise Company paid $2 850 on account. The effect of this transaction on the accounting equation is to _____.　　　　　　　　　　　　　　　　　(　　)
   A. decrease assets and decrease owner's equity
   B. increase liabilities and decrease owner's equity
   C. have no effect on total assets
   D. decrease assets and decrease liabilities

3. Which of these accounts has a normal debit balance?　　　　　　(　　)
   A. Rent Expense.
   B. Withdrawals.
   C. Service Revenue.
   D. Both A and B have a normal debit balance.

4. The ending cash account balance is $57 600. During the period, cash receipts equal $124 300. If the cash payments during the period total $135 100, then the

beginning Cash account must have _____. （　　）
A. $68 400
B. $46 800
C. $181 900
D. Cannot be determined from the information given

5. The principle or concept that holds that an entity will remain in operation for the foreseeable future is the _____. （　　）
   A. going-concern concept
   B. stable-monetary concept
   C. reliability principle
   D. cost principle

6. Which of the following is true of the accounting entity principle? （　　）
   A. Requires that sole proprietors have unlimited liability.
   B. Requires that partnership income be taxed at the partnership level.
   C. Means that business records should be kept separately from the owner's financial records.
   D. Requires that partnerships have written agreement.

7. Which of the following is another term for owner's equity? （　　）
   A. Net income.
   B. Expenses.
   C. Net assets.
   D. Revenues.

Exercises 1.2

Decide whether the statements are true or false. Write "T" for "True" and "F" for "False".

1. It is customary to include any amounts received from customers but has not yet earned as revenue in current liability. （　　）
2. Managerial accounting is governed by GAAP. （　　）
3. Current assets are presented in the order of liquidity or convertibility into cash; while current liabilities are listed in the order that they come due. （　　）
4. Retained earning represents exactly what the term implies: that portion of net income the company has retained. （　　）
5. Business firms whose accounting year ends on December 31 are said to be on a calendar-year basis. （　　）

6. The presentation of the owners' equity section is same for three types of business organization. (   )

Exercises 1.3

The following selected transactions were completed by ABC Service during December:

1. Received cash from owner as additional investment, $20 000.
2. Paid advertising expense, $520.
3. Purchased supplies of gas and oil for cash $780.
4. Received cash from cash customers, $1 500.
5. Charged customers for delivery services on account, $2 100.
6. Paid creditors on account, $470.
7. Paid rent for December, $1 000.
8. Received cash from customers on accounts, $1 810.
9. Paid cash to owner for personal use, $900.
10. Determined by taking an inventory that $650 of supplies of gas and oil had been used during the month.

Indicate the effect of each transaction on the accounting equation by listing the numbers identifying the transactions, 1 through 10, in a vertical column, and inserting at the right of each number the appropriate letter from the following list:

(1) Increase in one asset, decrease in another asset.
(2) Increase in an asset, increase in a liability.
(3) Increase in an asset, increase in capital.
(4) Decrease in an asset, decrease in a liability.
(5) Decrease in an asset, decrease in capital.

Unit Two

Forms of Business Ownership

Teaching Objectives

Upon completion of this chapter, you will:
1. Know the concept of sole proprietorships, partnerships and corporations and understand each form's advantages and disadvantages as well as their difference.
2. Know the accounting of each form.
3. Know how to account for stock transactions and dividends.

Vocabulary

sole proprietorship	独资企业
partnership	合伙
partner	合伙人
corporation	公司
own	拥有
amortize	摊销,分摊
distribution	分配
combine	联合
recognize	承认,认可
consolidate	巩固,加固
divide	划分
share	股份,份额
evidence	证实,证明
subtotal	小计
ordinarily	普通地

issuance	发行
common stock	普通股
preferred stock	优先股
shareholder (stockholder)	股东
dividend	股利/股息
preemptive right	优先权
owner's equity	所有者权益
par value stock	有面值股票
paid-in capital	实收资本
additional paid-in capital	多收资本,增收资本
issuing corporation	发行公司
retained earnings	留存收益
cash dividend	现金股利
stock dividend	股票股利
declaration of dividend	股利宣布,股利公告
dividend distribution	股利分配
stockholders' equity	股东权益

TEXT

There are basically three types or forms of business ownership structures: sole proprietorships, partnerships and corporations.

2.1 Sole Proprietorships

The vast majority of small businesses start out as sole proprietorships. These firms are owned by one person, usually the individual who has day-to-day responsibilities for running the business. Sole proprietors own all the assets of the business and the profits generated by it. They also assume complete responsibility for any of its liabilities or debts. In the eyes of the law and the public, you are one in the same with the business.

(1) **Advantages of a Sole Proprietorship**

①Easiest and least expensive form of ownership to organize.

②Sole proprietors are in complete control, and within the parameters of the law, may make decisions as they see fit.

③Sole proprietors receive all income generated by the business to keep or reinvest.

④Profits from the business flow directly to the owner's personal tax return.

⑤The business is easy to dissolve, if desired.

(2) **Disadvantages of a Sole Proprietorship**

①Sole proprietors have unlimited liability and are legally responsible for all debts against the business. Their business and personal assets are at risk.

②May be at a disadvantage in raising funds and are often limited to using funds from personal savings or consumer loans.

③May have a hard time attracting high-caliber employees or those that are motivated by the opportunity to own a part of the business.

2.2 Partnerships

A partnership is an unincorporated association of two or more individuals to carry on a business for profit. Many small businesses, including retail, service, and professional practitioners, are organized as partnerships.

The partners should have a legal agreement that sets forth how decisions will be made, profits will be shared, disputes will be resolved, how future partners will be admitted to the partnership, how partners can be bought out, and what steps will be taken to dissolve the partnership when needed.

(1) **Advantages of a Partnership**

①Partnerships are relatively easy to establish; however time should be invested in developing the partnership agreement.

②With more than one owner, the ability to raise funds may be increased.

③The profits from the business flow directly through to the partners' personal tax returns.

④Prospective employees may be attracted to the business if given the incentive to become a partner.

⑤The business usually will benefit from partners who have complementary skills.

(2) **Disadvantages of a Partnership**

①Partners are jointly and individually liable for the actions of the other partners.

②Profits must be shared with others.

③Since decisions are shared, disagreements can occur.

④Some employee benefits are not deductible from business income on tax returns.

⑤The partnership may have a limited life; it may end upon the withdrawal or death of a partner.

2.3 Corporations

A corporation is a legal entity, meaning it is a separate entity from its owners who are called stockholders. A corporation is treated as a "person" with most of the rights and obligations of a real person. A corporation is not allowed to hold public office or vote, but it does pay income taxes. It may be established as a profit making or nonprofit organization and may be publicly or privately held. The stock of a public company is traded on a stock exchange. There may be thousands, even millions, of stockholders in a public company. Stock of a privately held company is not traded on an exchange and there are usually only a small number of stockholders.

(1) **Advantages of a Corporation**

①Shareholders have limited liability for the corporation's debts or judgments against the corporations.

②Generally, shareholders can only be held accountable for their investment in stock of the company. (Note however, that officers can be held personally liable for their actions, such as the failure to withhold and pay employment taxes.)

③Corporations can raise additional funds through the sale of stock.

④Corporations may deduct the cost of benefits it provides to officers and employees.

(2) **Disadvantages of a Corporation**

①The process of incorporation requires more time and money than other forms of organization.

②Incorporating may result in higher overall taxes. Dividends paid to shareholders are not deductible from business income; thus it can be taxed twice.

2.4 Sole Proprietorship and Partnership Accounting

In most aspects, partnership accounting is similar to that in a sole proprietorship except there are more owners. Therefore, a separate capital account and drawing account is maintained for each partner. Partnerships recognize no salaries expense for services provided to the organization by the partner. Accounts paid to partners are recorded by debiting partner's drawing account.

1. Accounting for Initial Investments

Because ownership rights in a partnership are divided among two or more partners, separate capital and drawing accounts are maintained for each partner.

If a partner invested cash in a partnership, the cash account of the partnership is debited, and the partner's capital account is credited for the invested amount.

If a partner invested an asset other than cash, an asset account is debited, and the partner's capital account is credited for the market value of the asset. If a certain amount of money is owed for the asset, the partnership may assume liability. In that case an asset account is debited, and the partner's capital account is credited for the difference between the market value of the asset invested and liabilities assumed.

2. Allocation of Net Income

Net income or loss is allocated to the partners in accordance with the partnership agreement. In the absence of any agreement between partners, profits and losses must be shared equally regardless of the ratio of the partners' investments. If the partnership agreement specifies how profits are to be shared, losses must be shared on the same basis as profits. Net income does not include gains or losses from the partnership investment.

2.5 Accounting for Stock Transactions and Dividends

1. Stock Issued for Cash

Corporations may issue stock for cash. When a company such as Big City Dwellers issues 5 000 shares of its $1 par value common stock at par for cash, that means the company will receive $5 000 (5 000 shares × $1 per share). The sale of the stock is recorded by increasing (debiting) cash and increasing (crediting) common stock by $5 000. The entry is as follows:

Cash   5 000
    Capital Stock—Common Stock 5 000

2. Stock Issued in Exchange for Assets or Services

If corporations issue stock in exchange for assets or as payment for services rendered, a value must be assigned using the cost principle. The cost of an asset received in exchange for a corporation's stock is the market value of the stock issued. If the stock's market value is not yet determined (as would occur when a company is just starting), the fair market value of the assets or services received is used to value the transaction. If the total value exceeds the par or stated value of the stock issued, the value in excess of the par or stated value is added to the additional paid-in-capital (or paid-in-capital in excess of par, capital reserve – capital stock premium) account.

For example, The J Trio, Inc. , a start-up company, issues 10 000 shares of its $ 0. 50 par value common stock to its attorney in payment of a $ 50 000 invoice from the attorney for costs incurred by the law firm to help establish the corporation. The entry to record this exchange would be based on the invoice value because the market value for the corporation's stock has not yet been determined. The entry to record the transaction increases (debits) organization costs for $ 50 000, increases (credits) common stock for $ 5 000 (10 000 shares × $ 0. 50 par value), and increases (credits) additional paid-in-capital for $ 45 000 (the difference). Organization cost is an intangible asset, included on the balance sheet and amortized over some period not to exceed 40 years.

3. Dividends

The Board of Directors must authorize all dividends. A dividend may distribute cash, assets, or the corporation's own stock to its stockholders. Distribution of assets, also called property dividends, will not be discussed here. Before authorizing a dividend, a company must have sufficient retained earnings and cash (cash dividend) or sufficient authorized stock (stock dividend). Three dates are relevant when accounting for dividends:

(1) Date of Declaration

The date of declaration is the date the Board of Directors formally authorizes for the payment of a cash dividend or issuance of shares of stock. This date establishes the liability of the company. On this date, the value of the dividend to be paid or distributed is deducted from retained earnings.

(2) **Date of Record**

The date of record does not require a formal accounting entry. It establishes who will receive the dividend.

(3) **Date of Payment or Distribution**

The date of payment or distribution is when the dividend is given to the stockholders of record.

For example, on May 1, the Board of Directors of Triple Play authorized payment of a $50 000 cash dividend on June 30 to the stockholders of record on May 25. On May 1, the date of declaration, the value of the dividend to be paid is deducted from (debited to) Profit Distribution and set up as a liability in a separate dividends payable account.

Profit Distribution   50 000
    Dividend Payable   50 000

It should be noted that some companies use separate accounts called "Dividends, Common Stock" and "Dividends, Preferred Stock" rather than retained earnings to record dividends declared. If these accounts are used, a closing entry is made at the end of the period to decrease (debit) retained earnings and decrease (credit) "Dividends, Common Stock" and "Dividends, Preferred Stock" to zero out the balances in the dividend accounts and update the retained earnings balance.

On the date of payment when the cash is sent out to the stockholders, the dividends payable account is decreased (debited) and the cash account is decreased (credited).

Dividend Payable   50 000
    Cash   50 000

Once declared and paid, a cash dividend decreases total stockholders' equity and decreases total assets. Dividends are not reported on the income statement. They would be found in a statement of retained earnings or statement of stockholders' equity once declared and in a statement of cash flows when paid.

Exercises

Exercises 2.1 Multiple Choice

1. The economic resources of a business are called _____. ( )
   A. assets
   B. liabilities
   C. owner's equity
   D. receivables

2. Basically, the three forms of business ownership structures are the following except _____. ( )
   A. sole proprietorship
   B. partnerships
   C. corporations
   D. firm

3. All of the following are the advantages of a Sole Proprietorship except _____.
   ( )
   A. easiest and least expensive form of ownership to organize.
   B. the owners are in complete control, and within the parameters of the law, may make decisions as they see fit
   C. may have a hard time attracting high-caliber employees or those that are motivated by the opportunity to own a part of the business
   D. the owners receive all income generated by the business to keep or reinvest

4. A partnership is an unincorporated association of _____ individual(s) to carry on a business for profit. ( )
   A. only one
   B. two or more
   C. two
   D. three

5. Which one is the disadvantage of a corporation? ( )
   A. Some employee benefits such as owner's medical insurance premiums are not directly deductible from business income (only partially deductible as an adjustment).
   B. May be at a disadvantage in raising funds and are often limited to using funds from personal savings or consumer loans.
   C. The process of incorporation requires more time and money than other forms of

organization.

D. Shareholders can only be held accountable for their investment in stock of the company.

6. In a partnership, if a partner invested cash, the _____ of the partnership is debited, and the partner's _____ is credited for the invested amount. ( )

   A. capital account; cash account   B. asset account; capital account
   C. capital account; asset account   D. cash account; capital account

7. Which of the following forms of business organization is an "artificial person" that conducts its business in its own name? ( )

   A. Law firm.   B. Proprietorship.
   C. Partnership.   D. Corporation.

8. If we account for dividends on the date of payment when the cash is sent out to the stockholders, the dividends payable account is _____ and the cash account is _____. ( )

   A. debited; credited   B. debited; debited
   C. credited; credited   D. credited; debited

9. Three dates are relevant when accounting for dividends. They are all but _____. ( )

   A. date of declaration   B. date of opening
   C. date of payment   D. date of record

10. Once declared and paid, a cash dividend _____ total stockholders' equity and _____ total assets. ( )

    A. increases; decreases   B. decreases; decreases
    C. increases; increases   D. decreases; increases

Exercises 2.2 Record the Following Transactions.

1. ABC Corporation issues 5 000 shares of no-par common stock at $30 a share and at a later date issues 1 000 additional shares at $25. Please record the entries of no-par stock.

2. ABC Corporation issues 100 000 shares of common stock, par $5, for cash of

$ 6 per share. Please record this entry.
3. Mike and Brown form a partnership. Mike invests in the partnership totally $ 230 000, including land $ 60 000, building $ 100 000, inventory $ 60 000 and cash $ 10 000. Please record Mike's investment in the partnership.
4. After four months of operation, the partnership is in need of more cash, then Mike and Brown each make additional investment of $ 20 000. Please record these additional investments.

Exercises 2.3   Translations

1. The incorporated business, namely the corporation, is a legal entity. Stockholders are not personally liable for the debts of a corporation. Thus, the most that a stockholder may lose by investing in a corporation is the amount of his investment.
2. In general, business takes out of the three alternative legal forms: sole proprietorship, partnerships and corporations.
3. Amounts paid to partners are recorded by debiting the partner's drawing account.
4. As a result, a separate capital account and drawing account is maintained for each partner.
5. The Board of Directors must authorize all dividends. A dividend may distribute cash, assets, or the corporation's own stock to its stockholders.

Unit Three

Financial Statements

Teaching Objectives

Upon completion of this chapter, you will:
1. Know what financial statements are.
2. Understand why financial statements are prepared.
3. Know what retained earnings are.
4. Master balance sheet, income statement and cash flow statement's structure and function.
5. And relationship of each financial statement.

Vocabulary

financial statement	财务报表
assets	资产
liabilities	负债
owner's equity	所有者权益
revenue	收入,盈利
expense	费用,花费
net income	净收益
net loss	净损失
retained earning statement	留存收益表
cash flow statement	现金流量表
balance sheet	资产负债表
income statement	利润表

TEXT

The daily accounting information is normally detailed, specific, enormous and disperse. In order to get a clear picture of the financial position, performance and changes in the financial position of an enterprise, measures need to be taken to record, classify, summarize, and interpret the daily accounting data. The results finally are communicated to the decision-makers.

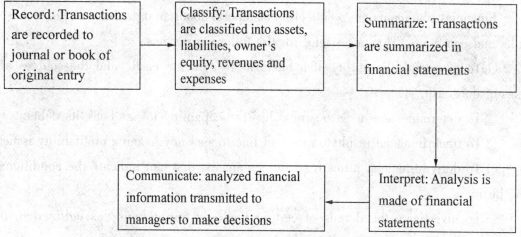

Chart 3.1 **Measures to Analyze Accounting Data**

In the communication stage, documents and forms are prepared to present the financial situation of the company. These are called financial statements. Financial statements are the final product of the accounting process, because users need to know how the business is doing to make economic decisions. Financial statements prepared for this purpose meet the common needs of most users. However, financial statements do not provide all the information that users may need to make economic decisions, since they largely portary the financial effects of past events and do not necessarily provide non-financial information.

The objective of financial statements is to provide information about the financial position, performance and cash flows of a business. Information about financial position is primarily provided in a balance sheet. Information about operating performance of the company is primarily portrayed in an income statement. Information on cash flow is provided by a cash flow statement. Balance sheet and income statement are the two basic financial statements that are most commonly used.

3.1 Definition

Financial statements are a collection of reports about an organization's financial results and condition. They are useful for the following reasons:

①To determine the ability of a business to generate cash, and the sources and uses of that cash.

②To determine whether a business has the capability to pay back its debts.

③To track financial results on a trend line to spot any looming profitability issues.

④To derive financial ratios from the statements that can indicate the condition of the business.

⑤To investigate the details of certain business transactions, as outlined in the disclosures that accompany the statements.

3.2 Purpose of Financial Statements by Business Entities

The objective of financial statements is to provide information about the financial position, performance and changes in financial position of an enterprise that is useful to a wide range of users in making economic decisions. Financial statements should be understandable, relevant, reliable and comparable. Reported assets, liabilities, equity, income and expenses are directly related to an organization's financial position.

Financial statements are intended to be understandable by readers who have a reasonable knowledge of business and economic activities and accounting and who are willing to study the information diligently. Financial statements may be used by users for different purposes:

①Owners and managers require financial statements to make important business decisions that affect its continued operations. Financial analysis is then performed on these statements to provide management with a more detailed understanding of the figures. These statements are also used as part of management's annual report to the stockholders.

②Employees also need these reports in making collective bargaining agreements (CBA) with the management, in the case of labor unions or for individuals in discussing their compensation, promotion and rankings.

③Prospective investors make use of financial statements to assess the viability of investing in a business. Financial analyses are often used by investors and are prepared by professionals (financial analysts), thus providing them with the basis for making investment decisions.

④Financial institutions (banks and other lending companies) use them to decide whether to grant a company with fresh working capital or extend debt securities (such as a long-term bank loan or debentures) to finance expansion and other significant expenditures.

⑤Government entities (tax authorities) need financial statements to ascertain the propriety and accuracy of taxes and other duties declared and paid by a company.

⑥Vendors who extend credit to a business require financial statements to assess the creditworthiness of the business.

⑦Media and the general public are also interested in financial statements for a variety of reasons.

3.3　Balance Sheet

The balance sheet shows the financial position of the business at a specific time. It reports assets (the resources a business owns) and claims to those assets. These claims are subdivided into two categories: claims of creditors (debts of the company) are called liabilities. Claims of owners (owner's interest in the company) are called owner's equity.

Table 3.1 Balance Sheet
December 31, 2007

unit: $

Assets		
Cash		21 000
Accounts Receivable		4 500
Equipment	40 000	
Less: Accumulated Depreciation	5 500	34 500
Total Assets		60 000
Liabilities		
Accounts Payable		4 000
Salaries Payable		2 000
Interest Payable		1 700
Notes Payable		19 500
Unearned Revenue		1 500
Total Liabilities		28 700
Owner's Equity		
Capital		29 700
Retained Earnings		1 600
Total Owner's Equity		31 300
Total Liabilities and Owner's Equity		60 000

3.4 Income Statement

The income statement shows the performance and profitability of a business for a given period of time. It's also called earning's statement. From the income statement, users of the financial reports can get a clear idea of the operating results or performance of the business in a certain period called the accounting period. Users are thus able to analyze the trend and causes for the increase or decrease in the business profits.

Income is increases in economic benefits during the accounting period in the form of inflows or enhancements of assets or decreases of liabilities that result in increases in equity, other than those relating to contributions from equity participants. The definition of income encompasses both revenue and gains, and revenue arises in the course of ordinary activities of an enterprise and is referred to by different names, such as sales, fees, interest, dividends, royalties, and rent.

The income statement lists the company's revenues followed by its expenses. The difference between them is then calculated. If the revenue is greater than the expenses, the result is shown as net income. Conversely, if expenses exceed revenues, the result is shown as a net loss. The income statement reports the results from operating the business for a period of time, such as a year.

Table 3.2 Income Statement
For the Year Ended December 31, 2007   unit: $

Revenues:	
Sale Revenue	708 255
Rent Revenue	600
Total Revenue	708 855
Expenses:	
Cost of Merchandise Sold	525 305
Selling Expenses	70 820
Administrative Expenses	34 890
Interest Expenses	2 440
Total Expenses	633 455
Net Income	75 400

3.5 Retained Earnings Statement

Retained earning is the net income retained in the corporation. Retained earnings statement is a link between the balance sheet and income statement in that it shows the changes of the owner's interest in the company over an accounting period and how (by aggregating the net income and dividends). It's a useful supporting statement for a business.

Table 3.3 Retained Earnings Statement

For the Year Ended December 31, 2007 unit: $

Beginning Balance	76 000
Plus: Net Income	3 700
	79 700
Less: Dividends	1 000
Ending Balance	78 700

3.6 Cash Flow Statement

Cash flow statement shows where the cash comes from and goes to in a business in an accounting period. It reports the movement of the cash in a business in three fields: operating activities, investing activities, and financing activities.

Table 3.4 Cash Flow Statement

For the Year Ended December 31, 2007   unit: $

Operating Activities	
Cash Received from Customers	718 000
Cash Received for Lnterest	17 000
Cash Paid for Salaries	(230 000)
Cash Paid for Rent	(125 000)
Cash Paid for Other Items	(300 000)
Cash Provided by Operations	80 000
Investing Activities	
Purchase of Land	(250 000)
Financing Activities	
Payment of Dividends	(35 000)
Decrease in Cash	(205 000)
Cash Jan. 1	400 000
Cash Dec. 31	195 000

3.7 Relationship of Financial Statements

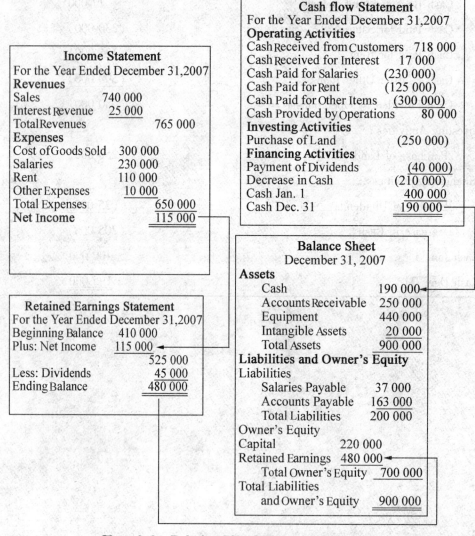

Chart 3.2 Relationship of Financial Statements

Cash balance goes to balance sheet; income statement balance goes to retained earnings statement, and retained earning balance goes to balance sheet.

Exercises

Exercises 3.1 Multiple Choice

1. An income statement reports _____.　　　　　　　　　　　　　　(　)
   A. the assets, liabilities, and owner's equity on a particular date
   B. the change in the owner's capital during the period
   C. the cash receipts and cash payments during the period
   D. the difference between revenues and expenses during the period

2. The following information about the assets and liabilities at the end of 2010 and 2011 is given below:

	2010	2011
Assets	$75 000	$90 000
Liabilities	36 000	45 000

   If net income was $1 500 and there were no withdrawals, how much did the owner invest?　　　　　　　　　　　　　　　　　　　　　　　　　　　　　(　)
   A. $4 500.　　　　　　　　　　　　B. $6 000.
   C. $45 000.　　　　　　　　　　　　D. $43 500.

3. The amount of net income shown on the income statement also appears on the _____.　　　　　　　　　　　　　　　　　　　　　　　　　　　　(　)
   A. statement of financial position
   B. balance sheet
   C. statement of owner's equity
   D. statement of cash flows

4. Please select the items which do not belong to the Balance Sheet.　　　(　)
   A. Long-term investment.　　　　　　B. Accounts receivable.
   C. Income tax expense.　　　　　　　D. Retained earnings.

5. In general, which is the basis of preparing a Balance Sheet?　　　　　(　)
   A. Assets = Liabilities + Owners' equity.
   B. Assets − Liabilities = Owners' equity.

C. Profits = Revenues − Expenses.

D. Revenues = Profits + Expenses.

6. The major elements of the income statement are _____. ( )

   A. revenue, cost of goods sold, selling expenses, and general expense

   B. operating section, cooperating section, discontinued operations, extraordinary items, and cumulative effect

   C. revenues, expenses, gains and losses

   D. all of these

7. Information in the income statement helps users to _____. ( )

   A. evaluate the past performance of the enterprise

   B. provide a basis for predicting future performance

   C. help assess the risk or uncertainty of achieving future cash flows

   D. all of these

8. Which of the following are reported in the stockholders' equity section of the balance sheet? ( )

   A. Revenues and expenses.

   B. Dividends and retained earnings.

   C. Common stock and dividends.

   D. Common stock and retained earnings.

9. Current assets are presented in the balance sheet in order of _____. ( )

   A. dollar amounts   B. liquidity

   C. solvency   D. the alphabet

10. For its most recent year, a corporation had beginning and ending accounts receivable balances of $50 000 and $60 000, respectively. The year's sales on account were $800 000. What was the amount of cash received from customers during the year? ( )

    A. $790 000.   B. $820 000.

    C. $810 000.   D. $800 000.

Exercises 3.2

1. The night manager of Majestic Limousine Service, who had no accounting background, prepared the following balance sheet for the company at February 28,

2001. The dollar amounts were taken directly from the company's accounting records and are correct. However, the balance sheet contains a number of errors in its headings, format, and the classification of assets, liabilities, and owner's equity.

\multicolumn{4}{c}{MAJESTIC LIMO}
\multicolumn{4}{c}{Manager's report}
\multicolumn{4}{c}{8 p. m. Thursday}
Assets		Owner's Equity	
J. Snow, Capital	162 000	Accounts Receivable	78 000
Cash	69 000	Notes Payable	288 000
Building	80 000	Supplies	14 000
Automobiles	165 000	Land	70 000
		Accounts Payable	26 000
	476 000		476 000

Required: Prepare a corrected balance sheet. Include a proper heading.

2. An inexperienced accountant for Fowler Company prepared the following income statement for the month of August 2001:

\multicolumn{3}{c}{FOWLER COMPANY}
\multicolumn{3}{c}{August 31, 2001}
Revenues:		
Services Provided to Customers		10 000
Investment by O. Fowler, Owner		5 000
Loan from Bank	15 000	30 000
Expenses:		
Payments to Long-term Creditors		8 000
Expenses Required to Provide		
Services to Customers		7 500
Purchase of Land	16 000	31 500
		1 500

Required: Prepare a revised income statement in accordance with generally accepted accounting principles.

Exercises 3.3

For each of the following items, state whether the item would be shown on the statement of cash flow as an operating, investing, financing activity.

A. payment of account payable

B. issuance of preferred stock for cash

C. payment of cash dividend

D. sale of long-term investment

E. collection of account receivable

F. issuance of long-term note payable to borrow cash

G. purchase of long-term investment

H. payment of wages to employees

I. cash sale of land investing

Exercises 3.4   Translation

1. With a properly prepared balance sheet, you can look at a balance sheet at the end of each accounting period and know if your business has more or less value, if your debts are higher or lower, and if your working capital is higher or lower.

2. It is a key figure for shareholders because it reveals the company's final income that can be distributed to shareholders and/or reinvested for future growth.

3. Current assets are cash or items that can be converted into cash within a year. Cash, accounts receivable, inventory, marketable securities, prepaid expenses, and short-term investment are all current assets.

4. A balance sheet is a snapshot of a business financial condition at a specific moment in time, usually at the close of an accounting period.

5. Depreciation means a part of the value of the asset is gradually transferred to the cost of products, or because of wear and tear, or technological obsolescence during its useful life.

Unit Four

Accounting Cycle

Teaching Objectives

Upon completion of this chapter, you will:
1. Master 8 steps of accounting cycle.
2. Know the concepts of journal, ledger, trial balance, prepaid expenses, unearned revenues, accrued revenue and accrued expense.
3. Know how to adjust and close entries.

Vocabulary

journal	日记账
ledger	分类账
trial balance	试算平衡表
adjust	（账项）调整
prepayment	预付费用
accrual	应计
prepaid expenses	预付费用
accrued revenues	应记收入
accrued expenses	应记费用
subcategory	二级分类
apportion	分摊,摊销
overstate	夸大,过多估计
understate	缩小,过少估计
deplete	耗尽,用光
wear and tear	（固定资产的）损耗
allocate	分摊,摊销

TEXT

The accounting cycle refers to the steps or procedures used repeatedly in a business to record and summarize accounting data. The steps in the accounting cycle include:

①Analyzing business transactions from source documents.
②Recording the effects of business transactions in journals.
③Posting to general (and subsidiary) ledger accounts from the journal.
④Making a trial balance.
⑤Adjusting some account balance.
⑥Preparing financial statements.
⑦Closing temporary accounts.
⑧Reversing some adjusting entries.

4.1 Journals & Ledgers

The sequence of accounting procedures used to record, classify, and summarize accounting information is often termed the accounting cycle. The accounting cycle begins with the initial recording of business transactions and concludes with the preparation of formal financial statements summarizing the effects of these transactions upon the assets, liabilities and owner's equity of the business.

1. Journals

The transaction occurred in a business can be directly entered into the accounts. But each account shows only the changes in that account, and because the debit and the credit sides of each transaction go to different accounts, it is very difficult to follow individual transactions. For example, the cash account contains only data on changes in cash and does not show the corresponding entry of the same transaction. How the cash is generated or how it is spent is not illustrated clearly. When a large number of transactions are involved in a business daily, errors in recording the transactions are hard to track down. This causes further mistakes in analyzing the evaluation of the business. A solution to this problem is to adopt a chronological record of the business transactions. This is called a journal. A journal is also called the book of original entry.

Explanations are provided to each transaction. Transactions are then transferred to the appropriate accounts to provide a clearer view on the change that happened to the accounting elements. Each transaction is a separate journal entry, and this process of recording transactions is called journalizing. The entries in the journal will be posted to another book called a ledger which will be discussed later.

The journal records the following information for each transaction:

①The transaction date.
②The names of the accounts debited and credited.
③An explanation of the transaction.
④The amounts debited and credited to each account.

Table 4.1 Journal

December 31, 2007   page1

Date	Account and Explanation	Post Ref	Debit	Credit
Mar. 2	Cash Accounts Receivable—Larry Sales on credit to Larry		50 000	50 000

◆Procedures of Recording

①Write the date with the month first and the day followed.

②Write the exact names of the accounts debited and credited under the heading "Accounts and Explanation". The name of the account debited is written at the beginning of the left margin of the column. The name of the account credited is written on the following line, indented about one inch. The explanation should be short but sufficient to explain the transaction and set it apart from other transactions.

③Write the debit amounts in the appropriate column corresponding to the accounts debited, and write the credit amounts accordingly.

④Skip a line after each journal entry.

⑤Nothing is recorded in the Post Ref (reference) column until the particular entry is posted to the general ledger, i. e. when the amounts are transferred to the related ledger accounts.

2. Ledgers

The ledger account provides a means of bringing together all the information about changes in a specific asset, a liability or owner's equity. It is the "reference book" of the accounting system and is used to classify and summarize transactions and prepare data for the financial statements. It is also a valuable source of information for managerial purposes. For example, the ledger account for the asset cash can give a clear record of the cash receipts, cash payments and current cash balance.

The account title and number appear at the top of the account form. The date column shows the date of the transactions as it does on the journal. The Item column is rarely used, because an explanation already appears on the journal. The Post Ref column is used to list the page number of journal in which the transaction is recorded. In the Balance column of the account, the new balance is entered each time the account is debited or credited. It is similar to the T-account. The advantage of a ledger over the T-account is that the current balance of the account is always available. However, because the easy-to-use nature of the T-account, it is often used to indicate the change of the ledger.

◆Posting

After the transactions have been entered in the journal, they must be transferred to the ledger. The procedure of transferring the data in the general journal account to the general ledger account is called posting. Its purpose is to summarize the effects of transactions on each individual asset, liability, owner's equity, revenue, and expense account.

In the posting procedure, each amount listed in the debit column of the journal is posted by entering it to the debit side of the corresponding account in the ledger, each amount listed in the credit column of the journal is posted to the credit side of a ledger account. The posting procedures for a journal entry are shown in the table below and the take the following steps:

①Transfer the date of the transaction from the journal to the ledger.

②Transfer the page number from the journal to the journal reference column of the ledger.

③Post the debit amount from the journal as a debit figure in the ledger account, likewise the credit amount.

④Enter the account number in the posting reference column of the journal once the figure has been posted to the ledger.

Table 4.2　Chart of Accounts

Balance Sheet	Income Statement
1. Assets	**3. Owner's Equity**
101 Cash	301 Paid-in Capital
102 Accounts Receivable	302 Retained Earnings
103 Notes Receivable	303 Withdrawals
104 Office Supplies	**4. Revenue**
105 Equipment	401 Sales Revenue
106 Inventory	402 Interest Revenue
107 Prepaid Insurance	**5. Expense**
108 Land	501 Salary Expense
109 Accumulated Depreciation	502 Telephone Expense
110 Intangible Assets	503 Supplies Expense
2. Liabilities	504 Advertising Expense
201 Accounts Payable	505 Rent Expense
202 Notes Payable	506 Gas Expense
203 Salaries Payable	507 Insurance Expense
204 Unearned Revenue	508 Depreciation Expense

4.2　Trial Balance

The aim of the trial balance is to make sure that for every debit entry, a corresponding credit entry has been made. Since equal amounts of debits and credits are entered in the account for every transaction, the total of the accounts with debit balance should equal the total of the accounts with credit balance.

The trial balance is a list of the account titles in the ledger with their respective debit and credit balance. It's prepared at the end of an accounting period after all transactions have been recorded in order to see if the total debit equals the total credit. Their procedure to prepare the trial balance is as follows.

①List all the account names in the trial balance in the order of assets, liabilities, owner's equity, expenses and revenues.

②Transfer debit balances from the ledger account to the left column of the trial balance and credit balances in the right column.

③Add the debits and credits and record the totals.

④Compare the totals to see if they're equal.

Table 4.3 ABC Service Company Trial Balance
November 30, 2011   unit: $

Accounts Title	Debits	Credits
Cash	3 800	
Office Equipment	2 000	
Accounts Payable		2 000
Capital		3 000
Service Revenue		1 000
Salaries Expense	200	
	6 000	6 000

4.3 Adjusting Entries

Adjusting entries are journal entries which are classified as either prepayments or accruals. Each of these classes has two subcategories.

◆ Prepayments

Prepaid expenses: expenses paid in cash and recorded as assets before they are used or consumed.

Unearned revenues: cash received as liabilities before revenue is earned.

◆ Accruals

Accrued revenues: revenues earned but not yet received in cash or recorded.

Accrued expenses: expenses incurred but not yet paid in cash or recorded.

Table 4.4 Adjustment at the End of Accounting Period

Type of Adjustment	Accounts Before Adjustment	Adjusting Entry
Prepaid expenses	Assets overstated Expenses understated	Dr. Expenses Cr. Assets
Unearned revenues	Liabilities overstated Revenues understated	Dr. Liabilities Cr. Revenues
Accrued revenues	Assets understated Revenues understated	Dr. Assets Cr. Revenues
Accrued expenses	Expenses understated Liabilities understated	Dr. Expenses Cr. Liabilities

In order to correctly measure a period's income and expense, adjusting entries are needed because they assign revenues to the period when they are earned and expenses to the period when they are incurred. With adjusting entries, related asset and liability accounts balances are corrected under the concept of accrual-basis. Adjusting entries are necessary before the financial statements are prepared.

After the trial balance is prepared, very frequently the debit and credit are not in balance because there are adjusting to be prepared to match the expenses and revenues actually occurred.

1. Prepaid Expenses

Payments of expenses that will benefit more than one accounting period are called prepaid expenses. Common prepayments are insurance, taxes, rents, and depreciation, etc. When expenses are prepaid, an asset account is increased to show the benefit that will be received in the future. At the end of each accounting period, apportion is needed to record the expenses that occurred in the current period.

Prior to the adjustment, assets are overstated and expenses are understated (the prepayments normally cover several accounting period: 3 months, 6 months, etc.), so an adjusting entry for prepaid expenses results in an increase (debit) to an expense account and a decrease (credit) to an asset account.

Example 4.1 Prepaid Insurance

Assume Target paid a $1 200 for a 3-month insurance. The payment was recorded as an increase in one asset—Prepaid Insurance and one decrease in another asset-Cash. Thus the entry would be:

Dr: Prepaid Insurance　　　　　　　　1 200
　　Cr: Cash　　　　　　　　　　　　　　1 200

At the end of the month, one third of the insurance coverage has expired or has been used. That is $400 of the Prepaid Insurance has been depleted. So the adjustment entry for this at the end of the month should be:

Dr: Insurance Expense　　　　　　　　400
　　Cr: Prepaid Insurance　　　　　　　　400

The accounting equation is affected as follows:

　　　　　Assets = Liabilities + Owner's Equity
　　　　　 -400　　　　　　　　　　 -400

Example 4.2 Supplies

Still Target: assume it purchased supplies costing $5 000. This is recorded by increasing the asset supplies and decreasing the asset cash.

Dr: Raw Material 5 000
  Cr: Cash 5 000

By the end of the month, a count of the inventory shows that $2 500 of the supplies has been used up. Therefore, adjusting entry is made as:

Dr: Mannfacturing Cost 2 500
  Cr: Supplies 2 500

The accounting equation is affected as following:

$$\text{Assets} = \text{Liabilities} + \text{Owner's Equity}$$
$$-2\,500 \qquad\qquad\qquad -2\,500$$

Example 4.3   Depreciation

Depreciation is a special kind of prepayment. It means the wear and tear on fixed assets that have long lives and will serve for years in a company, such as buildings, equipment, and motor vehicles. The period of service is called the useful life or service life of the asset. Because of the fact that the fixed assets are expected to provide service for many years, they are recorded as assets, rather than expenses, at the historical or actual cost. According to the matching principle, a portion of this cost should be reported as an expense during each period of the asset's useful life. Depreciation is the process of allocating the cost of an asset to expense over its useful life (see Unit 8 for on depreciation).

The acquisition of long-lived assets is essentially a long-term prepayment for services. So it's necessary to recognize the cost (expense) that has been used and to report the unused cost (asset) at the end of the accounting period. In order to do this, an account called Accumulated Depreciation is set up, which is a deduction of the assets account it offsets.

For example, if a company buys a piece of equipment for $1 million and expects it to have a useful life of 10 years, it will be depreciated over 10 years. Every accounting year, the company will expense $100 000.

Dr: Depreciation Expense 100 000
  Cr: Accumulated Depreciation 100 000

The accounting equation is affected:

$$\text{Assets} = \text{Liabilities} + \text{Owner's Equity}$$
$$-100\ 000 \qquad\qquad\qquad -100\ 000$$

2. Unearned Revenues

When payment is received for services to be provided in a future date, a liability account called Unearned Revenue is increased (credited) to recognize the obligation that is created. Items like prepaid rent from a customer, customer deposits for future service may result in unearned revenues. Unearned revenues are subsequently earned by providing service to the customer, hence the need for adjustment. The adjusting entry for unearned revenues results in a decrease (a debit) to a liability account and an increase (a credit) to a revenue account.

Example 4.4

Sears Corporation received $4 000 for services in advance supposed to be completed in 4 months. The payment was credited to Unearned Revenue. At the end of the month, through evaluation, a revenue of $1 000 has been earned in the current period. The following adjustment entries are made:

Dr: Unearned Revenue   1 000
    Cr: Service Revenue   1 000

This would affect the accounting equation in the following way:

$$\text{Assets} = \text{Liabilities} + \text{Owner's Equity}$$
$$\qquad\qquad -1\ 000 \qquad +1\ 000$$

3. Accrued Revenues

Revenues earned but not yet recorded at the statement date are called accrued revenues. Accrued revenues may accumulate (accrue) with the passing of time, as in the case of interest revenue. Thus an adjusting entry is required to show the receivable that exists. Prior to adjustment both assets and revenues are understated. An adjusting entry for accrued revenues results in an increase (a debit) to an asset and an increase (a credit) to a revenue account.

Example 4.5 Sears Corporation performed service for revenue fee of $300 which would not be received until later. Before cash is received, assets and owner's equity would be affected as follows:

$$\text{Assets} = \text{Liabilities} + \text{Owner's Equity}$$
$$+300 \qquad\qquad\qquad +300$$

Thus, the following adjusting entry is made:

Dr: Accounts Receivable   300
   Cr: Service Revenue   300

If the adjustment entry is not made, assets and owner's equity will be understated.

When the cash was received:

Dr: Cash   300
   Cr: Accounts Receivable   300

4. Accrued Expense

Expenses incurred but not yet paid or recorded are called accrued expenses. Interest, taxes, and salaries are common examples of accrued expenses. Accrued expenses result from the same factors as accrued revenues. Adjustments for accrued expenses are necessary to record the obligations that already existed. Prior to an adjustment, both liabilities and expenses are understated. Therefore, an adjusting entry for accrued expense results in an increase (a debit) to an expense account and an increase (a credit) to a liability account.

Example 4.6 Accrued Interest

Sears Corporation signed a three-month notes payable in the amount of $10 000 in October 1. The note requires interest at an annual rate of 12%. The amount of interest accumulation is determined by three factors: the face value of the note, the interest rate, and the term of the note. The interest is determined in the following way:

$$\text{Interest} = \text{Face Value of Note} \times \text{Annual Interest Rate} \times \text{Time in Terms of One Year}$$

The interest cost for a month would be: $\$10\,000 \times 12\% \times 1/12 = \$100$

Accounting equation would be affected as follows:

$$\text{Assets} = \text{Liabilities} + \text{Owner's Equity}$$
$$+100 \qquad -100$$

The following adjustment entry would be made at the end of the month:

Dr: Interest expense   100

   Cr: Interest Payable   100

Example 4.7   Accrued Salaries

Item like salaries and commissions are paid after the services have been performed. Still taking Sears Corporation, salaries payable represents an accrued expense and a related liability. Suppose Sears has accrued salaries to pay at the end of the month $2\,000. This accrual increases a liability, Salaries Payable, and an expense account, Salaries Expense, and has the following effect on the accounting equation:

$$\text{Assents} = \text{Liabilities} + \text{Owner's Equity}$$
$$+2\,000 \qquad -2\,000$$

The adjusting entry is:

Dr: Salaries Expense   2 000

   Cr: Salaries Payable   2 000

4.4   Closing Entries

Closing involves closing temporary accounts and transferring the data to an account called Income Summary. It is a non-financial statement account used only to facilitate the closing process. Revenues, expenses and dividends are temporary accounts. In contrast, asset, liability, and equity accounts are called real accounts, as their balances are carried forward from period to period. The closing process includes: ①Close the revenues and expenses to the income summary. ②Transfer the account balance for income summary to Retained Earnings. ③Close dividend straightly to Retained Earnings.

For example, current accounts shows National City has the following revenues and expenses information: revenues $35 000, expenses for the period: salary $ 800, advertising: $5 000, depreciation: $5 000, interest: $200; dividend for the period: $200.

①To close revenues and expenses into income summary

Dr: Revenue	35 000
Cr: Income Summary	35 000
Dr: Income Summary	11 000
Cr: Salaries Expense	800
Advertising Expense	5 000
Depreciation Expense	5 000
Interest Expense	200

②Now the income summary has a balance of $24 000 credit which will be carried over to Retained Earning

Dr: Income Summary	24 000
Cr: Retained Earnings	24 000

③To close the dividend

Dr: Retained Earnings	200
Cr: Dividend Payable	200

4.5　Adjusted Trial Balance

After adjusting and closing, the trial balance will be prepared again. This time it should be in perfect balance based on which financial statements are prepared.

Exercises

Exercises 4.1 Multiple Choice

1. Which of the following is not a characteristic of plant assets?　　　(　　)
   A. Tangible.   B. Long-lived.
   C. Unchanged outlook.   D. For resale.

2. Which of the following statements about a trail balance is incorrect?　(　　)
   A. It's primary purpose is to prove the mathematical equality of debits and credits after posting.
   B. It uncovers certain errors in the journalizing and posting.
   C. It is useful in the preparation of financial statements.
   D. It proves that all transactions have been recorded.

3. In the closing process all of the revenues and expenses account balances are transferred to the _____.　　　(　　)
   A. capital account
   B. income summary account
   C. retained earnings account
   D. dividends account

4. The post-closing trial balance consists only of _____.　　　(　　)
   A. asset and liability accounts
   B. temporary accounts
   C. revenue and expense accounts
   D. permanent accounts

5. Which of the following statements is True?　　　(　　)
   A. The credit side of an account implies something favorable.
   B. For a given account, total debits must always equal total credits.
   C. Transactions are initially recorded in a ledger account

D. Journalizing means entering the economic effect of each transaction in a journal in chronological order under the double-entry system.

6. Which book or document is a list of all accounts and their balances? (   )
   A. The journal.
   B. The trial balance.
   C. The ledger.
   D. The chart of accounts.

7. Which of the following statements is correct? (   )
   A. The chart of accounts is a list of all accounts with their balances.
   B. The trial balance is a list of all accounts with their balances, divided as debit or credit.
   C. The ledger is maintained in chart-of-accounts order.
   D. Both B and C are correct.

8. An adjusting entry could contain all of the following except _____. (   )
   A. a debit to Unearned Revenue
   B. a credit to Cash
   C. a debit to Interest Receivable
   D. a credit to Salary Payable

9. On July 31, $3 600 is paid for a one-year insurance policy. On December 31, the adjusting entry for prepaid insurance would include _____. (   )
   A. a debit to Insurance Expense, $3 600
   B. a credit to Prepaid Insurance, $3 600
   C. a debit to Insurance Expense, $1 500
   D. a credit to Prepaid Insurance, $2 100

10. On September 30, accounts payable had a normal balance of 2 300. During September, the account was credited for a total of 5 400 and debited for a total 3 900. What was the balance in the accounts payable at the beginning of September?
    (   )
    A. A 0 balance.
    B. An 800 debit balance.
    C. An 800 credit balance.
    D. A 3 800 debit balance.

Exercises 4.2

1. The following accounts show the first six transactions of the Gutierez. Construction Company. Prepare a journal entry (including written explanation) for each transac-

tion.

	Cash				Vehicles	
Nov. 1	120 000	Nov. 8	33 600	Nov. 30	9 400	
		Nov. 25	12 000			

	Land			Notes Payable	
Nov. 8	70 000		Nov. 25	12 000	Nov. 8	95 000

	Building			Accounts Payable	
Nov. 8	58 600		Nov. 21	480	Nov. 15	3 200

	Office Equipment			Joe Gutierrez, Capital	
Nov. 15	3 200	Nov. 21	480		Nov. 1	120 000
					Nov. 30	9 400

2. Louis Dixon, a dentist, begin his own dental practice. The practice was organized as a sole proprietorship. The business transactions during September are listed below.

Sept. 1　Dixon opened a bank account in the name of the business by depositing $50 000 cash., which he had saved over a number of years.

Sept. 10　Purchased a small office building for a total price of $182 400, of which $106 000 was applicable to the land and $76 400 to the building. A cash payment of $36 500 was made and a note payable was issued for the balance of the purchase price.

Sept. 15　Purchased a microcomputer system from Computer Stores, inc. for $4 680 cash.

Sept. 19　Purchased office furnishings, at a cost of ＄5 760. A cash down payment of ＄960 was made, the balance to be paid in future.

Required: Prepare journal entries to record the above transactions. Select the appropriate account titles from the following chart of accounts:

　　cash;　　office furnishings;　　notes payable;　　accounts receivable;　　land;　　accounts payable;　　building;　　Louis Dixon, Capital;　　Computer System

Exercises 4.3

Carrie Ford opened a new accounting practice called Carrie Ford, Public accountant, and completed these transaction during March 2011:

Mar. 1 Invested 25 000 in cash and office equipment that had a fair value (公允价值) of 6 000.

1 Prepaid 1 800 cash for three months' rent for an office.

3 Made credit purchase of office equipment for 3 000 and office supplies for 600.

5 Completed work for a client and immediately received 500 cash.

9 Completed a 2 000 project for a client, who will pay within 30 days.

11 Paid the account payable created on March 3.

15 Paid 1 500 cash for the annual premium on an insurance policy.

20 Received 1 600 as partial payment for the work completed on Match 9.

23 Completed work for another client for 660 on credit.

27 Carrie Ford withdrew 1 800 cash from the business to pay some personal expense.

30 Purchased 200 of additional office supplies on credit.

31 Paid 175 for the month's utility bill.

(1) Prepare journal entries to record the transaction.

(2) Finish the adjusting entries for the transaction above.

(3) Make the closing entries for the transaction above.

Unit Five

Current Assets

Teaching Objectives

Upon completion of this chapter, you will:
1. Understand the concept of cash and cash equivalents, as well as accounts receivable and inventory.
2. Learn some modes of internal controls over cash.
3. Know the allowance methods of recording bad debts.
4. Know the two kinds of inventory system.

Vocabulary

financial accounting	财务会计
economic resources	经济资源
entity	实体
economic benefits	经济利益
tangible	有形的
accounts receivable	应收账款
inventory	库存,存货
transaction	交易
current asset	流动资产
non-current asset	非流动资产
operating cycle	经营周期
cash equivalent	现金等价物
marketable securities	有价证券
notes receivable	应收票据
liquidity	流动性,清偿能力

money order	汇票
receipt	收据,收到的物(或款项),收入
disbursement	支出
internal control	内部控制
cash balance	现金余额
bank statement	银行对账单;银行结单
contra account	备抵账户
write off	冲销
direct write-off method	直接冲销法
the allowance method	备抵法
deficiency	缺点,不足,缺少
percentage-of-sales approach	销售额百分比法,或损益表法
percentage-of-receivables approach	应收账款余额百分比法
aging schedule	账龄分析法
outstanding	未偿还的,未清偿的
past due	过期
finished goods	产成品
semi-finished goods	半成品
goods in process or work in process	在产品
raw materials	原材料
periodic inventory system	实地盘存制
perpetual inventory system	永续盘存制
historical cost	历史成本
tax payable	应付税款
the specific identification method	个别认定法
the FIFO	先进先出法
the LIFO	后进先出法
weighted average	加权平均法
uncollectible	(*adj.*)(债务、款项等)未收回的;(*n.*)坏账

TEXT

In financial accounting, assets are economic resources. An asset is a resource controlled by the entity as a result of past events and from which future economic benefits are expected to flow to the entity.

Anything tangible or intangible that is capable of being owned or controlled to produce value and that is held to have positive economic value is considered an asset. Assets include such thing as cash, accounts receivable, inventory, supplies, equipment, buildings, land, etc. An accounting asset usually has the following three characteristics: ①it is expected to provide future economic benefits to the firm; ②it is owned or controlled by the firm; ③the firm acquired it as a result of a past transaction or event. The assets have been further classified into current assets and non-current assets, which will be discussed in the next unit.

Current assets are defined as cash and other assets that are reasonably expected to be realized in cash or to be sold or consumed within one year or within the normal operating cycle of the business, whichever is longer. In addition to cash and cash equivalent, current assets typically include temporary investments in marketable securities, notes receivable, accounts receivable, inventory and prepaid expense. Within the current asset category, the items are listed in the order of their liquidity, the most liquid first and the least liquid last. Cash is obviously the most liquid of all assets.

5.1 Cash and Cash Equivalents

Cash is money in the form of paper money or coins, besides it includes cash equivalents, such as checks, money orders, and money on deposit that is available for unrestricted withdrawal from banks and other financial institutions. Normally, you can think of cash as anything that a bank would accept for deposit in your account.

Cash is a very important component in the company, and from the prediction of cash flows, the users can determine the availability of cash to meet maturing obligations, the availability of cash to pay dividends, and the amount of idle cash that can safely be invested for future use.

Cash equivalents are short-term, highly liquid investment assets meeting two criteria: first, readily convertible to a known cash amount and second, sufficiently close to their due date so that their market value is not sensitive to interest rate change. Most businesses combine cash equivalents with cash as a single item on the balance sheet.

Cash is the most liquid asset of a business and a large portion of the total transactions of a business involves the receipt or disbursement of cash.

Cash is the most liquid asset of a business and a large portion of the total transactions of a business involves the receipt or disbursement of cash. Liquidity refers to a company's ability to pay for its near-term obligation. Cash and cash equivalents are liquid assets because they can be readily used to settle such obligation. A company needs liquid assets to effectively operate. In the balance sheet, cash is listed first among the current assets.

Because cash is more susceptible to theft than any other assets, for security purpose, an adequate system of internal control over cash is needed.

Because cash is more susceptible to theft than any other assets, for security purpose, an adequate system of internal control over cash is needed. Good accounting systems help in managing and controlling of cash. Effective management of cash includes measures that will:

①Provide accurate accounting for cash receipts, cash payments and cash balances;

②Prevent losses from fraud or theft;

③Maintain a sufficient amount of cash at all times to make necessary payments, plus a reasonable balance for emergencies;

④Prevent unnecessarily large amounts of cash from being held idle in bank accounts which produce no revenues.

Some major internal controls over cash transactions and cash balances are discussed here.

First, also the most important control, the handling of cash should be separated from the recording of cash. That is to say, employees who handle cash should not have access to the accounting records, and accounting personnel should not have access to cash. That's because when two or more people are involved, it becomes more difficult for theft or errors to occur. Cash could be stolen, and certain employees could cover up the shortage by falsifying the accounting records, if the cash records are maintained by those who also have access to the cash itself.

Second, it is required that all the cash be deposited daily in the bank. This means to handle cash is the personal responsibility, and it is focused on the individual who is assigned to make the regular deposit. Moreover, this can prevent the accumulation of a large amount of cash, by which even the most trusted employee can be tempted.

Third, all payments should be better made by check except that the small payment by a petty cash fund. As we know, payments made with pocket cash are quickly forgotten and easily concealed. In contrast, when they are made by check, payments are well documented, both in our personal check registers and by our bank. Payments should never be made out of cash receipts.

Fourth, it is required that the validity and amount of every expenditure be verified before a check is issued in payment, and separating the function of approving expenditures from the function of signing checks.

Last, promptly reconcile bank statements with the accounting records.

5.2 Accounts Receivable

Accounts receivable also known as Debtors, is money owed to a business by its clients (customers) and shown on its Balance Sheet as an asset. It also implies oral promises of the purchaser to pay for goods and services sold, and it is normally collectible within a period of 30 to 60 days and represents "open account" resulting from short-term extensions of credit. Therefore, accounts receivable appears on the balance sheet immediately after cash and cash equivalents.

Two accounting problems associated with accounts receivable are: (1) recognizing accounts receivable; (2) valuing accounts receivable.

First, initial recognition of accounts receivable is relatively straightforward. A service organization records an account receivable when it renders service on credit. A vendor sells goods, it increases both the Accounts Receivable and Prime Operating Revenues. Sales discounts decrease accounts receivable. The merchandiser may offer terms that encourage early payment by rendering a discount. For instance, terms of 2/10, n/30 provide the buyer with 2% discount if it pays within 10 days. If the buyer chooses to pay within the discount period, the merchandiser reduces its accounts receivable. Sales returns also decrease accounts receivable. The purchaser might find some of the items unacceptable and choose to return the unwanted ones. The vendor decreases Accounts Receivable upon receipt of the returned goods.

Second, once businesses record accounts receivable in the accounts, how should they report receivables in the financial statements? Businesses report receivables on the balance sheet as an asset. Determining the amount to report is sometimes difficult because some accounts receivable will be uncollectible.

Sometimes, companies sell goods on long-term installment plans, requiring 12, 24, or even 48 months to collect the entire amount receivable from the customer. By concept, the normal period of time required to collect accounts receivable is part of a company's operating cycle. Therefore, accounts receivable arising from normal sales transactions usually are classified as current assets, even if the credit terms extend beyond one year.

If a company has receivables, this means the company has made a sale but it has to collect the money from the buyers. Few companies that extend credit to customers are immune to credit losses. Sometimes, there might be some buyers who fail to pay their debts; therefore, these accounts receivables would be uncollectible. Since it is so, when do the receivables become uncollectible? Actually, there is no general rule for determining when the receivables become uncollectible. In fact, one of the most significant indications of partial or complete uncollectibility is the bankruptcy of the debtor. Other indications include the closing of the customer's business and the failure of repeated attempts to collect.

If those credit losses happen, they will be tied to an appropriately titled account such as Bad Debts Expense (or Uncollectible Accounts Expense) or Loss from Uncollectible Accounts (or Loss from Doubtful Accounts).

Allowance for Bad Debts is the estimated amount of accounts receivable that will not be collected. It is the provision for possible uncollectibility associated with accounts receivable, or we can say, Allowance for Bad Debts is a contra asset account.

Bad debts should be written off against Allowance for Bad Debts or charged to current profit or loss, if such allowance is not set up. When an accounts receivable is written off as uncollectible, the customer still has an obligation to pay.

There are two methods for recording those uncollectibles. One is called direct write-off method. Under this method, bad debt expense is recorded when an account is determined to be uncollectible and no adjustment entry is recorded at the end of the period to estimate uncollectibles. Any entry to write off the uncollectible account is as follows:

Dr: Uncollectible Accounts Expense　　　　　　× × × ×
　　Cr: Accounts Receivable　　　　　　　　　　× × × ×

The advantage of this method is that it is simple and convenient to apply, and the deficiency of this method lies in that it mismatches revenues and expenses unless the write-off occurs in the same period as the related sales.

As there is no way of telling in advance which accounts receivable will prove to be uncollectible, it is not possible to credit the accounts of specific customers for our estimate of probable uncollectible accounts. Therefore, another practical alternative is to credit a separate account, known as Allowance for Uncollectible Accounts, with the amount estimated to be uncollectible. This method estimates the total bad debts that are expected to result from the sales in the current period, and records the expense during the same period as the related sale. For example, a company estimates that ¥1 000 of the accounts receivable will be uncollectible. Therefore, a debit of ¥1 000 is made to Uncollectible Accounts Expense (or doubtful accounts expense or bad debt expense) and a credit of ¥1 000 is made to Allowance for Uncollectible Accounts. So any entry like that is as follows:

Dr: Uncollectible Accounts Expense　　　　　　× × × ×
　　Cr: Allowance for Uncollectible Accounts　　× × × ×

This is the theoretically correct method. The advantage of this method is that it follows conservatism, which understates the assets and revenues, and overstates the liabilities and expenses. The estimates are based on the following three methods.

First, it is the percentage-of-sales approach, which is also called income statement approach. This method is widely used for estimating uncollectible accounts in practice, because it is simple to apply. Businesses often use this method to estimate uncollectibles periodically during the year and then adjust the allowance account at year-end in relationship to the accounts receivable balance. When this basis is used, the amount of uncollectible accounts in past years relative to total sales provides a percentage of estimated uncollectibles. This percentage may be modified by expectations based on current experience. Since doubtful accounts occur only with credit sales, it would seem logical to develop a percentage of doubtful accounts to credit sales of past periods. This percentage is then applied to credit sales of the current period. To illustrate, if 2% of sales are considered doubtful in terms of collection and sales for the period are ¥100 000, the charge for Uncollectible Accounts Expense would be 2% of the current period's sales, or ¥2 000. The entry for this period would be simply:

Dr: Uncollectible Accounts Expense　　　　　2 000
　　Cr: Allowance for Uncollectible Accounts　　2 000

Second, it is the percentage-of-receivables. Instead of using a percentage of sales to estimate uncollectible accounts, companies may base their estimates on a percentage of total accounts receivable outstanding. This method emphasizes the relationship between the accounts receivable balance and the allowance for doubtful accounts. For example, if total accounts receivable are ¥50 000 and it is estimated that 3% of those accounts will be uncollectible, then the allowance account should have a balance of ¥1 500(¥50 000×3%). If the allowance account already has a ¥600 credit balance from prior periods, then the current-period adjusting entry would be:

  Dr:Uncollectible Accounts Expense   900
    Cr:Allowance for Uncollectible Accounts 900

  Third, it is aging schedule (or aging method). This method classifies outstanding accounts receivable in terms of how long each has been outstanding. The aging of accounts receivable method applies a percentage to each class to estimate the amount of total receivables due that will not be collected. This method is the most commonly used method, and is more reliable, because it draws attention to the specific accounts that are actually past due. Individual accounts are analyzed to determine those not yet due and those past due. Past-due accounts are classified in terms of the length of the period past due. An analysis of accounts receivable based on past experience indicates that the following bad debt losses are likely to occur for each group:

Age Interval	Percent uncollectible
0~30 days	2%
31~60 days	4%
61~90 days	10%
Over 90 days	30%

On December 31, 2010, the following aged accounts receivable information is available:

Age Interval	Amount Uncollectible	Percent	Allowance
0~30 days (past due)	25 000	2%	500
31~60 days	15 000	4%	600
61~90 days	5 000	10%	500
Over 90 days	3 000	30%	900
Total	48 000		2 500

Assume that the existing unadjusted balance in the allowance for uncollectible accounts is ￥1 000(credit). Just as with the previous method based on a percentage of total receivables outstanding, Uncollectible Accounts Expense is debited and Allowance for Uncollectible Accounts is credited for an amount bringing the allowance account to the required balance.

The adjusting entry would be:

Dr:Uncollectible Accounts Expense   1 500

    Cr:Allowance for Uncollectible Accounts   1 500

This method provides the most satisfactory approach to the valuation of receivables at their net realizable amounts. Furthermore, data developed through aging receivables may be quite useful to management for purposes of credit analysis and control. On the other hand, application of aging method may involve considerable time and cost.

The percentage-of-receivables and the aging method are also called balance sheet method. They are both focus on the total estimated uncollectibles, which is the balance in allowance for uncollectible accounts.

The difference between the percentage-of-sales approach and the balance sheet approach lies in whether the balance of the allowance for uncollectible accounts in prior accounting period needs to be considered in current period or not. Under the income statement approach, the accountants don't need to consider the balance in the allowance in prior year, whereas under the balance sheet approach, the accountants must calculate the current balance of allowance for uncollectible accounts, which should equal to the amount of allowance, happened in current accounting period deducting or adding the balance of prior accounting period.

5.3 Inventory

Inventory refers to merchandise, finished goods, semi-finished goods, goods in process, and all kinds of materials, and so on that held for sale in the normal course of business and in the case of a manufacturer, goods in production or to be placed in production. In other words, it is composed of the items that have been purchased in order to be sold. For example, in a supermarket, milk is its inventory, but a shopping cart is not. In a manufacturing company, there are three different types of inventory: raw materials, work in process, and finished goods.

Raw materials are the basic materials from which a product is manufactured or made. For a knife company, one of the raw materials is steel. Raw materials can be obtained directly from natural sources; however, most of them are purchased from other companies and represent the finished products of the suppliers. For a paper factory, high-quality, acid-free paper is its finished product, while for a book publishing company it is the raw material.

Work in process includes a large of unfinished items for products in a production process. These items are not yet completed but either just being fabricated or waiting in a queue for further processing. The term is used in production and supply chain management.

Something bought as a "raw material" is used to manufacture a product. A thing that is not completed during the manufacturing process is called "work in process". When the manufacturing of the thing is completed but it is not yet sold or distributed to the end-user, then it is called a "finished goods", such as cars, computers, which are the manufactured products awaiting sale.

Inventory costs consist of all costs involved in purchasing the inventories and preparing them for sale. Proper calculation of inventory cost is absolutely critical for making production, pricing, and strategy decisions. All costs incurred in producing and getting inventories ready to sell should be added to inventory cost. The costs associated with the selling effort itself are expenses of the period. Companies record inventories at their original costs. The costs of inventory items include all expenditure for the goods incurred to their existing condition and location. The costs consist of the invoice price, transportation-in, insurance while in transit and other expense for the goods to the place of business.

The inventory figure appears in both the balance sheet and the income statement. In the balance sheet, the inventory is often the largest current asset. In the income statement, the ending inventory is subtracted from the cost of goods available for sale to determine the cost of goods sold during the period. How can a business determine, at the end of a year, a month, or other accounting period, the quantity and the cost of the goods remaining on hand?

How can management determine the cost of the goods sold during the period? These amounts must be determined before either a balance sheet or an income statement can be prepared. In fact, the determination of inventory value and of the cost of goods sold may be the most important single step in measuring the profitability of a business. There are two methods that are used to determine the inventory quantity as well as the cost of goods sold and the two alternative approaches to the determination of inventory and of cost of goods sold are called the perpetual inventory system and the periodic inventory system.

Consider the last time you made a purchase. Did the business where you made the purchase keep a record of what item they sold you, or did they just record the selling price? With a traditional cash register system, the seller records only the sales price; the seller has no record of how many units of a particular inventory item have been sold. Accountants call this type of system a periodic inventory system, because the only way to verify what inventory has been sold and what remains is to do a periodic physical count.

Under the periodic inventory system, the enterprises do not need to keep a continuous record of the inventory on hand, and at the end of accounting period, the enterprises make physical count of the inventory on hand and apply the unit cost to determine the cost of the ending inventory. And when it is used, inventory purchases are recorded as they occur, but the ending balance in the inventory account and cost of goods sold is not determined until the end of the period after an inventory count is taken. This method is often used for relatively inexpensive goods. A convenience store without cash registers does not keep a daily running record of every loaf of bread and every key chain that it sells. Instead, the business counts its inventory at some regular interval to determine the quantities on hand. Restaurants and small retails stores also use the periodic system which is becoming less and less popular as more businesses keep their inventory records by computer.

Example 5.1 ABC company purchased $4 000 merchandise on credit on June 4. Later the company sold the merchandise $5 000 on account and cost of goods sold is $3,000 on June 16. At the end of June, it took a physical inventory and found its ending inventory was $900 (assuming beginning inventory was $300).

On June 4, the entry is:

Dr. Merchandise Inventory	4 000	
Cr. Accounts Payable		4 000

On June 16, the entry should be:

Dr. Accounts Receivable	5 000	
Cr. Prime Operating Revenues		5 000

At the end of the month, the gross margin should be $1 600, that is:

$$[5\ 000 - (4\ 000 + 300 - 900)] = 1\ 600$$

The alternative to a periodic system is a perpetual inventory system. Under perpetual inventory system, an enterprise keeps a continuous record in the inventory account, recording inventory when items are sold, and both the selling price and the type of item sold are recorded for each sale. This system achieves control over the inventory. A barcode scanning system is an example of a perpetual inventory system. When an enterprise chooses this system, the seller knows the number of each item sold and the number that should still be in inventory. Even in a perpetual system, the enterprise counts inventory at least once a year. The physical count establishes the correct amount of ending inventory for the financial statements and also serves as a check on the perpetual records. For example, it is useful in revealing the amount of inventory shrinkage—inventory lost, stolen, or spoiled.

Example 5.2 Just as the above-mentioned Example 5.1, under perpetual inventory system, the entry is the same on June 4. On June 16, the entry should be:

Dr. Accounts Receivable		5 000
Cr. Prime Operating Revenues		5 000
Dr. Cost of Goods Sold		3 000
Cr. Merchandise Inventory		3 000

The gross margin at the moment sold inventory is $2,000 ($5 000 - $3 000).

The following illustrates the comparison between the periodic inventory system and the perpetual inventory system.

◆Periodic Inventory System:

① does not keep a running record of all goods bought and sold.

② inventory counted at least once a year.

◆Perpetual Inventory System:

① keeps a running records of all goods bought and sold.

② inventory counted at least once a year.

Before the widespread use of computers in accounting, only companies that sold a limited number of products of relatively high value used periodical inventory systems. However, since computers have made the record-keeping chore much easier, an increasing number of firms are switching from periodic to perpetual system.

Once a year, businesses take the physical inventory count required by a periodic system. However, most businesses need more current information about their inventory levels to protect against stockouts or over-purchasing and to aid in preparation of monthly or quarterly financial data. As a consequence, many businesses take advantage of a modified perpetual inventory system. This system provides detailed inventory records of increases and decreases in quantities only—on dollar amounts. It is only a memorandum device outside the double-entry system, which helps in determining the level of inventory at any point in time.

Whether a business keeps a perpetual system in quantities and dollars amounts or in quantities only, or has no perpetual inventory record at all, it probably takes a physical inventory once a year. No matter what type of inventory records businesses use, they all face the danger of loss and error. Waste, breakage, theft, improper entry, failure to prepare or record requisitions, and other similar possibilities may cause the inventory records to differ from the actual inventory on hand. As a result, all businesses need periodic verification of the inventory records by actual count, weight, or measurement, with the counts compared with the detailed inventory records. A company corrects the records to agree with the quantities actually on hand.

Insofar as possible, businesses should take the physical inventory near the end of their fiscal year, to properly report inventory quantities in their annual accounting reports. Because this is not always possible, however, physical inventories taken within two or three months of the year would be satisfactory, if a business keeps detailed inventory records with a fair degree of accuracy.

Inventories are normally accounted for at historical cost, as the cost principle requires. Historical cost of inventory purchased includes the purchase consideration, transportation, loading and unloading, expenses, insurance, reasonable damage or loss incurred in transit, preparatory expenses incurred before warehousing and taxes payable. There are four generally acceptable methods that a company may use to account for inventories: specific identification; first-in, first-out (FIFO); last-in, first-out (LIFO); weighted average.

Specific identification, which is also called specific-unit-cost method, is usually used when a company buys goods that are easy to identify. Suppose Elmon Music Company acquires three 64-inch TV sets at costs of $700, $750, and $800, respectively. During the year, two sets are sold at $1 200 each. On December 31, the $750 set is still on hand. The ending inventory is $750, and the cost of goods sold is $1 500 ($700 + $800).

This method most naturally fits operations that involve somewhat differentiated products of a relatively high unit value. This kind of items could be ships, airplanes, equipment, automobiles, jewels, and real estate, etc. When we use this method, it is always because that some specific cost is an important determinant of the sales prices and because the goods are unique. That is to say, specific identification is almost feasible when the volume of sales is low and the cost of individual items is high. This method may appear logical, and it might be used in the purchase and sale of high-priced articles, such as automobiles and works of art, but it is not used by many companies because of two definite disadvantages. First, it is often difficult and impractical to keep track of the purchase and sale of individual items. Second, when a company deals in items that are identical but that it bought at different costs, deciding which items were sold becomes arbitrary, thus, the company can raise or lower income by choosing the lower- or higher-cost items.

FIFO method assumes that first goods purchased are the first goods sold so that the ending inventory is priced at the latest purchase price. In these cases, FIFO most nearly matches the flow of costs to the probable flow of goods. For example, ABC Company sells computers and at a moment it had four identical MAC on hand—two MAC costing $ 6 000 each (that were purchased first) and two same type of MAC costing $ 8 000 each (that were bought by the company after the first ones). Customers do not care which one to buy since the four computers and prices are totally the same. If the company wants to increase its cost of goods sold, it will use $ 8 000 as the cost of goods sold.

The distinguishing feature of this method is that the oldest purchased are transferred to the cost of the goods sold, while the most recent costs remain in inventory. Over the last few year, we have lived in an inflationary economy, which means that most prices tend to rise over time. When purchase costs are rising, the FIFO method assigns lower costs to the cost of goods sold and the higher (more recent) costs to the goods remaining in inventory. By assigning lower costs to the cost of goods sold, FIFO usually causes a business to report somewhat higher profits than would be reported under the other inventory valuation methods. Some companies favor the FIFO method for financial reporting purposes, because their goal is to report the highest net income possible. For income tax purposes, however, reporting more income than necessary results in paying more income taxes than necessary.

LIFO is that the cost of the inventories purchased last is charged to the cost of goods sold. This method is based on the assumption that the units sold are the last items received. During a period of rising prices, the use of the last-in, first-out method will result in a less amount of net profit than the other methods and that is regarded as the most conservative of the inventory methods during a period of rising prices. The reason is that the cost of the most recently bought goods most nearly approximates their cost of replacement. Therefore, it can be argued that the use of this method matches current costs with current revenues. There is also the practical advantage of a saving in income taxes. In a period of deflation or falling price levels, the effect described above is reversed and the LIFO method yields the highest amount of net profit.

In the example above, the cost of goods sold would be $ 8 000. This approach does not match the usual flow of goods in a business and it is canceled in our country now.

Weighted average method is sometimes called average-cost method. This method means that the average unit cost is included in the cost of goods sold and it is based on the assumption that goods sold should be charged at an average cost, with the average being weighted by the number of units acquired at each price. In other words, to determine the weighted average cost, you need to add all the costs of the inventories on hand and divide the result by the number of inventories. This approach is best suited to operations that involve a large volume of undifferentiated goods stored in common areas. In the example above, it would be:

$$(6\ 000 \times 2 + 8\ 000 \times 2) / 4 = 7\ 000$$

Exercises

Exercises 5.1 Multiple Choice

1. The inventory costing method that is based on the assumption that costs should be charged against revenue in the order in which they were incurred is ( )
   A. FIFO   B. LIFO
   C. Average Cost   D. Perpetual Inventory
2. The cost of ABC company on inventory purchase is $ 250 000 during the year and its ending inventory is $ 20 000, its beginning inventory of $ 100 000. The com-

pany's cost of goods sold is _____.　　　　　　　　　　　　(　　)
   A. $ 170 000　　　　　　　　　　B. $ 270 000
   C. $ 330 000　　　　　　　　　　D. $ 370 000
3. If merchandise inventory is being valued at cost and the price level is steadily rising, the method of costing that will yield the highest net income is _____.
　　　　　　　　　　　　　　　　　　　　　　　　　　　　　　(　　)
   A. LIFO　　　　　　　　　　　　B. FIFO
   C. Average Cost　　　　　　　　　D. Periodic Inventory
4. The accounts receivable of ABC company has a balance of $ 100 000 and allowance for doubtful accounts has a balance of $ 7 000 at the end of a fiscal year. The expected net realizable value of the accounts receivable is _____.
　　　　　　　　　　　　　　　　　　　　　　　　　　　　　　(　　)
   A. $ 7 000　　　　　　　　　　　B. $ 93 000
   C. $ 100 000　　　　　　　　　　D. $ 107 000
5. _____ is the most liquid asset of a business and a large portion of the total transactions of a business involves the receipt or disbursement of it.　　(　　)
   A. Cash　　　　　　　　　　　　B. Liability
   C. Inventory　　　　　　　　　　D. Notes
6. There are two methods for recording the uncollectible. One is called _____ and another is _____.　　　　　　　　　　　　　　　　　　(　　)
   A. LIFO; FIFO
   B. periodic system; perpetual system
   C. average method; LIFO
   D. direct write-off method; allowance method
7. Which items are not included in computing cost of goods sold?　　(　　)
   A. Ending inventory.　　　　　　　B. Freight-in.
   C. Beginning balance.　　　　　　D. Beginning inventory.
8. In a supermarket, _____ is its inventory, but _____ is not.　(　　)
   A. milk; a shopping cart　　　　　B. bread; milk

C. a shopping cart; milk   D. none of them

9. For a chair manufacturing company, _____ is not its raw material.   (   )
   A. wood   B. nail
   C. plastic   D. screw driver

10. Merchandise inventory includes: (   )
    A. all goods owned by a company and held for sale.
    B. all goods in transit.
    C. all goods on consignment.
    D. only damaged goods.

Exercises 5.2   Record the Following Transactions.

1. On December 10, (1) ABC Company purchased 100 units of inventory on account for $20 per unit; (2) on December 20, the company sold 50 units of inventory for cash at $30 per unit. (using periodic method)

2. ABC Company (1) recognized $4 000 of sales revenue earned on account; (2) collected $2 000 cash from accounts receivable; (3) recognized $800 of bad debt expense for accounts receivable that are expected to be uncollectible in the future.

3. The balance of ABC Company is $600 000 and the Allowance for Doubtful Debt is $300 at the end of 2011. The percentage is 0.3%. At 2012, the balance of ABC Company is $500 000, Allowance for Doubtful Debt is $2 000. Record adjusting entry for 2011 and 2012.

Exercises 5.3   Translations

1. In the balance sheet, cash is listed first among the current assets, because it is the most current and liquid of all assets.

2. Prepaid expenses shall be amortized according to period benefiting, and the balance shall be shown separately in accounting statement.

3. Accountants define cash a money on deposit in banks and any items that banks will accepts for immediate deposit. These items include not only coins and paper money,

but also checks and money orders. On the other hand, notes receivable, IOUs, and postdated checks are not accepted for immediate deposit and are not included in the accountant's definition of cash.

4. 有价证券应按取得时的实际成本记账，应当以账面余额在会计报表中列示。当期的有价证券收益，以及有价证券转让所取得的收入与账面成本的差额，计入当期损益。

5. 在生产性企业，存货主要包括三个类别：原材料、在产品和产成品。在资产负债表中，这三项存货均包括在流动资产部分。

Unit Six

Non-Current Assets

Teaching Objectives

Upon completion of this chapter, you will:
1. Know the concept of non-current assets, including long-term investment, fixed assets, and intangible assets.
2. Master the of the types of long-term investment: investments in equity securities.
3. Know the four mainly used depreciation methods: straight-line method, units-of-production method, sum-of-the-years'-digits (SYD) method and double-declining balance method.
4. Know the main forms of intangible assets, such as copyright, patents, trademark, trade names, and franchise.

Vocabulary

long-term assets	长期资产
depreciation	折旧
freight costs	运费
fair market value	公允价值
capital expenditures	资本性开支
revenue expenditures	收益性开支
depreciation base	折旧基数
the original cost	原始成本
the salvage value	残值
straight-line method	直线法
sum-of-the-years' digits method	年限总和法
declining balance method	余额递减法

the double-declining balance method	双倍余额递减法
book value	账面价值
scrap value	残值
long-term investment	长期投资
investment in equity securities	股权投资
investment in debt securities	债权投资
cost method	成本法
equity method	权益法
consolidation	合并报表
investee	被投资人
franchises	特许经营；特许权
trademark	商标
tangible assets	有形资产
plant assets	固定资产
operating expense	经营费用
useful life	使用年限
residual value	残值
amortization	摊销
wear out	磨损
installation cost	安装费
depreciation method	折旧方法
accelerated methods	加速折旧法
carrying value	账面价值
acquisition cost	购置成本
depreciation rate	折旧率
physical substance	实物形态
depreciable amount	应计折旧金额
impairment	减值

TEXT

Compared with current assets such as cash, bank accounts, inventory, and accounts receivable which are described as liquid assets and expected to be turned into cash within one year, non-current assets are not expected to be fully realized or consumed within a year or the company's operating cycle, whichever is longer. Instead, those assets will be consumed within a period longer than a year of their acquisition, so non-current assets are also called long-term assets. Characterized by high economic value, many accounting periods, and a wide range of forms, those non-current assets refer to long-lived assets that are consumed in the operation of a business and are not intended for sale to customers.

Non-current assets normally may be further divided into the following three classes: firstly, long-term investments; secondly, fixed assets (or property, plant, and equipment, also called PPE); thirdly, intangible assets (without physical substance).

6.1 Long-term Investment

A company may invest excess cash not needed for current operations in securities consisting of stocks or bonds of another company. The investments purchased with the intention of holding them for more than a year are long-term investments on a balance sheet. There are two features of long-term investments, compared with short-term investments. Firstly, the pay-off period is over a year. Secondly, to affect and control the companies invested to realize long-term strategy of development to accumulate matching amount of fund to meet special needs of the business is the main goal of investments.

There are normally two aspects about long-term investment, that is, investments in equity securities and investments in debt securities. Equity securities are described as securities representing ownership interests such as common, preferred or other capital stock. When equity securities are purchased, their costs include the purchase price of the securities plus other fees related to the purchase, such as brokerage fees, transfer costs, and taxes.

1. Investments in Equity Securities

Accounting for those investments in equity securities includes cost method, equity method and the consolidation. When using cost method, the percentage of stock that the investors held should be less than 20%. In this case, the investor has little or no influence over the investee. Under this method, an investment in equity securities is carried at its historical cost, and revenue is recorded and reported as dividends received. The cost method is criticized because it does not measure current fair value.

To illustrate, assume that ABC Company purchased 5 000 shares of XYZ Company as long-term investment, $20 per share, on January 20, 2009. The total amount is $100 000, which is 10% of the investee's total capital. At the end of 2009, XYZ Company reported a net profit of $200 000, including $50 000 as dividends distributed and ABC Company received dividends $20 000. In 2011, ABC Company sold those stocks at the price of $30. The entries to record this transaction would be as follows:

On Jan. 20, 2009, shares were purchased:

Dr: Long-term Investment in Equity Securities—Cost	100 000
Cr: Cash in Bank	100 000

At the end of 2011, dividends were received:

Dr: Cash in Bank	20 000
Cr: Dividend Receivable	20 000

In 2011, shares were sold:

Dr: Cash in Bank	150 000
Cr: Long-term Investment—Stock Investment	100 000
Investments Income—Stock Investment	50 000

When using equity method, the investor's holdings should between 20% and 50%. In this case, the investor has a significant influence over the operating and financial policies or decisions of the company it has invested in. Ability to exercise significant influence can be determined in a number of ways, including representation on the board of directors, participation in policy making processes, intercompany material and interchange of managerial personnel. Given this influence, the investor adjusts the value of its equity investment for dividends received from, and the earnings (or losses) of, the corporation whose stock has been purchased. The dividends received are accounted for as a reduction of the investment value because dividends are a partial return of the investor's investment.

To illustrate, assume The Sisters, Inc. acquired 30% of the stock of ABC GROUP for $72 000 on Jan. 1, 2010. During the year, ABC GROUP paid dividends totaling $30 000 and had net income of $150 000. Under the equity method, the $9 000 in dividends ($30 000 × 30%) received by The Sisters, Inc. would decrease the Investment in ABC GROUP account rather than be reported as dividend revenue. The same account would increase $45 000 for The Sisters, Inc. 30% share of net income ($150 000 × 30%) as they treat their share of net income as revenue. At the end of the year, the balance in the Investment in ABC GROUP account would be $108 000.

The entries by The Sisters, Inc. to record the acquisition of ABC GROUP stock, receipt of dividends, and share of net income are as follows.

On Jan. 1, 2010, acquiring 30% of ABC GROUP stock:
Dr:Long-term Investment in Equity Securities—Investment Cost   72 000
　Cr:Cash in Bank   72 000

On Dec. 31, 2010, dividends received—ABC GROUP
Dr:Cash in Bank   9 000
　Cr:Long-term Investment in Equity Securities—Profit and Loss Adjustment
                                                                9 000

On Dec. 31, 2010, share of net income—ABC GROUP
Dr:Long—term Investment in Equity Securities—Profit and Loss Adjustment
                                                                45 000
　Cr:Investment Profits   45 000

When using consolidation, the investor's holdings should be 50% or beyond 50%.

In this case, the investor has a controlling interest over the investee, and the two entities as one are prepared consolidated financial statements for accounting purposes.

The company that owns greater than 50% of another entity is called the parent company, while the company whose stock is owned is called the subsidiary company. A parent company uses the equity method to account for its investment in its subsidiary. When financial statements are prepared, the assets and liabilities (balance sheet), revenues and expenses (income statement), and cash flows (cash flow statement) of both the parent company and subsidiary company are combined and are shown in the same statements.

These statements are called consolidated balance sheets, consolidated income statements, and consolidated cash flow statements—together they are called consolidated financial statements—and represent the financial position, results of operations, and cash flows of the parent company and any other companies it controls.

2. Investments in Debt Securities

Long-term investment in debt securities is another form of long-term term investment. The so-called debt securities normally are investments in bonds issued by the government or a corporation, which include government securities, municipal securities, corporate bonds, convertible debt, and all securitized debt instruments.

At the time of purchasing a bond, the acquisition costs vary with different forms of purchasing: at face value, a premium, or a discount. Any dividends received on interest that received on bond investments are classified as Other Revenue on an income statement because they do not represent revenue earned from operations.

When purchasing a long-term investment in bonds, we debited an asset account entitled Long-term Investment in Bonds, and any premium or discount is amortized whenever bond interest earned is recorded. Amortization of a premium requires a credit to the investment account and amortization of a discount requires debit to the investment account, therefore, on the maturity date of bonds, the investment account will have a balance that is equal to the face value of the bonds.

For example, if ABC Company purchases five of the 10%, ten-year $1 000 bonds issued by XYZ Company on July 1, 2010 for $5 000 and pays broker's fees of $50, the entry to record the purchases would include both the purchase price and broker's fees in the cost of the investment.

July 1, 2010, purchase of XYZ Company bonds:
Dr:Held-to-Maturity Investment-Cost   5 050
    Cr:Cash   5 050

The bonds pay interest every December 31 and June 30. When the semiannual interest is received on December 31, 2010, the entry to record cash increases (debits) and increases (credits) of the interest revenue for $250 (5 000 × 10% ×6/12).

Dec. 31, 2010, Interest earned on bonds:
Dr:Cash   250
    Cr:Investment Income   250

6.2 Fixed Assets

Fixed assets are also called property, plant, and equipment assets (known as PPE), which are long-term or relatively permanent tangible assets used in the normal business operations. They are owned by the business and are not held for sale in normal operations. Real estate, building structure (offices, factories, warehouses), automobiles, and equipment (machinery, furniture, tools) are good examples of fixed assets.

Fixed assets are titles used to classify tangible non-current assets that a company uses in the normal operations of its business. Alternative terms are plant assets, and operational assets. To be included in this category, an asset must have three characteristics:

Firstly, the asset must be held for use and not for investment. Only assets used in the normal course of business should be included. However, the asset does not have to be used continuously; therefore machinery owned for standby purpose in case of breakdown is included. In contrast, idle land or buildings should not be included and should be categorized separately as an investment.

Secondly, the asset must have an expected life of more than one year. The asset represents a bundle of future service that the company will receive over the life of the asset. To be included in property, plant, and equipment, the benefits must extend for more than one year or the operating cycle, whichever is longer.

Thirdly, the asset must be tangible in nature. There must be a physical substance that can be seen and touched. In contrast, intangible assets such as goodwill or patents do not have a physical substance. Unlike raw materials, generally, property, plant, and equipment do not change their physical characteristics and are not incorporated into the product. That is to say, fixed assets are existing entities which can be felt. They are different from intangible assets, accounts receivable, and other receivables.

Fixed assets are mainly classified into two groups: depreciable assets and non-depreciable assets. Depreciable assets are fixed assets with physical substance, which are expected to be used during more than one accounting period and have limited useful life. The objective of depreciation is to allocate the cost of each fixed asset as expense with reasonable and systematic distribution methods and among the economic years in which it is used. The expense should be recorded in income statement to identify the profit or loss of enterprises correctly. For example, buildings, equipment, and machinery all belong to depreciable assets. Non-depreciable assets include the fixed assets which have been finished depreciating and continue to be used, the land which is valued separately and recorded as fixed asset and the fixed asset held for sale.

1. Acquisition Costs of Fixed Assets

When a transaction is made for cash, cost is easy to determine. In this case, the asset is the cash paid for it plus the possible expenditures for freight, insurance while in transit, installation, and other necessary related costs. If a debt incurred in the purchase of the asset, the interest charges are not a cost of the asset but are a cost of borrowing the money to buy the asset. They are, therefore, an expense for the period. An exception to this principle is that interest costs during the construction of an asset are properly included as a cost of the asset.

The acquisition costs of fixed assets include all expenditures reasonable and necessary to get them in place and ready for use. Expenditures such as freight, insurance while in transit, and installation are included in the cost of the asset because these expenditures are necessary for the asset to function. Costs not necessary for getting an asset ready for use do not increase the asset's usefulness and should not be included in its cost. For example, the cost of installing and testing a machine is a legitimate cost of the machine; however, if the machine is damaged during installation, the cost of repairing it is an operating expense rather than a cost of the machine.

In conclusion, the costs of acquiring fixed assets include sales taxes, freight, installation, repairs (used assets), reconditioning (used assets), insurance while asset is in transit, assembling, modifying for use, testing for use, and permits from government agencies. On the other hand, the costs of fixed assets exclude costs of vandalism, mistakes in installation, uninsured theft, damage during unpacking and installing and fines for not obtaining proper permits from government agencies.

2. Depreciation

Land has an unlimited life and therefore can provide unlimited services. On the other hand, other fixed assets such equipment, buildings lose their ability as time goes by, to provide services. As a result, the costs of equipment, buildings should be transferred to expense accounts in a systematic manner during their expected useful lives. This periodic cost expiration is called depreciation. In other words, fixed assets can bring certain economic benefits to businesses in the future; however, the service potentials are limited. With the use of fixed assets in operating, the service potentials will decrease and even disappear. Depreciation is a way to measure and reflect these changes of service potentials. Depreciation differs from most expenses in that it does not require a cash payment when it is recorded. That is to say, depreciation does not influence cash flows, but it does affect the current profit or loss.

The basic objective of depreciation is to achieve the matching principle, that is to say, to offset the revenue of an accounting period with the costs of the goods and services being consumed in the effort to generate that revenue.

There are mainly two factors causing a decline in the ability of a fixed asset to provide services. One is physical depreciation caused by wear and tear from use and from the action of the elements decreases usefulness. The other one is functional depreciation caused by inadequacy and obsolescence decreases usefulness.

Depreciation during each fiscal period measures the amount of the asset cost or expense charged to that period. The entry to record depreciation expense consists of a debit to Depreciation Expense and a credit to Accumulated Depreciation. When determining the amount of depreciation expense, three factors are considered. These three factors are the fixed asset's initial cost, its expected useful life, and its estimated value at the end of its useful life. The last factor is also called the residual value, scrap value, salvage value. For the methods used in computing depreciation expense, there are a number of different types. In practice, the four mainly used depreciation methods are straight-line method, units-of-production method, sum-of-the-years'-digits method, and double-declining balance method. These four methods are illustrated as follows.

(1) **Straight-line Method**

The straight line method is the most extensively used and most conservative method to compute depreciation charge. This method is based on the assumption that depreciation depends only on the passage of time, and asset's economic revenue is the same each year. Besides, the repair and maintenance cost is also the same for each period. Under the straight-line method, the depreciation expense is allocated equally to each period of the asset's useful life. Thus the depreciation amount is the same for each year. The formula of this method is as follows:

$$\text{Annual depreciation amount} = \frac{\text{Original Cost-Estimated Net Residual Value}}{\text{Estimated Years of Useful Life}}$$

Example 6.1 Assume that a company's automobile costs $10 000 and has an estimated residual value of $1 000 at the end of its estimated useful life of five years. In this case, the annual depreciation would be 20 percent of depreciable cost or $1 800 under the straight-line method. This calculation is $1 800 ((10 000 − 1 000)/5).

The straight-line method is particularly suitable for buildings, machinery, pipelines, etc.

(2) **Units-of-production Method**

This units-of-production method determines depreciation expense based on the amount the asset is used. The length of life of an asset is expressed in a form of productive capacity. The initial cost less any residual value is divided by productive capacity to determine a rate of unit-of-production depreciation per unit of usage. Units of usage can be expressed in quantity of goods produced, hours used, number of cuttings, miles driven or tons hauled, for instance.

The depreciation expense of a period is determined by multiplying usage by a fixed unit-of-production rate of usage. This depreciation method is commonly used when asset usage varies from year-to-year.

The following formula is used to calculate depreciation under this method:

$$\text{Depreciation Amount} = \frac{\text{Number of Units Produced}}{\text{Life in Number of Units}} \times (\text{Original Cost} - \text{Salvage Value})$$

Example 6.2 A plant costing $110 million was purchased on April 1, 2010. The salvage value was estimated to be $10 million. The expected production was 150 million units. The plant was used to produce 15 million units till the year ended December 31, 2010. Calculate the depreciation on the plant for the year ended December 31, 2011.

Solution:

Depreciation = (15/150) × ($110 million − $10 million) = $10 million

This method is similar to straight-line method except that life of the asset is estimated in terms of number of operations or number of machine hours etc.

(3) Sum-of-the-years'-digits (SYD) Method

Sum of the years' digits method of depreciation is one of the accelerated depreciation techniques which are based on the assumption that assets are generally more productive when they are new and their productivity decreases as they become old. The formula to calculate depreciation under SYD method is:

$$\text{SYD Depreciation} = \text{Depreciable Base} \times \frac{\text{Remaining Useful Life}}{\text{Sum of the Years' Digits}}$$

In the above formula, depreciable base is the difference between original cost and salvage value of the asset and sum of the years' digits is the sum of the series:
1, 2, 3, $\cdots$, n; where "n" is the useful life of the asset in years.

Sum of the years' digits can be calculated more conveniently using the following formula:

$$\text{Sum of the Years' Digits} = \frac{n(n+1)}{2}$$

Example 6.3 If an asset has original cost of \$1 000, a useful life of 5 years and a salvage value of \$100, compute its depreciation schedule.

Solution:

First, determine years' digits. Since the asset has useful life of 5 years, the years' digits are: 5, 4, 3, 2, and 1.

Next, calculate the sum of the digits: $5 + 4 + 3 + 2 + 1 = 15$.

The sum of the digits can also be determined by using the formula $n(n+1)/2$ where n is equal to the useful life of the asset. The example would be shown as $5(5+1)/2 = 15$.

Depreciation rates are as follows:

5/15 for the 1st year, 4/15 for the 2nd year, 3/15 for the 3rd year, 2/15 for the 4th year, and 1/15 for the 5th year.

Table 6.1 Calculate the Depreciation Expense at the End of Year unit: $

Book Value at Beginning of Year	Total Depreciable Cost	Depreciation Rate	Depreciation Expense	Accumulated Depreciation	Book Value at End of Year
1 000 (Original Cost)	900	5/15	300 (900×5/15)	300	700
700	900	4/15	240 (900×4/15)	540	460
460	900	3/15	180 (900×3/15)	720	280
280	900	2/15	120 (900×2/15)	840	160
160	900	1/15	60 (900×1/15)	900	100 (Scrap Value)

(4) Double-declining Balance Method

Declining-balance method utilizes a depreciation rate that is some multiple of the straight-line method. When the rate is two times of the straight-line depreciation rate, we call it double-declining balance method. Thus when straight-line depreciation rate is 8%, double declining balance rate will be 2 × 8% = 16%. In other words, using this method, the Book Value (or Carrying Value) at the beginning of each period is multiplied by a fixed Depreciation Rate which is 200% of the straight line depreciation rate, or a factor of 2.

The double-declining balance method is a popular form of accelerated depreciation. This method does not consider the estimated salvage value in determining the depreciation rate or in computing the periodic depreciation. However, an asset cannot be depreciated beyond the estimated salvage value. Depreciation expense is highest in the first year, and becomes smaller each subsequent year.

Declining balance depreciation is calculated by the following formula:

Depreciation Amount = Depreciation Rate × Book Value of Asset

Depreciation rate is given by following formula:

Depreciation Rate = 2 × Straight-line Rate

To illustrate the double-declining balance method, here is another example:

Suppose a business has an asset with $1 000 original cost, $100 salvage value, and 5 years useful life.

First, calculate straight-line depreciation rate. Since the asset has 5 years useful life, the straight-line depreciation rate equals (100%/5) 20% per year. With double-declining balance method, as the name suggests, double that rate, or 40% depreciation rate is used.

The table below illustrates the double-declining balance method of depreciation.

Table 6.2 Calculation of the Depreciation Expense Using Double-declining Balance Method

unit: $

Book value at beginning of year	Depreciation rate	Depreciation expense	Accumulated depreciation	Book value at end of year
1 000 (original cost)	40%	400	400	600
600	40%	240	640	360
360	40%	144	784	216
216	20%	58	842	158
158	20%	58	900	100 (scrap value)

Calcuate the Depraciation Expense Using Dpuble delining Balance Method.

Note that the fixed rate is always applied to the carrying value of the previous year. Next, the depreciation is greatest in the first year and declines each year after that. Finally, the depreciation in the last year is limited to the amount necessary to reduce carrying value to salvage value. For the depreciation in the last year, a subtraction might be needed in order to prevent book value from falling below estimated Scrap Value.

Both the sum-of-the-years'-digits method and double-declining balance method belong to accelerated depreciation method, which results in higher charges to depreciation expense in the early years of the asset's life and, therefore, lower reported net income than straight-line depreciation in those early years. These methods, which are based on the passage of time, assume that many kinds of plant assets are most efficient when new, so they provide more and better services in the early years of useful life. It is consistent with the matching rule to allocate more depreciation to the early years than to later years, if the benefits or services received in the early years are greater.

6.3 Intangible Assets

The term intangible assets is used to describe assets which are used in the operation of the business but no physical substance, and are non-current. Current assets such as accounts receivable or prepaid rent are not included in the intangible classification, even though they are lacking in physical substance.

Intangible assets are either acquired in a business combination or developed internally. In case of acquisition in a business combination, such assets are recorded at their fair value, while in case of internally generated intangible assets, the assets are recognized at the cost incurred in R&D phase. In relation to the development of internally generated intangible assets there are two phases: research phase and development phase. Research phase includes all activities and costs incurred before the intangible asset is commercially feasible, while the development phase includes all activities and costs incurred after the asset is established to be commercially feasible. All costs in research phase are expensed in the period incurred while costs incurred in development phase are capitalized.

Intangible assets include copyrights, patents, trademark, franchise etc.

1. Copyrights

Copyrights are granted by the government, giving the owner the exclusive right to reproduce and sell an artistic or published work. Copyrights extend for the life of the creator plus 50 years or useful life, whichever is shorter. The cost of a copyright consists of the cost of acquiring and defending it.

2. Patents

Patents are exclusive rights issued by the government that enables the recipient to manufacture, sell or otherwise control his or her invention for a period of 20 years from the date of filing the application. The initial cost of a patent is the cash or cash equivalent price paid when the patent is acquired. The cost of the patent should be amortized over its 20-year legal life or its useful life, whichever is shorter.

3. Trademark and Trade Names

Trademarks include corporate logos, and product names that have been registered with the government and serve to identify specific companies and products. All expenditures associated with securing and defending trademarks and trade names are amortizable.

4. Franchise

Franchise operations have become so common in daily life that we often don't realize we are dealing with them. In fact, these days it is difficult to find a non-franchise business in a typical shopping mall. The purchaser of a franchise license receives the right to sell certain products or services and to use certain trademarks or trade names. These rights are valuable because they provide the purchaser with immediate customer recognition. Many fast-food restaurants, hotels, gas stations, and automobile dealerships are owned by individuals who have paid a company for a franchise license. The cost of a franchise license is amortized over its useful life, often its contractual life.

Amortization of intangible assets is the process of expensing out intangible assets over their useful life. It is in effect the depreciation of intangible assets. Some intangible assets have indefinite or unlimited useful life. Such assets are not amortized. Others have a definite useful life and are amortized over their useful life. Most of intangible assets are amortized using straight line method. Useful life is the shorter of legal life and economic life. For example, suppose Innovative Gadgets Ltd. patented one of their products at a cost of $100 000. The patent is enforceable for 10 years, so the legal life is 10 years. However, the company expects to produce the patented product for only 5 years and expects to replace it with an advanced version at the end of 5 years. The company uses straight line method of amortization. The company is required to amortize the patent over 5 years which is the shorter of legal life and economic life and hence per year amortization would be $20 000 ($100 000/5).

Although intangible assets with indefinite useful life are not amortized, they are periodically tested for impairment.

Exercises

Exercises 6.1 Multiple Choice

1. Depreciation means _____.   (   )
    A. the physical deterioration of an asset
    B. the decrease in the market value of an asset
    C. the allocation of the cost of a plant asset to expense to reflect the use of asset services
    D. the systematic write-off of the cost of a natural resource over its productive life
2. The straight-line method of depreciation _____.   (   )
    A. should be used in a period of inflation because it accumulates, at a uniform rate, the fund for the replacement of the asset
    B. is the best method to use for income tax purposes
    C. ignores fluctuations in the rate of asset usage
    D. generally gives best results because it is easy to apply

3. Which of the following answers is not belong to fixed assets?   (　)
   A. property   B. plant
   C. equipment   D. accounts receivable
4. Copyrights, patents, trademark, trademark, and franchise are all belong to
   _____.   (　)
   A. intangible assets   B. tangible assets
   C. current assets   D. Short-term assets
5. What is the amount of depreciation, using the sum-of-the-years'-digits method for the second year of use for equipment costing $9 600, with an estimated residual value of $600 and an estimated life of 3 years?   (　)
   A. $2 000.   B. $3 000.
   C. $4 000.   D. $6 000.
6. Please select which components should less from the value of plant assets.
                                                                   (　)
   A. Merchandise inventory.   B. Income tax payable.
   C. Accumulated depreciation. D. Retained earnings.
7. In accounting, which of the following factors is not an estimate to determine the depreciation of a plant asset?   (　)
   A. Cost.   B. Useful life.
   C. Salvage value.   D. Total units of output.
8. A purchase of office equipment for cash of 130 was recorded as an addition to office equipment and an addition to liabilities. By what amounts are the accounts under-or overstated as a result of this error? ("understated" means too low, and "overstated" means to high.)   (　)
   A. assets, understated 130; liabilities, overstated 130
   B. office equipment, understated 260; liabilities, overstated 130
   C. office equipment, overstated 130; liabilities, overstated 130
   D. assets, overstated 130; liabilities, overstated 130

9. If an accountant forgot to record depreciation on office equipment at the end of an accounting period, which of the following would be true regarding the statement prepared at that time?   (　　)

   A. Assets are overstated and owner's equity is understated.

   B. The assets and owner' equity are both understated.

   C. The assets are overstated, net income is understated, and owner's equity is overstated.

   D. The assets, net income and owner's equity are overstated.

10. In China Accelerated depreciation methods are used primarily in _____. (　　)

   A. income tax returns

   B. the financial statements of small businesses

   C. the financial statements of publicly owned corporations

   D. companies with computer-based accounting systems

Exercises 6.2

1. Fill in the following blanks.

   (1) Fixed assets, also called PPE, include _____, _____, and _____.

   (2) There are classes of non-current assets: _____, _____. and _____.

   (3) Practically, the four mainly used depreciation methods are _____, _____, _____ and _____.

   (4) The sum-of-the-years'-digits method and double-declining balance method belong to _____.

   (5) Intangible assets include copyrights, _____, _____, and franchise.

2. A truck with an estimated life of four years was obtained on March 31, 2000, for $11 000. The estimated residual value of the truck is $1 000, and the service life is estimated at 100 000 miles. Calculate depreciation for year 2000 and year 2001 using methods in the following blanks, where appropriate. (Year 2000 = 20 000; Year 2001 = 40 000)

Method	Year 2000	Year 2001
Straight-line	(1) $	(2) $
Double-declining Balance	(3) $	(4) $
Units of Output (here miles driven)	(5) $	(6) $

Exercises 6.3 Record the following transactions:.

1. Johnson's Company purchased a set of equipment, and its cost totally is $51 500 including cash purchase price $50 000, insurance during shipping $500, installation and testing $1 000. Johnson's Company purchased this factory machinery for cash, please record this acquisition.

2. Assume ABC Company has an old pickup truck that originally cost $10 000, the balance of accumulated depreciation is $7 000, so this truck now has a book value of $3 000. ABC Company sold this old truck with a fair market value of $6 000 and receive cash. How to record this transaction?

3. Hony Company purchased a delivery truck for $24 000, and the estimated residual value of this truck is $3 000. The estimated life of the truck is 7 years. If the straight-line method is used for its depreciation, then how to record the depreciation of this delivery truck for the third year?

Exercises 6.4 Translations

(1) There are normally two aspects about long-term investment, that is, investments in equity securities and investments in debt securities.

(2) In China practice, items that have a unit price over 2 000 yuan and that have useful lives of more than one year should be treated as fixed assets, even though they are not directly used in production and operating activities.

(3) The term intangible assets is used to describe assets which are used in the operation of the business but no physical substance, and are non-current.

(4) The intangible assets are long term in nature and subject to amortization.

(5) Amortization of intangible assets is the process of expensing out intangible assets over their useful life.

Unit Seven

Current Liabilities

Teaching Objectives

Upon completion of this chapter, you will:
1. Know the concept of current liabilities.
2. Know the classification of current liabilities and know how to account for each form.

Vocabulary

current liabilities	流动负债
account payable	应付账款
note payable	应付票据
dividend payable	应付股利
dividend declaration	股利宣告
unearned revenue	预收收入
income taxes payable	应付所得税
temporary differences	暂时性差异
permanent differences	永久性差异
contingencies	或有事项
contingent assets	或有资产
contingent liabilities	或有负债
non-taxable revenues	免税收入
non-deductible expense	不可扣除费用
non-current liabilities	非流动负债
acquisition	购置;获得

credit terms	信用期限;信贷条件;赊销付款条件
economic benefits	经济利益
outflow	流出
enterprise	企业
contract	合同
supplier	供应商
investor	投资人
operating cycle	经营周期
short-term borrowings	短期借款
accrued liabilities	应计负债
interest payable	应付利息
income taxes	所得税
face value	票面价值
principal	本金
working capital	营运资金;营运资本
maturity	到期
liquidation	清偿;清算;偿还
account payable	应付账款
open account	往来账户;未清结的账目;赊销
receipt	收据;收入;收到
title	所有权;权利
retail	零售
invoice	发票
cash discount	现金折扣
turnover	周转;营业额;流通量
administrative expense	管理费用
financial expenses	财务费用
inventory	存货;库存
promissory notes	本票
payee	收款人
interest rate	利率
insurance policy	保险单
prime operating revenue	主营业务收入
board of directors	董事会

TEXT

What is a liability is not a simple question to solve. It seems obvious that liabilities include more than debts arising from borrowing. The acquisition of goods or services on credit terms gives rise to liabilities and is much like borrowing. Less similarly, they may result from the imposition of taxes, withholdings from employees' wages and salaries, and dividend declarations, etc.

In accounting, liabilities are defined as probable future sacrifices of economic benefits arising from present obligations of a particular entity to transfer assets or provide services to other entities in the future as a result of past transactions or events. Thus, liabilities represent existing obligations for a business to part with its resources in the future. Liabilities are obligations of the company; they are amounts owed to creditors for a past transaction and they usually have the word "payable" in their account title. Its essence is a kind of financial debt that must be repaid in a certain period of time.

All liabilities have certain characteristics in common, and there are five key points. First, "probable" means that business is full of uncertainty and it is likely or most likely to be true. Second, the amount of the outflow of economic benefits in the future can be measured reliably. Thirdly, "present obligation" is a duty committed by the enterprise under current circumstances. Obligations that will result from the occurrence of future transactions or events are not present obligations and shall not be recognized as liabilities. Fourthly, "transfer assets or provide services" means that most liabilities involve an obligation to transfer assets or provide services in the future. Last, "past transactions or events" means that liabilities arise from transactions or events that have already happened.

Most liabilities are for a definite dollar amount, clearly stated by contract. Along with owner's equity, liabilities can be thought of as a source of the company's assets. They can also be thought of as a claim against a company's assets. For example, a company's balance sheet reports assets of $100,000 and Accounts Payable of $40,000 and owner's equity of $60,000. The sources of the company's assets are creditors/suppliers for $40,000 and the owners for $60,000. The creditors/suppliers have a claim against the company's assets and the owner can claim what remains after the accounts payable have been paid.

In financial statements, liabilities are reported on the balance sheet and normally have credit balances. Liabilities are usually classified into two categories according to the time of the company holding the liabilities: current liabilities and non-current liabilities (long-term liabilities). The proper classification of liabilities provides useful information to investors and other users of the financial statements. It may be regarded as essential for allowing outsiders to consider a true picture of an organization's fiscal health.

7.1 Definition of Current Liabilities

A liability is considered current if it is due within 12 months from the date of balance sheet or within the normal operating cycle, where this is longer than 12 months. That is to say, if the company's normal operating cycle is longer than 12 months, a liability is considered current if it is due within the operating cycle. In other words, for most businesses, operating cycle is less than one year, but not always and current liabilities are short obligations that are expected to be paid in the next year or in the next operating cycle. Another requirement for classification as a current liability is the expectation that the debt will be paid from current assets (or through the rendering of service). Liabilities that do not meet these conditions are classified as long-term liabilities. Current liabilities are a critical link in the operating cycles of most firms. In the course of day-to-day operations, firms incur short-term obligations to suppliers, employees, and other entities. The cash received from sales of goods and services to customers is then used to pay these obligations, as they are due.

The most common examples of current liabilities are accounts payable, short-term borrowings, notes payable, the current portion of long-term debt, dividends payable, accrued liabilities (such as interest payable, income taxes payable and payroll liabilities) and unearned revenue. Since current liabilities are payable within a relatively short time, they generally are shown on the balance sheet at their face value, which is the amount of cash needed to discharge the principal of the liabilities. The current liabilities are usually listed at the top or first classification in the "liabilities and owner's equity" section of the balance sheet. In some instances, current liabilities are listed as a group immediately after current assets with the total of the current liabilities deducted from the total current assets to obtain "working capital". Within the current liabilities section the accounts may be presented in order of maturity, according to amount (largest to smallest), or in order of liquidation preference.

7.2　Accounts Payable

Under current economic circumstances, most goods and services can be purchased on credit. Account payable is the term that refers to the amount of money that a business has to pay its creditors within a certain period of time. They are the most commonly seen current liabilities and often refer to trade accounts payable. Accounts payable represent balances owed to others for goods, supplies, and services purchased on open account. Accounts payable arise because of the time lag between the receipt of services or acquisition of title to assets and payment for them. More than 90% of major U.S companies show accounts payable as a separate line item under current liabilities on their balance sheet. The size of the balance in accounts payable can be an important indicator of a company's financial condition, especially in the retail industry where suppliers are heavily relied upon to provide goods.

Example 7.1　On August 12th, Vila restaurant purchased 50 dining chairs form ROI furniture store on credit, the price is $100 each, and the payment would be made within 15 days. The entries for Vila restaurant on this transaction are:

August 12th, when receiving the dining chairs:

Dr: Fixed Assets—Furniture 5 000
　Cr: Account Payable 5 000

August 22nd, when paying for the dining chairs:

Dr: Account Payable 5 000
　Cr: Cash 5 000

Example 7.2　If Jim's Company purchased office supplies from supplier on credit, invoice for a total $20 000. The sum of the accounts was presented as a current liability on Jim's balance sheet. The journal entry is as follows:

Dr. Administrative Expenses—Office Supplies 20 000
　Cr. Accounts Payable 20 000

When Jim's Company paid the bill, Jim's Company should record as follows:

Dr. Accounts Payable 20 000
　Cr. Cash 20 000

Account payable result from credit purchase normally takes no interest, because the credit sales is a promoting approach made by the seller. Sometimes, the seller even offers a cash discount to encourage customer for prompt payment. Taking the cash discount benefits both side of the transaction, the buyer saves money and the seller receive payment earlier for turnover.

Example 7.3　On July 15th, Collins High school purchased 700 notebooks form Reba stores on account, the total price is $2 700, the credit term of the transaction is 2/10, n/30. the entries for Collins High school on this transaction are:

July 15th, when receiving the notebooks:

Dr: Administrative Expense—Office Supply 2 700
　Cr: Account Payable 2 700

July 23rd, when paying for the notebooks:

Dr: Account Payable 2 700
　Cr: Financial Expenses—Cash Discount 54
　　Cash 2 646

Accounts payable are often associated with inventory purchases. Most accounting systems are designed to record liabilities when the goods are received or, practically, when the invoices are received.

7.3　Short-term Borrowings

Short-term borrowings usually cash owed by a company to banks or other loan companies, according to the needs of production and operation of the company. Its repayment period is usually from 30 days to one year, and it belongs to financing activities in cash flow statement. At the maturity date (when the borrowing is due), the borrowing company repays the principal as well as the interest subordinated to the principal.

Example 7.4　Suppose that on September 1, 2019, Kally Company borrows $100 000 from Commercial Bank and will repay the principal as well as a three-month interest of totally $3 000 (that is $1 000 for each month) at maturity date. The journal entry to record this transaction is provided below.

On September 1, 2019, Kally Company receives cash from bank.

Dr. Cash in Bank　　　　　　　　　　　　　　100 000
　Cr. Short-term Borrowings　　　　　　　　　　　　100 000

At the end of each month, the company should make provision for interest expenses for the month. For all the three months, the entries here are the same for each month.

Dr. Financial Expenses—Interest Expenses　　　1 000
　Cr. Interests Payable　　　　　　　　　　　　　　1 000

At maturity date, the company repays the principal $100 000 and interest $3 000 to the bank.

Dr. Short-term Borrowings　　　　　　　　　　100 000
　　Interests Payable　　　　　　　　　　　　　3 000
　Cr. Cash in Bank　　　　　　　　　　　　　　　　103 000

7.4　Short-term Notes Payable

　　Short-term notes payable are debts in the form of written promissory notes. Notes payable are issued whenever bank loans are acquired. Other transactions which may give rise to notes payable include the purchase of real estate or costly equipment, the purchase of merchandise, and the substitution of a note for a past-due account payable. The borrower is the maker of the note and the lender is the payee (note holder). The maker of the note promises to pay the face amount of the note at the maturity date, which is also called due date. Notes payable usually require the borrower to pay an interest expenses. Accounting for interest expenses is easiest if the interest rate is stated separately from the principal amount of the note. Notes payable are recorded in either a short-term notes payable account or a long-term notes payable account, depending on when it must be repaid. Short-term notes payable may be interest-bearing or non-interest-bearing. Current notes payable are normally trade notes payable, which are short-term obligations to suppliers who keep these written promissory notes. In China, notes payable only refer to trade notes payable. Companies borrow funds from banks or other lenders frequently by signing an agreement. It is called short-term borrowings rather than notes payable in Chinese practice.

　　A common scenario would entail the borrowing of money in exchange for the issuance of a promissory note payable. The note will look something like this:

Promissory note

For value received, the undersigned promises to pay to the order of Bass Code, Inc.

The sum of ——Five Thousand and Seven Hundred Dollars——

Along with annual interest of 7% on the unpaid balance. This note shall mature and be payable along with accrued interest, on June 30, 2012

January 1, 2012　　　　　　　　　　　　　　　　　　　　　　Bachir Kane

Issue Date　　　　　　　　　　　　　　　　　　　　　　　Maker Signature

Example 7.5 The promissory note above shows that Bachir Kane has agreed to pay to Bass Code $5 700 plus interest of $199.5 on June 30, 2012. The interest represents 7% of $5 700 for half of one year (January 1st through June 30th).

January 1st, recording the amount borrowed:

Dr. Cash   5 700
　Cr. Notes Payable   5 700

June 30th, when the note was paid, the difference between the carrying amount of the note and the cash necessary to pay that note is reported as interest expenses. The journal entry should be as follows:

Dr. Notes Payable   5 700
　　Financial Expenses—Interest Expenses   199.5
　Cr. Cash   5 899.5

Example 7.6 John's Company could not pay its past-due $15 000 accounts to Simon's Company. As a compromise, on April 1st, Simon's Company agreed to accept three-month, 12%, $15 000 note of John's Company in granting an extension on the due date of the debt.

John's Company recorded the issuance of the note on April 1 as follows:

Dr. Accounts Payable—Simon's Company   15 000
　Cr. Notes Payable   15 000

At each end of the three months-April, May, and June, John's Company recorded the following entry:

Dr. Financial Expenses—Interest Expenses   150
　Cr. Interests Payable   150

Note that the note does not pay off the debt. Rather, the form of the debt is merely changed from accounts payable to notes payable. Simon's Company should prefer holding the note to the account, because, in case of default, the note is very good written evidence of the debt's existence and its amount.

When the note becomes due, John's Company will give Simon's Company a check for $450 and record the payment of the note and its interest with this entry:

On July 1, John's Company paid Simon's Company the principal and interest expenses.

Dr. Notes Payable 15 000
    Financial Expenses—Interest Expenses 450
    Cr. Cash 15 450

If companies borrow funds from banks or other financial institutions by signing notes, it is financing activities in cash flow statement.

In the above example, assume that on April 1, Simon's Company lent money to accept the three-month, 12%, $15,000 note of John's Company.

John's Company recorded the issuance of the note on April 1 as follows:

Dr. Cash 15 000
    Cr. Notes Payable 15 000

7.5 Unearned Revenue

A firm may receive cash before providing goods or performing services to customers. Because the firm has an obligation to render the services or provide the goods, this cash is a kind of liability and these advance payments by customers are called unearned revenues in accounting. In China, Advances from Customers is also often used besides the account title of Unearned Revenues. Unearned revenue ordinarily is classified as a current liability because activities involved in earning revenue are part of the firm's normal operating cycle. Otherwise, they should be classified as non-current liability. Examples include selling magazine subscriptions in advance, selling gift-cards, selling tickets well before a scheduled event. Although Unearned Revenue takes the title of "Revenue", but it is a liabilities account which is presented in current liability section of the balance sheet. In the cash flow statement, cash from advances from customers is considered as an operating activity. At the same time, advance to suppliers is the buyer's current assets.

Normally for a transaction, the amount of unearned revenue is equal to the revenue actually earned later. That is because, when the products and services were completely delivered, the obligation of seller against customer has been fulfilled; and in accordance with revenue recognition principle, it is also the time point to recognized revenue. Thereby, as the products or services completely offered, the unearned revenue would be converted in the realized sales or service revenue.

Example 7.7 Flora flower store receives a payment of $600 in advance from Mr. Roberts on July 20th. This payment is made for the flower decoration to be used on July 26th, Mrs. Roberts birthday party. The entries for the flower store on this transaction are:

July 20th, when the payment received:

Dr.　Cash　　　　　　　　　　　　　　　　　　　　600

　　Cr.　Unearned Revenue　　　　　　　　　　　　　600

July 26th, when the flower decoration has delivered:

Dr.　Unearned Revenue　　　　　　　　　　　　　　600

　　Cr.　Prime Operating Revenue　　　　　　　　　 600

Example 7.8 Suppose a customer pays $3 600 on March 1st for an insurance policy to protect her delivery vehicles for six months. The entries for insurance company on this transaction are:

Initially, the insurance company records this transaction as the increase of an asset—cash, and the increase of a liability—unearned revenue.

March 1st, when the payment received:

Dr.　Cash　　　　　　　　　　　　　　　　　　　　3 600

　　Cr.　Unearned Revenue　　　　　　　　　　　　　3 600

After one month, the insurance company makes an entry to record the decrease of unearned revenue and the increase of service revenue by an amount equal to one sixth of the initial payment. As one sixth of the insurance service has been offered, thus one sixth of the service revenue is realized.

March 31st, when one month of insurance service was offered:

Dr. Unearned Revenue	600
Cr. Prime Operating Revenue	600

From an accounting perspective, unearned revenue is a double-edged sword. The early cash flow to the firm is advantageous for any number of activities, such as paying interest on debt to purchasing more inventories. However, by accepting unearned revenue, the firm has then entered a legal obligation to deliver on the terms of the payment.

7.6 Dividends Payable

Businesses pay dividends as a way of returning cash to their shareholders and a liability (dividends payable) is created when the board of directors of a corporation declares a dividend to be paid to the stockholders. Dividends payable is classified as a current liability on the balance sheet because dividends are usually paid within several weeks of declaration. A dividend to stockholders or shareholders involves two entries. The first entry was recorded on the date that the board of directors declares the dividend, when the account Profits Distribution is debited and Dividends Payable is credited for the amount of the dividend that will be paid.

Example 7.9 Hayward Corporation's board of directors declares a quarterly dividend of $2 for each of the firm's 100 000 outstanding common shares on April 1st, which will be paid on April 25th to the shareholders. The entries for Hayward Corporation on this event are:

April 1st, recording the declaration of the quarterly dividend:

Dr. Profits Distribution	200 000
Cr. Dividend Payable	200 000

April 25th, recording the payment of the quarterly dividend:

Dr. Dividend Payable	200 000
Cr. Cash	200 000

Dividends payable is different than other current liabilities, since dividends payable represents funds the owners owe to themselves. Nevertheless, from the standpoint of the business as an economic entity, dividends payable do represent a legal obligation like any other. A dividend payable is a liability on a company's balance sheet, but it does not affect the statement of cash flow until the company actually issues the dividend checks. Cash dividend payments affect the financing activities section of the statement of cash flow.

7.7 Accrued Liabilities

Accrued liabilities happen when the recognition of expenses to be paid in a future period. In fact, certain expenses are incurred by the business before they are actually paid, which causes accrued liabilities, so it is also called accrued expenses. Examples of accrued liabilities include taxes payable, interest payable, salaries payable, etc. As accrued expenses stem from recording of expenses, the timing and amounts of these liabilities are governed by the matching principles. All businesses incur accrued liabilities. However, in most cases, this kind of liability normally does not accumulate to large amounts. In balance sheet, it is usually combined with accounts payable, rather than being listed separately.

1. Interest Payable

Interest is the cost of borrowing and increases with the passage of time. It is often created by deposit taking, short or long-term loans and bonds payable. When enterprises enter into a long-term financing agreement, they would be committed to paying a large amount of interest in the future. It is measured by the transaction amount and contract interest rate. As liabilities arise from past transactions, the interest payable is the unpaid interest, which has already accrued. At any balance sheet date, however, only a small portion of this total interest obligation represents a liability. At the end of each accounting period, any accrued interest payable is recorded by debiting Interest Expense and crediting Interest Payable.

Example 7.10 Assume that John borrows $500 000 from its bank for period of five years at an annual interest rate of 12%. Though the principal amount of this borrowing will not be due for five years, interest is still to be paid monthly—on the first date of each month. The interest amount of this borrowing is $60 000 per year (500 000 × 12%). During the five years, John will have a liability for only one month's interest—the interest which has accrued since the last interest payment date. Thus, John's balance sheet normally will show accrued interest payable of only $5 000(60 000 × 1/12)

At the end of each month, to record the accrued interest:
Dr. Financial Expenses – Interest Expenses   5 000
    Cr. Interest Payable   5 000

If the John pay the interest expenses at the end of each month:
Dr. Interest Payable   5 000
    Cr. Cash   5 000

If this debt has called for the accrued interest to be paid on the last day of each month, John's balance sheet would include no liability for accrued interest payable. A borrower's contractual obligation to pay interest in future periods is not yet a liability and does not appear in the borrower's balance sheet. However, this information may be of significant importance to investors and creditors evaluating a company's solvency and its ability to finance future growth. For this reason, accounting principles require a company to disclose the terms of major borrowing arrangements in the notes which accompany their financial statements.

To determine the amount of a company's interest expense for the year, the reader of financial statements should look in the income statement, not the balance sheet. For information about the company's interest obligations in future years, the reader must study the notes which accompany the financial statements.

2. Tax Payable

Enterprises must fulfill their tax obligations in accordance with state regulations and various taxes should be paid by enterprises on their operating income. Tax Payable shows the amount that an entity owes government units for taxes. Here taxes include value-added tax, income tax, consumption tax, resources tax, land value added tax, house property tax, vehicle tax, land use tax and so on. These taxes payable shall be recognized and accrued on an accrual basis. Profitable companies are required to pay income tax equal to a portion of their taxable income. At the end of each accounting period, income tax expense is estimated and recorded in an adjusting entry, shown as below:

Dr. Income Tax Expenses
    Cr. Income Taxes Payable

7.8 Contingent Liabilities

Contingencies are financial transactions that may take place in the future and affect the financial standing of a company, but cannot be accurately predicted or guaranteed. To allow fair comparison of financial accounts of different companies, accounting standards will set down rules on the handling of specific issues such as contingencies.

Contingent liability is obligation that is dependent upon the occurrence of non-occurrence of one or more future events to confirm either the amount payable, or the payee, or the date payable, or even its existence; that is, determination of one or more of these factors is dependent on a contingency. Contingent liabilities do not cover every possible cost a business could face. It is a potential obligation that results from an existing condition or situation whose final resolution depends on some future event. Generally, the amount of a contingent liability must be estimated; the actual amount cannot be determined until the event that confirms the liability occurs. Moreover, in many cases, the actual person or company to whom payments will be made is not known until the future event occurs. The general threshold is that contingent liabilities relate to the business activities of the company, rather than wider risks, such as damage caused by extreme weather events or military action. There are numerous examples of contingent liabilities. Legal disputes give rise to contingent liabilities, environmental contamination events give rise to contingent liabilities, product warranties give rise to contingent liabilities, and so forth. An automobile guarantee and other product warranties are examples of contingent liabilities that usually are recorded on a compány's books. The matching principle requires the expense to be recorded in the period of the sale, not when the repair is made. The contingency is not reported on the balance sheet, but rather in the footnotes.

A company will recognize the related obligation of a contingency as a liability when the obligation fulfills the following conditions:

(1) The obligation is present obligation of the company;

(2) It is probable that an outflow of economic benefits from the company will be required to settle the obligation;

(3) A reliable estimate can be made of the amount of the obligation.

If the amount of the obligation is unsure, the amount should be best estimate of the expenditure required to settle the liability. If there is a range of expenditure required to settle the liability, the best estimate should be determined in terms of the average of the lower and upper limit of the range. Where there is no a range of expenditure required to settle the liability, the best estimate should be determined in accordance with the following methods:

(1) Where the contingency involves a single item, the best estimate should be determined according to the most likely outcome;

(2) Where the contingency involves several items, the best estimate should be determined by weighting all possible outcomes by their associated probabilities.

A business should disclose the following contingent liabilities in the notes of financial statements:

(1) Contingent liabilities arising from discounted commercial acceptance bills of exchange;

(2) Contingent liabilities arising from pending litigation or arbitration;

(3) Contingent liabilities arising from guarantees provided for the debts of other businesses; and

(4) Other contingent liabilities (excluding those contingent liabilities of which the possible of any outflow of economic benefits is remote).

For those contingent liabilities, which should be disclosed, a business should disclose the following:

(1) The cause of the contingent liabilities;

(2) An estimate of the expected financial effect of the contingent liabilities (if the estimate cannot be made, the reason should be stated);

(3) The possibility of any reimbursement.

Exercises

Exercises 7.1 Multiple Choice

1. Liabilities are classified on the balance sheet as current or _____.   (   )

    A. Deferred   B. Unearned

    C. Non-current   D. Accrued

2. Most companies pay current liabilities _____.   (   )

    A. Out of current assets

    B. By issuing interest-bearing notes payable

    C. By issuing shares

    D. By creating long-term liabilities

3. Typical current liabilities include _____.   (   )

    A. Prepayments by customers

    B. Travel advances to employees

C. The principal portion of a mortgage note that is due beyond one year or the operating cycle, whichever is longer

D. Accumulated depreciation

4. Current liabilities are debts that are expected to be satisfied within _____. ( )

   A. one year
   B. the normal operating cycle
   C. one year or operating cycle, whichever is shorter
   D. one year or operating cycle, whichever is longer

5. Which of the following would most likely be classified as a current liability? ( )

   A. Mortgage payable
   B. Bonds payable
   C. Dividends payable
   D. Five-year notes payable

6. Notes payable usually require the borrower to pay _____. ( )

   A. Interest
   B. Revenue
   C. Prepayments
   D. Contingencies

7. On January 1, 20 × 1, Hillcrest Company, a calendar-year company, issued $80 000 of notes payable, of which $20 000 is due on January 1 for each of the next four years. The proper balance sheet presentation on December 31 20 × 1 is _____. ( )

   A. Current Liabilities, $80 000
   B. Long-Term Liabilities, $80 000
   C. Current Liabilities, $20 000; Long-Term Liabilities, $60 000
   D. Current Liabilities, $60 000; Long-Term Liabilities, $20 000

8. Contingent liabilities are those liabilities _____. ( )

   A. whose final resolution depends on some future event
   B. whose amount can be reasonably estimated
   C. such as pending litigation
   D. all of the above

9. Contingent liabilities should be recorded in the accounts when _____. ( )
   A. It is probable that the future event will occur
   B. The amount of the liability can be reasonably estimated
   C. Both (A) and (B)
   D. Either (A) or (B)
10. East Bank agrees to lend The Custom Brick Company Ltd $100 000 on 1 January. The Custom Brick Company Ltd signs a $100 000, 8%, 9-month note. The entry made by The Custom Brick Company Ltd on 1 January to record the proceeds and issue of the note is _____. ( )

    A. Interest Expense   6 000
       Cash   94 000
           Notes Payable   100 000
    B. Cash   100 000
           Notes Payable   100 000
    C. Cash   100 000
       Interest Expense   6 000
           Notes Payable   106 000
    D. Cash   100 000
       Interest Expense   6 000
           Notes Payable   100 000
           Interest Payable   6 000

Exercises 7.2

Indicate the effect of each transaction below on the accounting equation. After each transaction is properly recorded, compute new subtotals for the Assets, Liabilities, and Owners' Equity, being sure to maintain the equality of the equation. Use the following format:

Example: Issued 4 000 shares of $100 par value common stock for $600 000 cash.

Transaction Number	Assets	=	Liabilities	+	Owners' Equity
Example	+ $600 000				+ $600 000
Subtotal	$600 000				600 000

a. Received $12 000 for a magazine subscription to be delivered to customers over the next year.
b. Paid $7 000 in advance for one year of insurance.
c. Purchased for $500 000 cash a building the firm will use for office space.
d. Paid $15 000 to an advertising agency for a promotional campaign that will start in one month.
e. Bought $115 000 of merchandise inventory on account.
f. Paid $65 000 to the supplier for inventory purchase in (e) and gave a note for the remaining $50 000.
g. Loaned $30 000 to an officer and accepted a 90-day note as evidence of the loan.
h. Bought $42 000 of merchandise for cash.
i. Borrowed $75 000 from the bank.
j. Issued ten shares of $100 par value common stock in settlement of an account payable of $26 000.
k. The company agrees to buy four trucks six months from now for $178 000.

Exercises 7.3

The following transactions (a ~ g) occurred during January. For each transaction, make the appropriate journal entry to record the transaction.

a. The firm collected the note receivable of $8 000 and the related accrued interest of $1 000 on January 2nd.
b. Paid the note payable for $16 000 and the related accrued interest of $800 on January 2nd.
c. Paid the December 31st balance in Accounts Payable on January 15th.
d. Issued $80 000 of bonds at face value and used the proceeds to pay for an addition to the building on January 20th.
e. Acquired merchandise inventory costing $30 000 on January 21st with payment of

$16 000 in cash and the remainder due in 30 days on open account.
f. Sold the plot of land costing $15 000 for $15 000 on January 25th.
g. Issued an additional 400 shares of common stock for $125 per share on January 28th. The par value of the stock is $100.

Unit Eight

Non-Current Liabilities

Teaching Objectives
Upon completion of this chapter, you will know:
1. What non-current liabilities are.
2. The time value of money.
3. What bonds payable are and the classification of bonds payable.
4. Accounting for bonds payable (at face value; at discount; at premium).

Vocabulary

non-current liabilities	非流动负债
time value	时间价值
simple Interest	单利
compound Interest	复利
future Value	终值
present Value	现值
annuity	年金
bonds Payable	应付债券
serial bonds	分期偿还债券
convertible bonds	可转换债券
callable bonds	可回收债券
registered bonds	记名债券
coupon bond	有息债券
market rate	市场利率
face value	面值
issued at discount	折价发行
issued at premium	溢价发行

TEXT

8.1　Definition of Non-Current Liabilities

Non-current liabilities, also called long-term debts, are company's obligations that extend beyond the current year or alternatively beyond the current operating cycle, including long-term notes payable, bonds payable, mortgages payable, and obligations under capital leases. Accounting for non-current liabilities is complex because payments of interest, or in some cases payments of principal and interest, are periodically made over periods.

8.2　Time Value of Money

The time value of money is the value of money figuring in a given amount of interest earned over a given amount of time. The time value of money is the central concept in finance theory, it impacts business finance, consumer finance, and government finance.

Time value of money results from the concept of interest, which means money available at the present time is worth more than the same amount in the future due to its potential earning capacity. Because of this universal fact, we would prefer to receive money today rather than the same amount in the future.

For example, assuming a 5% interest rate, $100 invested today will be worth $105 in one year (that is $100 multiplied by 1.05). Conversely, $100 received one year from now is only worth $95.24 today (that is $100 divided by 1.05), assuming a 5% interest rate as well.

1. Simple Interest and Compound Interest

The calculation of interest involves three elements: Principle, Interest rate, and Time. Principal is the beginning amount of borrowing or investment; interest rate is the percentage of the outstanding principle; time is the duration that the principal is outstanding. Let's take a look at the calculation of different type of interest.

◆Simple Interest

Simple interest is the interest that is paid on beginning principal only. It is means the principal basis for calculating interest will not increase with time, and the interest payment for each period will remain the same amount.

Example 8.1 if one were to receive 5% interest on a beginning value of $100, the first year interest would be:
$$100 \times 0.05 = 5$$

Continuing to receive 5% interest on the original $100 amount, over five years the growth of the original investment would like:

Year 1: 5% of 100 = 5; 5 + 100 = 105
Year 2: 5% of 100 = 5; 5 + 105 = 110
Year 3: 5% of 100 = 5; 5 + 110 = 115
Year 4: 5% of 100 = 5; 5 + 115 = 120
Year 5: 5% of 100 = 5; 5 + 120 = 125

Therefore, by applying simple interest on $100 beginning value would receive $5 each year and eventually receive $25 interest for 5 years.

◆Compound Interest

Compound interest is the interest paid on beginning principal and any additional accumulated principal. It's good to receive compound interest, but not so good to pay compound interest. With compound interest, interest is calculated not only on the beginning interest, but on any interest accumulated in the meantime.

Example 8.2 If one were to receive 5% compound interest on a beginning value of $100, the first year interest would be the same as simple interest on the $100, or $5. The second year, though, interest would be calculated on the beginning amount of year 2, which would be $105. So the interest would be:

$$105 \times 0.05 = 5.25$$

This provides a balance at the end of year two of $110.25. If this were to continue for 5 years, the growth in the investment would like:

Year 1: 5% of 100.00 = 5.00; 5.00 + 100.00 = 105.00
Year 2: 5% of 105.00 = 5.25; 5.25 + 105.00 = 110.25
Year 3: 5% of 110.25 = 5.51; 5.51 + 110.25 = 115.76
Year 4: 5% of 115.76 = 5.79; 5.79 + 115.76 = 121.55
Year 5: 5% of 121.55 = 6.08; 6.08 + 121.55 = 127.63

If you comparing the growth graphs of simple and compound interest, investments with simple interest grow in a linear fashion and compound interest results in geometric growth. So with compound interest, the further in time an investment is held the more dramatic the growth becomes.

Instead of calculating interest year-by-year, it would be simple to see the future value of an investment using a compound interest formula. The formula for compound interest is:

$$P_n = P_0(1+i)^n$$

P_n = Value at end of n time periods

P_0 = Beginning Value

i = Interest

n = Number of years

Take Example 8.2 for instance, if one were to receive 5% compounded interest on $100 for five years, to use the formula, simply plug in the appropriate values and calculate.

$$P_n = 100 \times (1.05)^5 = 127.63$$

For most of the accounting practice, interests of notes, borrowing and investment are determined on the compound interest basis.

2. Future Value and Present Value of a single amount

◆Future Value of a single amount

Future value (FV) is the value of money at a specific date in the future. To be more accurate, it measures the nominal future sum of money that a given sum of money is "worth" at a specified time in the future assuming a certain interest rate, or more generally, rate of return; it is calculated by current value multiplied by the accumulation function. The value does not include corrections for inflation or other factors that affect the true value of money in the future.

For a single amount, its future value with compound interest can always be calculated using the preceding formulation:

$$FV = P_0(1+i)^n$$

Example 8.3 Suppose that you invest \$5 000 today and it will earn 8% interest annually. How much will you have in 4 years?

$$FV = 5\,000 \times (1+8\%)^4 = 6\,802$$

There in the formulation, the $(1+i)^n$ part is the future value factor that is used to multiply beginning values for future value, and in the future value table include values of this factor corresponding to various rates and periods. To find the future value of a present amount, locate the appropriate number of years and the appropriate interest rate, take the resulting factor and multiply it times the beginning value.

◆Present Value of a single amount

Present value (PV), also known as present discounted value, is the reciprocal of future value. is simply the reciprocal of compound interest. Another way to think of present value is to adopt a stance out on the time line in the future and look back toward time 0 to see what was the beginning amount.

For a single amount, its present value with compound interest can always be calculated using the following formulation:

$$PV = FV/(1+i)^n \text{ or } PV = FV(1+i)^{-n}$$

Example 8.4   if you think you can sell an asset for $25 000 in five years and you think the appropriate discount rate is 5%, how much would you be will to pay for the asset today?

$$PV = 25\ 000 / (1 + 5\%)^5 = 19\ 588.15$$

There in the formulation, the $1/(1+i)^n$ or $(1+i)^{-n}$ part is the present value factors that is used to multiply future value for present value. Notice that the present value factors are all less than one. Therefore, when multiplying a future value by these factors, the future value is discounted down to present value. The present value table is used in much the same way as the previously discussed future value tables, locate the appropriate number of years and the appropriate interest rate, take the resulting factor and multiply it times the future value.

3. Future Value and Present Value of an annuity

An annuity (A) is an equal, annual series of cash flows. Annuities may be equal annual deposits, equal annual withdrawals, equal annual payments, or equal annual receipts. The key is equal, annual cash flows.

When cash flows occur at the end of the year, this makes them an ordinary annuity (End of year cash flows), if the cash flows were at the beginning of the year, they would be an annuity due (beginning of year cash flows). In this section we will discuss about ordinary annuity only.

An annuity has three essential characteristics:

①Annuity has equal time period (normally one year);
②Annuity has equal amount for each time period
③Annuity has equal interest rate compounded or discounted for each interest period.

◆Future Value of an annuity

The Future value of an ordinary annuity (FA) is the value that a stream of expected or promised future payments will grow to after a given number of periods at a specific compounded interest.

Assume annual deposits of $100 deposited at end of year earning 5% interest for three years.

Year 1: 100 deposited at end of year = 100.00
Year 2: 100 × 0.05 = 5; 5.00 + 100 + 100 = 205.00
Year 3: 205 × 0.05 = 10.25; 10.25 + 205 + 100 = 315.25

The Future value of an ordinary annuity could be solved by calculating the future value of each individual payment in the series using the future value formula and then summing the results. A more direct formula is:

$$FA = A[(1+i)^n - 1]/i$$

Again, there are tables for working with annuities. There in the formulation, the $[(1+i)^n - 1]/i$ part is the future value of annuity factors to be used in calculating annuities due. The future value of annuity table works the same way as the previous tables. Look up the appropriate number of periods, locate the appropriate interest, take the factor found and multiply it by the amount of the annuity.

Example 8.5 The national savings fund promises a monthly 0.75% return if you deposit $100 per month for 15 consecutive years. What amount will be accumulated after those 15 years?

$$FV = 100 \times [(1+0.75\%)^{180} - 1]/0.75\% = 37\,840.58$$

Example 8.6 Willy has just bought a house. She estimates that the roof will have to be renewed at a cost of $25 000 after 20 years. To cover these costs, she intends to save an equal amount of money at the end of each year, earning 6% annual interest rate. How much is such a yearly annuity?

$$25\,000 = A \times [(1+6\%)^{20} - 1]/6\%$$
$$A = 679.61$$

◆ Present Value of an annuity

The Present value of an ordinary annuity is the value of a stream of expected or promised future payments that have been discounted to a single equivalent value today. It is extremely useful for comparing two separate cash flows that differ in some way. PA can also be thought of as the amount you must invest today at a specific interest rate so that when you withdraw an equal amount each period, the original principal and all accumulated interest will be completely exhausted at the end of the annuity.

The Present value of an ordinary annuity could be solved by calculating the present value of each payment in the series using the present value formula and then summing the results. A more direct formula is:

$$PA = A[1-(1+i)^{-n}]/i$$

Example 8.7 calculate the present value of a 4 - year, \$3 000 per year annuity at 6% interest rate.

$$PA = 3\,000 \times [1-(1+6\%)^{-4}]/6\% = 10\,395.32$$

There in the formulation, the $[1-(1+i)^{-n}]/i$ part is the present value of annuity factors. Look up in the present value annuity table the appropriate number of periods, locate the appropriate interest, take the factor found and multiply it by the amount of the annuity.

Example 8.8 Pete considers buying a house. Currently, he rents a place for \$1 000 a month. The current monthly interest rate on mortgages is 0.5%. His planning period is 20 years. If he doesn't want to increase his housing costs, what amount of mortgage is available for his purchase?

$$PA = 1\,000 \times [1-(1+0.5\%)^{-240}]/0.5\% = 139\,580.8$$

8.3 Bonds Payable

Bonds have many different kinds, and each has its particular feature. Some bonds can be converted into common stock at the bondholder's option, known as convertible bonds. Others that are subject to redemption at a stated amount prior to maturity at the option of the issuer, are called callable bonds. Furthermore, there are secured bonds and unsecured bonds depending on whether bonds have specific assets pledged as collateral; term bonds and serial bonds depending on whether maturing at a specified date or maturing in installments; registered bonds and bearer bonds depending on whether they are issued in the name of owner. Whatever kind, bonds are a form of interest-bearing notes payable.

If the contractual interest rate (often called nominal interest rate) equals the market interest rate (called effective interest rate) by coincidence, bonds are sold at face value. However, this seldom happens because market interest rates change daily, which makes it hardly possible for a company to estimate the exact market interest rate of selling bonds when printing the bond certificates. As a result, bonds are more often sold at an amount different from face value. They are sold at a discount if the contractual interest rate is lower and sold at a premium in case the market interest rate is lower. The amortization of bonds premiums and discounts should be recorded and reported separately in each accounting period in either Straight-line Method or Effective Interest Method. Accordingly, the sale of bonds at a discount does not represent the issuer's bad financial situation, nor does the sale of bonds at premium mean outstanding financial strength. 1 Long-term creditors are particularly interested in a company's ability to pay due interest and the ability to pay back the face value at maturity. The following two ratios can be of some referential value for the investors:

(1) **Debt to Total Asset Ratio**

It is calculated by dividing total liabilities (current and long-term) by total assets. Higher debt to total asset ratio indicates the greater possibility that the company fails to pay out the bonds at due time.

(2) **Times Interest Earned Ratio**

This ratio computed by dividing income before income taxes and interest expense by interest expense, implies the company's ability to pay interests as they come due or the extent of which earnings are available to meet interest payments. A lower times interest earned ratio means that less earnings are available to meet interest payments and the business is less possible to increase the interest rates.

The bond payable is issued security for the purpose of raising fund and promise to pay back within a certain period of time. It is a written certificate. The basic elements of the bond payable are as follows:

(1) The face value of the bond;

(2) The issuing price of the bond;

(3) The repayment period;

(4) The date of paying the interest;

(5) The band rate.

The face value of a bond and its face interest rate are fixed. If the issuing price is less than the face value, the bonds are issued at a discount; if the issuing price is more than the face value, the bonds are issued at a premium; if the issuing price is equal to the face value, the bonds are issued at par.

Example 8.9 B Company issued 3-year long-term bond at face value of ¥40 000 000 in July, 2019, the repayment of principal and interest was made on maturity date. The raised money was used for the construction and operation of fixed assets, and the annual rate of the bond was 8%.

(1) When the fund was received:

Dr. Cash in Bank   40 000 000
    Cr. Bonds Payable Face Value   40 000 000

(2) When the interests was accrued at the end of 2019:

Dr. Construction in Progress   1 600 000 (40 000 000 × 8% × 1/12 × 6)
    Cr. Bonds Payable—Interest Accrued   1 600 000

(3) When the interest and principal were paid off on maturity date:

Dr. Bonds Payable —Face Value   40 000 000
    —Interest Accrued   9 600 000 (4 000 000 × 8% × 3)
    Cr. Cash in Bank   49 600 000

Exercises

Exercises 8.1

1. The time period for classifying a liability as current is one year or the operating cycle, whichever is ( )
   A. longer
   B. shorter
   C. probable
   D. possible

2. To be classified as a current liability, a debt must be expected to be paid ( )
   A. out of existing current assets
   B. by creating other current liabilities
   C. within 2 years
   D. both A and B

3. Golden Shirley Company borrows $108 000 on September 1, 2016 from Ohio State Bank by signing a $108 000, 11% payable semiannually, one-year note. What is the accrued interest at December 31, 2019? ( )
   A. $11 880
   B. $3 960
   C. $108 000
   D. $5 940

4. The term used for bonds that are issued in the name of the owner is ( )
   A. bearer bonds
   B. registered bonds
   C. secured bonds
   D. callable bonds

Exercises 8.2

Assume that Green Company raises cash $100 000 from the bonds issued with a face value of $100 000. Please record the transaction in the accounting entries of "Cash" and "Bonds payable".

Dr. _____ _____
   Cr. _____ _____

Unit Nine

Owners' Equity

Teaching Objectives

Upon completion of this chapter, you will:
1. Know shareholders' rights and privileges.
2. Know what treasury stock and retained earnings are.
3. Know how to account for stock issues.

Vocabulary

common stock	普通股
preferred stock	优先股
treasury stock	库存股
outstanding stock	流通股
stockholder	股东
paid-in capital	实收资本
additional paid-in capital	多收资本
dividend	股利
cash dividend	现金股利
stock dividend	股票股利
par value	面值
face value	面值
stated value	设定价值
market value	市场价值
retained earnings	留存收益

corporation	公司
shareholder	股东,股票持有者
corporate charter	公司章程
liquidation	结算,清算
no-par value	无面值
stated value	设定价值
date of declaration	宣告日
date of record	登记日
date of payment	支付日

TEXT

9.1 Shareholders' Rights and Privileges

1. Common Stock

Common stock represents ownership in a corporation. A single share of stock is a piece of ownership of the corporation. If a corporation issues 10 shares of stock, each share represents 10 percent of its ownership. If the corporation issues 100 shares each share represents 1 percent of the ownership. This share entitles the owner to a vote in corporate decisions as well as a piece of the profits of the company. Of course, most companies issue millions of shares of stock, so each share represents only a tiny piece of the company. These shares are also able to be transferred. Which is what you are doing every time you place a trade.

Common stock dividends may be paid in cash, stock or property. The most common payment method is a cash dividend. The board of directors determines whether or not to pay dividends to common shareholders. Increases or reductions most frequently depend on how well the company is performing. In a weak economy, the company may even suspend dividends until its balance sheet improves.

Should the corporation issuing the stock go bankrupt and have to sell its assets, common stockholders will receive the assets, but only after all other creditors, bondholders and preferred stockholders receive them first.

Rights of Common Stockholders:

①Vote in the election of board of directors at annual meeting.

②Share the corporate earnings through receipt of dividends.

③Keep same percentage ownership when new shares of stock are issued.

④Share in assets upon liquidation, In proportion to their holdings.

2. Preferred Stock

Preferred stock also represents ownership in a corporation. Preferred stock gives its owners certain preferences superior to those of common stock. The following rights are those most often associated with preferred stock issues.

① Preference as to dividends.

② Preference as to assets at liquidation.

③ Convertible into common stock.

To obtain the above rights, preferred shareholders cannot vote or share other specified rights.

A preference as to dividends is not assurance that dividends will be paid. It is merely assurance that the stated dividend rate or amount applicable to the preferred stock must be paid before any dividends can be paid on the common stock.

Preferred stock may have either a par value or no-par value.

Par value stock is capital stock that has been assigned a value per share in the corporate charter. The par value may be any amount selected by the corporation. Generally, par value is a very small amount that bears no relationship to its market price. For example, a company has a par value of $1.25, while its recent market price may have risen to $80 per share.

The dividend payments of preferred stock are a fixed percentage of the par. For example, if the par value of a stock share was $100 with a 6 percent annual dividend rate, the annual dividend would be $6 on that share. In recent years, some companies have also begun issued preferred shares with variable rates tied to interest rates.

9.2 Accounting for Stock Issues

When a corporation is organized, the charter will state how many shares of common and preferred stock are authorized. Often more stock is authorized than is intended to be Issued. This will make future expansion possible without having to apply for more shares. When stock is issued for cash, usually Cash is debited and the particular stockholders' equity accounts are credited. For instance, if par value common stock is issued, Common Stock is credited. If common stock is issued at a premium, "Additional Paid-in Capital, Common Stock" is credited for the premium.

Example 9.1 To illustrate, we assume that B Company Company was approved to incorporate. So on March 1 B Company Company issued 80 000 shares of $10 par common stock for $25 pershare. The entry to record the stock issuance would be:

Dr. Cash (80 000 ×25)   2 000 000
  Cr. Common Stock (80 000 ×10)   80 000
     Additional Paid-in Capital, Common Stock (80 000 ×15)
                                                            1 200 000

If the par-value stock was preferred stock, the entry would be:
Dr. Cash (80 000 ×25)   2 000 000
  Cr. Preferred Stock (80 000 ×10)   800 000
     Additional Paid-in Capital, Preferred Stock (80 000 ×15)
                                                            1 200 000

If the issued stock is no-par with a stated value, the entries are just the same. See the following example:

Example 9.2 Assume that B Company Company's authorized stock was no-par stock with a stated value of $1 per share, and that 400 000 shares were issued for $5 per share. The entry would be:

Dr. Cash (400 000 × 5)　　　　　　　　　　　　　　2 000 000
　　Cr. Common Stock(400 000 × 1)　　　　　　　　　　400 000
　　　　Additional Paid-in Capital—Common Stock(400 000 × 4)
　　　　　　　　　　　　　　　　　　　　　　　　　　1 600 000

9.3　Accounting for Treasury Stock

When a corporation wants some of its stocks back from investors, it may purchase some of its outstanding stocks. There are several reasons for a corporation to buy back its stocks. First, the management may want the stocks to be used as bonuses or stock-option plan for employees. Second, the management may feel that the stocks are traded at an unusually low price. Thirdly, the corporation may want the stocks for use in purchasing another company. Fourthly, the corporation may want to increase reported earnings per share by reducing the number of shares of stocks outstanding.

Note that treasury stock is not considered an asset because a corporation cannot own part of itself. Treasury stock is usually accounted for on a cost basis, that is, the stock is debited as cost (market value) on the date of repurchase, not at its par or stated value.

Example 9.3 Suppose that 1 000 shares of the $10 par common stock were required by B Company Company for $60 per share. The entry to record the acquisition would be:

Dr. Treasury Stock—Common stock　　　　　　　　60 000
　　Cr. Cash　　　　　　　　　　　　　　　　　　　　60 000

(purchased 1 000 shares of treasury stock at $60 per share.)

9.4 Retained Earnings

The increase in stockholder's equity arising from profitable operations is called retained earnings. At the end of the year the balance of the income account is closed into the retained earnings account. If a corporation has sufficient cash, a distribution of profits may be made to stockholders. Distributions of this nature are termed dividends and decrease both total assets and total stockholders' equity. Thus, the amount of the company since the date of incorporation minus any losses and all dividends.

In corporations, withdrawals must be accomplished more formally. The board of directors, elected by stockholders, must meet and "declare a dividends" before a distribution which can be made to the stockholders. Dividends are profits paid to the stockholders as a return on their investment. The following three dates are important to the dividend process.

① Date of declaration: Date a dividend is declared by the board of directors.

② Date of record: Stockholders who own the stock as of a certain date are entitled to receive the dividend.

③ Date of payment: Date dividend checks will be mailed to stockholders of record.

Declaration of dividends reduces the retained earnings portion of the owners' equity of the corporation and creates a liability called dividends payable. Payment of the dividend eliminates the liability and reduces assets (usually cash).

Some of the major transactions related to retained earnings are as follows:

(1) Cash dividends

Cash dividends reduce retained earnings and become a current liability when declared. Three requirements for the payment of a cash dividend are: retained earnings, an adequate cash position and dividend action by the board of directors. Dividends are paid only through action by the board of directors. An entry to record the transactions is as below:

On the declaration date:

Dr. Retained earnings　　　　　　　　　　　　　× × ×

　　Cr. Dividends payable—Cash dividends　　　× × ×

On the payment date:

Dr. Dividends payable　　　　　　　　　　　　× × ×

　　Cr. Cash　　　　　　　　　　　　　　　　　× × ×

(2) **Stock dividends**

Stock dividend is a term used to describe a distribution of additional shares of stock to a company's stockholders in proportion to their present holdings, which present a transfer of retained earnings to the appropriate stock. An important distinction must be drawn between a cash dividend and a stock dividend. A cash dividend reduces both assets and stockholders' equity. A stock dividend causes no change in assets or in total stockholders' equity. Each stockholder receives additional shares, but his or her percentage ownership in the corporation is no larger than before.

On the declaration date:

Dr. Retained earnings　　　　　　　　　　　　　× × ×

　　Cr. Dividends payable—Stock dividends　　　× × ×

On the payment date:

Dr. Dividends payable—Stock dividends　　　　× × ×

　　Cr. Capital stock　　　　　　　　　　　　　　× × ×

Exercises

Exercises 9.1

1. "Earnings" is another name for Net Profits. If earnings haven't been distributed as dividends, it should have been retained in the company. The name of this portion of number listed in the balance sheet is _____. 　　　　　　(　　)

　　A. paid-in capital　　　　　　　　B. retained earnings

C. dividend D. cash

2. Preferred stock may not have priority over common stock except in _____.
   ( )
   A. voting   B. conversion
   C. dividends   D. liquidate assets

3. _____ can not vote in the election of board of directors at annual meeting.
   A. Common stockholders   B. Debenture holders
   C. Preferred stockholders   D. Creditors

Exercises 9.2

If ABC Company declared to issue dividend per share at ¥0.5, and the company has outstanding stock of 1 000 000, then the dividend should be _____.

If ABC Company owned shares of 100 000 in its earlier stage, the market price was ¥200 per share. After the management of the business issued a 20% stock dividend, the amount of outstanding stock will be _____ (increased/ decreased /unchanged). Cash will be _____ (increased/decreased/unchanged). The market price per share willbe(increased/decreased/ unchanged).

Exercises 9.3

Carey Corporation, organized on July 1 with an authorization of 10 000 shares of common and preferred stock, respectively. If the corporation issues 8 000 shares at $40 par value for cash and 1 000 shares of 10% preferred stock at $100 par, make a journal entry to record the stockholders' investment and receipts of cash.

Dr. _____   _____
   Cr. _____   _____

Unit Ten

Financial Statement Analysis

Teaching Objectives
Upon completion of this chapter, you will:
1. Understand the basic forms of financial statement analysis.
2. Horizontal Analysis, Vertical Analysis, Ratio Analysis.

Vocabulary

acid-test ratio	酸性测试比率,速动比率
average days' inventory on hand	存货平均周转天数
average days' sales uncollected	应收销售款平均收现天数
base amount	基数
base period	基期
capital structure	资本结构
current ratio	流动比率
debt ratio	负债比率
efficiency ratio	效能比率,效率比率
equity ratio	股东权益比率,产权比率
financial statement analysis	财务报表分析
horizontal analysis	水平分析,横向分析
inventory turnover	存货周转率
liquidity ratio	流动比率
profitability ratio	盈利率
quick assets	速动资产
ratio analysis	比率分析
solvency analysis	偿债能力分析
vertical analysis	垂直分析,纵向分析

TEXT

10.1 Horizontal Analysis

Financial statement analysis pertains to managerial accounting. It involves transforming data into useful information and using analytical tools to help users make better business decisions. The users include decision makers both internal and external to the company. The internal users of accounting information are managing executives and administrators in the company. The purpose of financial statement analysis for these executives is to provide information for their scientific decisions and for the company's efficiency improvement. It helps reduce guesses and intuition. External users are those who are not directly involved in operating the company. They include shareholders, bankers, customers, suppliers, regulators, lawyers, etc. External users rely on financial statement analysis to make better and more informed decisions to pursue their own goals.

For example, the board of directors use the information of financial statement analysis to monitor the management's decisions. Employees and unions use this information in labor negotiations. Shareholders and creditors use this to assess the company's prospects in their investing and lending decisions. Suppliers use the information in establishing credit terms. Customers analyze financial statements in deciding whether to establish supply relationships. Public utilities set customer rates by analyzing financial statements. And auditors use financial statements analysis in assessing the "fair presentation" of their clients' financial statement numbers.

Horizontal analysis compares amounts for two or more successive periods. It involves the left-to-right movement of our eyes as we view comparative financial statements. Horizontal analysis begins with the computation of changes from the previous year to the current year in both dollar amounts and percentages.

1. Computation of dollar changes and percent changes

We can compute the dollar change for a financial statement item as:

Dollar change = Analysis period amount − Base period amount

In the formula, analysis period is the point of time under analysis, and base period is the point of time used for comparison. Often the previous year is used as the base period.

We compute the percent change by dividing the dollar change by the base period amount and then multiplying this quantity by 100%:

Unit Product Cost = (Analysis period amount − Base period amount)/Base period amount × 100%

2. Example of dollar changes and percent changes

An example of dollar and percent changes is given in the form of comparative financial statements for Lott Law Firm. Now we will show you the comparative financial statement to compute the dollar changes and percent changes, with February as the analysis period, January as the base period.

Example 10.1

Table10.1 Lott Law Firm
Comparative Balance Sheet

February 28, February and January of 2019   unit: $

	February	January	Dollar Changes	Percent Changes
ASSETS				
Current Assets				
Cash and cash equivalents	42 657	7 307	35 350	483.78%

Continued Table 10.1

	February	January	Dollar Changes	Percent Changes
Notes receivable	550		550	
Supplies	120	500	380	
Total current assets	43 327	7 807	35 520	454.98%
Non-current Assets, Net	47 000	2 000	45 000	2 250.00%
Total Assets	90 327	9 807	80 520	821.05%
LIABILITIES AND CAPITAL				
Lliabilities				
Current Liabilities				
Accounts payable	25 400	400	25 000	6 250.00%
Bank service charge payable	400		400	
Utilities payable	80		80	
Tax payable	16 512		16 512	
Total current liabilities	42 392	400	41 992	10 498.00%
Non-current Liabilities				
Bonds payable				
Mortgages payable				
Total non-current liabilities				
Total Liabilities	42 392	400	41 992	10 498.00%
Capital				
Beginning capital, Ted Lott	9 407	8 000	1 407	17.59%
Increase in capital	38 528	1 407	37 121	2 638.30%
Ending capital, Ted Lott	47 935	9 407	38 528	409.57%
Total Liabilities and Capital	90 327	9 807	80 520	821.00%

Continued Table 10.1

	February	January	Dollar Changes	Percent Changes
Fees Income	60 000	3 500	56 500	1 614.29%
Expenses				
Sales expenses	460	200	260	130.00%
General expenses	4 100	1 400	2 700	192.86%
Financial expenses	400	23	377	1 639.14%
Total Expenses	4 960	1 623	3 337	205.61%
Income before tax	55 040	1 877	53 163	2 832.33%
Less Income tax (30%)	16 512		16 512	
Net Income	38 528	1 877	36 651	1 952.64%

Note that when a negative amount appears in the base period and a positive amount in the ally's period (or vice versa), we cannot compute a meaningful percent change. Also, when there is no value in the base period, no percent change is computable. Finally when an item has a value in the base period and zero in the analysis period, the decrease is 100 percent.

After the dollar changes and percent changes are computed, we then try to identify the reasons for the changes though some of the growth figures are amazing and incredible for Lott Law Firm.

10.2 Vertical Analysis

Vertical analysis involves the up-down movement of our eyes as we review common-size financial statements. In vertical analysis, percentages are also used. They are used to show the relationship of a part (individual or a group of financial statement items) to a total (base amount) in a single financial statement. On a balance sheet the total figure (base amount) would be total assets, or total liabilities and owner's equity. On an income statement the viand total figure would be the net revenues or net sales. The total figure equals to 100% and otter the percentage of each part is computed in relation to that total. The resulting statement of percentages is called a common-size statement. This kind of percentage is called common-size percent and this way of analysis is also called common-size analysis.

1. Common-size statements

Since common-size statements show the percentages of the parts to the total, the common-size percents are the key point. A common-size percent is calculated by taking each individual financial statement amount under analysis and dividing it by its base amount:

Common size percent = Analysis amount/Base amount × 100%

2. Example of common-size financial statements

Common-size balance sheets and common-size income statements make up the common-size financial statements.

◆Example of common-size balance sheet

In the common-size balance sheet, a common-size percent for each asset, liability and owner's equity is computed using the total assets as the base amount. When a company's successive balance sheets are presented in this way, changes of assets, liabilities, and owner's equity are apparent. Example 10.2 shows a common-size comparative balance sheet (统一度量式财务报表(又称为"百分比式")) for Lott Law Firm.

Example 10.2

Table 10.2 **Lott Law Firm**
Common-size Comparative Balance Sheet
February 28, February and January of 2019   unit: $

	Feb.	Jan.	Common-size Percents	
			Feb.	Jan.
ASSETS				
Current Assets				
Cash and cash equivalents	42 657	7 307	47.23%	74.50%
Notes receivable	550		0.60%	
Supplies	120	500	0.13%	5.10%
Total current assets	43 327	7 807	47.97%	79.61%
Non-current Assets, Net	47 000	2 000	52.03%	20.39%
Total Assets	90 327	9 807	100.00%	100.00%
LIABILITIES AND CAPITAL				
Liabilities				
Current Liabilities				
Accounts payable	25 400	400	28.12%	4.07%
Bank service charge payable	400		0.44%	
Utilities payable	80		0.09%	
Tax payable	16 512		18.28%	

Continued Table 10.2

	Feb.	Jan.	Common-size Percents	
			Feb.	Jan.
Total current liabilities	42 392	400	46.93%	4.07%
Non-current Liabilities				
Bonds payable				
Mortgages payable				
Total non-current liabilities				
Total Liabilities	42 392	400	46.93%	4.07%
Capital				
Beginning capital, Ted Lott	9 407	8 000	10.41%	81.57%
Increase in capital	38 528	1 407	42.65%	14.35%
Ending capital, Ted Lott	47 935	9 407	53.07%	95.92%
Total Liabilities and Capital	90 327	9 807	100.00%	100.00%

Some information that stands out includes (1) a decrease in cash and cash equivalents (74.5% to 47.23%), therefore currents assets are affected (from 79.61% down to 47.97%), (2) an increase in non-current assets (20.39% to 52.03%) and accounts payable (4.07% to 28.12%); (3) a decrease in ending capital (95.92% to 53.07%). Causes for all these increases and decreases have to be carefully examined and explained.

◆Example of common-size income statement

Our analysis also benefits from an examination of a common-size income statement. The amount of revenues is usually the base amount, 100%. Each common-size income statement item appears as a percent of revenues. Example 10.3 shows the common-size comparative income statement（百分比比较利润表）for Lott Law Firm.

Example 10.3

Table 10.3 Lott Law Firm
Common-size Comparative income Satement
As of the month of February, February and January of 2019   unit: $

	Feb.	Jan.	Common-size Percents	
			Feb.	Jan.
Fees Income	60 000	3 500	100.00%	100.00%
Expenses				
Sales expenses	460	200	0.77%	5.71%
General expenses	4 100	1 400	6.83%	40.00%
Financial expenses	400	23	0.67%	0.66%
Total Expenses	4 960	1 623	8.27%	46.37%
Income before tax	55 040		91.73%	
Less: Income tax (30%)	16 512		27.52%	
Net Income	38 528	1 877	64.21%	53.63%

This example shows that Lott's expense, as a percent of revenues, is very low (8.27%) compared with other industry. This is because the February income statement cannot show the whole picture of Lott Law Firm. Anyway there is a sharp decrease in operating expenses (5.71% to 0.77%) and in general expenses (40% to 6.83%). Financial expenses are estimated and shown in the Feb. income statement because the bank statement has not arrived at the firm. Most important of all the income tax expense is incurred (from zero to 27.52%). But net income increases steadily (from 53.63% to 64.21%).

10.3 Ratio Analysis

Ratios are the popular and widely used tools in financial statement analysis. Through ratio analysis, the meaningful relationships between the financial statement items are apparent and the areas that need further attention can be uncovered. Ratios help us detect the present condition and future trend. So they, like other analysis tools, are usually future-oriented.

The usefulness of ratios depends on skillful interpretation that is the most challenging aspect of ratio analysis. In this section we will describe a set of financial ratios and show how they are applied. The ratios selected are grouped into liquidity and efficiency ratios, solvency ratios, and profitability ratios.

1. Liquidity and efficiency ratios

Liquidity refers to a company's ability to meet short-term or unexpected cash needs. Efficiency refers to how productive a company is in using its assets. Both liquidity and efficiency are important in our analysis. If a company fails to meet its current obligations, its continuity is doubtful. For example, if the owner of a business possesses unlimited liability (as in a proprietorship or a partnership), a lack of liquidity endangers their personal assets. To creditors, delays in collecting interest and principal payments would occur if a company lacks liquidity. Also, a company's customer and supplier relationships are affected by short-term liquidity problems.

◆Working capital and current ratio

Working capital is the amount of current assets less current liabilities. A company needs sufficient amount of working capital to meet current debts, carry inventory, and grant cash discounts.

When evaluating a company's working capital, we need to consider the current ratio that relates current assets to current liabilities. See as follows:

$$\text{Current ratio} = \text{Current assets} / \text{Current liabilities}$$

Taken from Example 10.1, the current ratios for Lott Law Firm are:

February, 2019

43 327/42 392 = 1.02/1

January, 2019

7 807/400 = 19.5/1

The January current ratio is high, which suggests a strong liquidity position. A high ratio means a business is able to meet its current obligation. But an excessively high ratio means the company has invested too much in current assets, which is not considered an efficient use of funds because current assets do not generate much additional revenue. A low ratio is considered an immediate danger in its ability to meet obligations. The generally accepted current ratio is 2:1. But for service business like Lott Law Firm a current ratio of 1:1 is also acceptable since it carries little or no inventory other than supplies. On the other hand, a company selling high-priced goods requires a higher ratio. This is due to the difficult in judging customer demand.

◆ Acid-test ratio

Acid-test ratio, also called quick ratio is used to measure short-term debt-paying ability. The acid-test ratio is computed as:

$$\text{Acid-test ratio} = \text{Quick assets} / \text{Current liabilities}$$

Quick assets include cash, short-term investments, accounts receivable, and notes receivable. These are the most liquid types of current assets. Taken from Example10.1, the acid-test ratios for Lott Law Firm are:

	February, 2019	January, 2019
Cash and cash equivalents	42 657	7 307
Notes receivable	550	

Total quick assets   43 207   7 307
Total current liabilities   42 392   400
Quick assets/Current liabilities 43 207/42 392 = 1.02∶1   7 307/400 = 18.3∶1

◆ Accounts receivable turnover

Accounts receivable turnover measures how frequently a company turns its receivables into cash. This is computed as:

Accounts receivable turnover = Net sales/Average accounts receivable

For B Company Company there is only one accounting period, so we can get nowhere the average accounts receivable. Nor there are accounts receivable amounts for Lott Law Firm. So let's take MK's 2018 and 2019 financial data for illustration. See Talbe 10.4.

Table 10.4　MK Comparative Balance Sheet

May 31, 2019 and 2018   unit: $

	2019	2018	Dollar Changes	Percent Changes
Assets				
Current assets				
Cash and equivalents	445 421	262 117	183 304	69.9%
Accounts receivable, less allowance for doubtful accounts of 57 233 and 43 372	1 754 137	1 346 125	408 012	30.3%
Inventory	1 338 640	931 151	407 489	43.8%
Deferred income taxes	135 663	93 120	42 543	45.7%
Prepaid expenses	157 058	94 427	62 631	66.3%
Total current assets	3 830 919	2 726 940	1 103 979	40.5%
Property, plant, and equipment	922 369	643 459	278 910	43.3%

Continued Table 10.4

	2019	2018	Dollar Changes	Percent Changes
Identifiable intangible assets and goodwill	464 191	474 812	10,621	2.2%
Deferred income taxes and other assets	143 728	106 417	37 311	35.1%
Total assets	5 361 207	3 951 628	1 409 579	35.7%
Liabilities and Shareholders' Equity				
Current liabilities				
Current portion of non-current debt	2 216	7 301	5 085	69.6%
Notes payable	553 153	445 064	108 089	24.3%
Accounts payable	687 121	455 034	232 087	51.0%
Accrued liabilities	570 504	480 407	90 097	18.8%
Taxes payable	53 923	79 253	25 330	32%
Total current liabilities	1 866 917	1 467 059	399 858	27.3%
Non-current debt	296 020	9 584	286 436	2 988.7%
Deferred income taxes and other liabilities	42 132	43 285	1 153	2.7%
Commitments and contingencies				
Redeemable preferred stock	300	300	0	0.0%
Shareholders' equity				
Common stock at stated value:				
Class A convertible—101, 711 and 102 240 shares outstanding	152	153	1	0.7%

Continued Table 10.4

	2019	2018	Dollar Changes	Percent Changes
Class B—187 559 and 185 018 shares outstanding	2 706	2 702	4	0.1%
Capital in excess of stated value	210 650	154 833	55 817	36.0%
Foreign currency translation adjustment	31 333	16 501	14 832	89.9%
Retained earnings	2 973 663	2 290 213	683 450	29.8%
Total shareholders' equity	3 155 838	2 431 400	724 438	29.8%
Total liabilities and equity	5 361 207	3 951 628	1 409 579	35.7%

Table 10.5 **MK Comparative Income Statement**

For Years Ended May 31, 2019 and 2018   unit: $

	2019	2018	Dollar Changes	Percentage Changes
Revenues	9 186 539	6 470 625	2 715 914	42.0%
Cost and Expenses				
Costs of goods sold	5 502 993	3 906 746	1 596 247	40.9%
Selling and administrative	2 303 704	1 588 612	715 092	45.0%
Interest expense	52 343	39 498	12 845	32.5%
Other income/expense, net	32 277	36 679	4 402	12.0%
Total costs and expenses	7 891 317	5 571 535	2 319 782	41.6%
Income before income taxes	1 295 222	899 090	396 132	44.1%
Income taxes	499 400	345 900	153 500	44.4%
Net Income	795 822	553 190	242 632	43.9%
Net income per common share	2.68	1.88	0.8	42.6%
Average number of common and common equivalents shares	297 000	293 608		

With these data, MK's 2019 accounts receivable turnover is computed as:

$$\frac{9\ 186\ 539}{(1\ 754\ 137 + 1\ 346\ 125)/2} = 5.93 \text{ times}$$

MK's accounts receivable turnover was 5.9 times, similar to other competing companies. If accounts receivable are collected quickly, the accounts receivable turnover will be high. A high turnover is favorable because it means the company need not apply large amounts of capital to accounts receivable. But accounts receivable turnover can also be very high if credit terms are too restrictive, which will negatively affect the sales amount.

◆ Average days' sales uncollected

This ratio measures the average time taken to collect receivables. It is computed as (using the information in Table 10.4, Table 10.5):

$$\text{Average days' sales uncollected} = \text{Days in year/Receivable turnover}$$
$$= 365 \text{ day}/5.93 \text{ times}$$
$$= 61.55 \text{ days}$$

◆ Inventory turnover

If a company wants to know how long it holds its merchandise before selling it, the ratio of inventory turnover will surely answer the question. It is calculated with the following formula:

$$\text{Inventory turnover} = \text{Cost of goods sold/Average inventory}$$

Again let's take Table 10.4, Table 10.5 for illustration:

$$\text{Inventory turnover} = \frac{5\ 502\ 993}{(931\ 151 + 1\ 338\ 640)/2}$$
$$= 4.8 \text{ times}$$

A company with a high turnover requires a smaller investment in inventory.

◆ Average days' inventory on hand

This ratio measures the average days taken to sell inventory. Following the above-mentioned, average days' inventory on hand for MK is calculated as follows:

$$\text{Average days' inventory on hand} = \text{Days in year/Inventory turnover}$$
$$= 365 \text{ day}/4.8 \text{ times}$$
$$= 76 \text{ days}$$

This formula estimates that MK's inventory will be turned into receivables (or cash) in 76 days, which is not considered quite fast.

◆Total assets turnover

Total assets turnover describes the ability of a company to use its assets to generate sales. It is calculated with:

$$\text{Total asset turnover} = \text{Revenues/Average total assets}$$

The usual practice of averaging total assets is to add up both the beginning and ending assets of accounting period and divide the total by two. Taking the information from the above Table 10.4, Table 10.5, this ratio is computed as:

$$\text{Total asset turnover} = \frac{9\ 186\ 539}{(5\ 361\ 207 + 3\ 951\ 628)/2}$$
$$= 1.97 \text{ times}$$

2. Solvency ratios

Solvency refers to a company's long-run financial ability to cover long-term obligations. Analysis of capital structure is the key point in evaluating solvency. Here, we will show the tools of solvency analysis. Our analysis is concerned with a company's ability both to meet its obligations and to provide security to its creditors over the long run.

◆Debt ratio

This ratio assesses the portion of assets contributed by owners and the portion contributed by creditors. It expresses the total liabilities as a percent of total assets. This is computed as:

$$\text{Debt ratio} = \text{Total liabilities/Total assets} \times 100\%$$

◆Equity ratio

The equity ratio expresses the total owner's equity as a percent of total assets. This is computed as:

Equity ratio = Total owners equity/Total assets × 100%

3. Profitability ratios

Profitability refers to a company's ability to produce profits. Profitability is also relevant to solvency. Profitability is of special interest to all of us. Then let's discuss the importance of profitability in our financial statement analysis.

Net profit margin (净利率) Net profit margin reflects a company's ability to earn a net income from sales. It is calculated in the formula as follows:

Net profit margin = Net income/Revenue × 100%

◆Return on total assets

This ratio measures the overall earning power or profitability of a company. It is calculated in the formula as below:

Return on total assets = Net income/Average total assets

Take the information in Table 10.4, Table 10.5, MK's 2019 return on total assets is:

$$\frac{795\ 822}{(5\ 361\ 207 + 3\ 951\ 628)/2} \times 100\% = 17.1\%$$

The 17.1% return on total assets is favorable compared to most businesses.

◆Return on equity

This ratio measures the rate of return on owners' equity. It tests a firm's efficiency at generating profits from every dollar of net assets, and shows how well a company uses its invested dollars to generate earnings. It is calculated in the formula as below:

Return on equity (ROE) = Net income/Total owners' equity × 10%

Using the information in Table 10.4, Table 10.5, MK's 2019 return on equity is:

$$\text{Return on equity (ROE)} = \frac{795\ 822}{3\ 155\ 838} \times 100\% = 25.2\%$$

4. DuPont analysis

By breaking ROE into three main components: profit margin, total assets turnover and leverage factor (财务杠杆), DuPont analysis is an overall analysis of a company's ROE. Breaking the ROE into distinct parts, managers or investors can examine how effectively a company is using equity, since poorly performing components will drag down the overall figure. It is calculated in the formula as follows:

Return on equity (ROE) = Return on total assets × Equity multiplier

Return on total assets = Profit margin × Total asset turnover

Equity multiplier = Total assets/Owners' equity

Based on the above, the calculation formula is:

$$ROE = \frac{\text{Net income}}{\text{Revenue}} \times \frac{\text{Revenue}}{\text{Total assets}} \times \frac{\text{Total assets}}{\text{Owners' equity}}$$

$$= \text{Profit margin} \times \text{Total asset turnover} \times \text{Equity multiplier}$$

Taking data from Talbe 10.4, Table 10.5, MK's 2019 ROE is calculated as follows:

$$\text{Return on equity (ROE)} = \frac{795\,822}{9\,186\,539} \times \frac{9\,186\,539}{5\,361\,207} \times \frac{5\,361\,207}{3\,155\,838}$$

$$= 8.66\% \times 171.3\% \times 1.698$$

$$= 25.19\%$$

Applying the DuPont analysis, we get the same result of ROE. But this method helps us do a better analysis with other ratios.

Besides the ratios introduced above, we have other ratios to be used to analyze financial statements.

Exercises

Exercises 10.1

1. Financial statement analysis helps users make _____ business decisions.

2. Financial statement analysis helps reduce _____ and _____.
3. External users rely on financial statement analysis to make better and more _____ decisions to pursue their own goals.
4. Horizontal analysis involves the _____ movement of our eyes as we view comparative financial statements.
5. Vertical analysis involves the _____ movement of our eyes as we review common-size financial statements.
6. Common-size statements show the _____ of the parts to the total. A common-size percent is calculated by taking each individual financial statement amount under analysis and dividing it by its _____ amount.
7. The usefulness of ratios depends on _____, which is the most challenging aspect of ratio analysis.
8. Liquidity refers to a company's ability to meet _____ or _____ cash needs.
9. Efficiency refers to how _____ a company is in using its assets.

Exercises 10.2

Use horizontal analysis to compute the amount and percentage changes for the income statement below, with the year 2019 as the analysis period. (Round the percentage changes to one decimal place.)

Tallman Works, Inc.

Comparative Income Statement

For the Years Ended December 31, 2019 and 2018   unit: $

	2019	2018	Dollar changes	Percentage Changes
Net sales	180 000	145 000	_____	_____%
Cost of goods sold	112 000	88 000	_____	_____%
Gross margin	68 000	57 000	_____	_____%
Sales expenses	40 000	30 000	_____	_____%
Operating income	28 000	27 000	_____	_____%

	2019	2018	Dollar changes	Percentage Changes
Interest expenses	4 000	5 000	_____	_____ %
Income before income taxes	24 000	22 000	_____	_____ %
Income taxes, 30%	7 200	6 600	_____	_____ %
Net income	16 800	15 400	_____	_____ %
Earnings per share (10 000 shares outstanding)	1.68	1.54	_____	_____ %

Exercises 10.3

Use vertical analysis to express the comparative balance sheet. (Round computations to one decimal place.)

Longman Works, Inc.

Common-size Comparative Balance Sheet

December 31, 2019 and 2018   unit: $

	2019	2018	Common-size Percents	
			2019	2018
Assets				
Current assets	24 000	20 000	_____ %	_____ %
Property, plants, and equipment (net)	130 000	100 000	_____ %	_____ %
Total assets	154 000	120 000	100%	100%
Liabilities and Stockholders' Equity				
Current liabilities	18 000	22 000	_____ %	_____ %
Non-current liabilities	90 000	60 000	_____ %	_____ %
Stockholders' equity	46 000	38 000	_____ %	_____ %
Total liabilities and stockholders' equity	154 000	120 000	100%	100%

Exercises 10.4

1. Using the information in Table 10.3, calculate the current ratio for Longman Works, Inc. in year 2018.
2. Using the information in Table 10.4, calculate the acid-test ratio for MK in the year 2019 and 2018.
3. Using the information in Table 10.4, calculate the debt ratio for MK in the year 2019.
4. Using the information in Example 10.1, calculate the profit margin for Lott Law Firm in February and January.

Part II　参考译文

Part II 参考论文

第一单元 会计概述

会计被称为商业语言。每一个拥有资金、机器和建筑物等资源的营利性商业组织都运用"会计"这个词,通过它可以为这些商业组织提供其所拥有的资源使用情况相关的财务信息。此外非营利性的组织也会使用"会计"来衡量他们的经济活动。

1.1 会计的定义

会计可以被定义为一个信息系统。这个信息系统可以对各项经济事件进行识别、记录并起到沟通作用。这样就可以为具有相关利益的使用者提供决策支持。会计还有另外一个定义。会计可以记录、报告、分析企业财务活动,并提供财务属术语反映出商业信息。早期会计侧重于传统的记录功能,相比之下,现代会计更侧重于计划、控制、预算和预测。

1.2 会计信息的使用和分类

会计信息是用来满足两类信息使用者的需求的:一类是外部使用者,他们虽然不经营企业,但是他们是企业利益的直接相关人,譬如所有者、投资者、债权人和经纪人;另一类是来自于企业内部的使用者,包括经理、雇员和工会等企业中的具有直接关系的人。

因此会计也被分为两种类型:财务会计和管理会计。财务会计主要编制财务报告和财务报表,这些数据是为企业以外的使用者编制的,也称为对外会计。而管理会计则主要是向企业内部的管理层提供决策信息,由于管理会计基本上是在企业内部使用,因此也称为内部会计。

1.3 会计基本假设和会计准则

为了发展会计准则,一系列假设和原则被用作会计活动中的基本准则,称为"一般公认会计准则"(GAAP)。这些假设和原则也构成了国际性的财务报告的基础。

1. 会计假设

（1）货币计量假设

货币单位假设要求会计账目只能记录可以用货币表示的内容。该假设对财务报告具有重要意义。因为货币交换是经济业务交易的基础，所以以货币来衡量经济业务是有意义的。但是，这也意味着投资者、债权人和管理者所需的某些重要信息不会在财务报告中报告，因为它们无法用金钱来衡量。

例如，客户满意度对每项业务都很重要，但不容易用美元来量化，因此不会在财务报表中报告。

（2）经济实体假设

经济实体假设也称为会计实体假设。经济实体假设指出，每个经济实体都必须分别进行记录和说明。有鉴于此，每个经济实体的会计账目必须独立于其他企业和企业所有者。

这意味着公司是与所有者分开的独立实体，其会计账户仅反映公司的财务活动，而不反映所有者的交易。必须确保公司的所有交易及其过程都记录在公司的财务报告中。特别是，必须确保排除所有者的交易。例如，如果您是Dove的股票持有人，那么您在个人银行账户中拥有的现金量不会在Dove的财务报告中报告。

（3）会计期间假设

会计期间假设规定，企业应为各自的交易进行会计处理并准备不同时间段的财务报表。换句话说，企业的日常被人为地分为相等的短时间段，以使其更容易计算利润并反映企业的财务状况。这称为会计期间，通常为一个月、一季度或一年。该原理是对先前假设的重要补充。

（4）持续经营假设

持续经营假设指出，除非提供足够的负面证据阻止该业务，否则该业务将在可预见的未来继续运营。此假设可确保以连续方式准备资产评估、计提折旧和会计报告。

2. 原则

（1）历史成本原则

它要求记录的是资产在获得时按成本或购置时所发生的支出，而不是平均的市场价值记录。这也适用于负债的记录。例如，如果沃尔玛以300 000美元的价格购买一块土地，则该土地的成本将在财务报告中以此金额报告，无论其市值增加了多少。该原则保证了信息的真实性，从而消除了主观和潜在有偏差的市场价值的机会，但这没有什么关系。

（2）收入确认原则

该原则要求在实际实现收入时以及在发生支出时（而不是在收到现金时）记录收入或支

出。这种会计方式称为权责发生制会计。

(3) 充分披露原则

该原则要求披露所有可能对财务报表产生影响的情况和事件。如果重要项目无法在财务报表中直接合理地报告,则应对其进行注释。

(4) 匹配原理

该原则要求收入必须与会计中的相关费用或成本相匹配。支出不是在执行工作或产品被生产出来时确认,而是在工作或产品创造实际收入时进行确认。此原理有助于计算特定会计期间的净收入或亏损。

1.4 会计要素和会计等式

会计旨在反映企业运营资金的流动。为了实现这一目标,建立账户以提供有关这些资金流动的有用信息。账户是会计系统中的一个元素,用于衡量、分类和汇总业务活动。

1. 会计要素

(1) 会计要素的定义

会计要素是指记账对象的基本分类以及记账对象的计算规则。它们用于反映和确定业务运营结果的目的。

(2) 会计要素分类

从静态角度来说,企业所拥有的任何形式的经济资源(在会计中称为资产)都有特定的来源。

它们不只是出现。通常,企业有两种可以获得资金的方式:第一,是企业外部(称为债权人)的贷款,这类资产只能在规定的时间内使用,并且需要在到期时偿还。另一类是所有者对企业的投资,可以长期使用。它参与利润分配,这将增加或减少业务资产。前者在会计术语中称为负债,后者被称为所有者权益。资产、负债和所有者权益是资产负债表中包含的三个基本的会计要素。

从动态角度来讲,企业的经营活动将不可避免地导致企业资本价值的变化。资本的消耗和回收分别称为费用和收入。两者在损益表中列出。

根据其经济内容,会计要素可以分为资产、负债、所有者权益、收入、支出。账户的经济内容是指会计对象的特定内容。这种分类有助于了解每个账户的计算和监管内容,并有助于分析财务报表。

◆资产

对资产来说,更完整的定义是:企业拥有或控制的,具有一定货币价值的,有望使未来业务受益的一切经济资源,例如现金、土地、建筑物等。就资产的流动性而言,资产可分为三大类:流动资产;不动产,工厂和设备(固定资产);无形资产。

流动资产是指预期在一年内或超过一年的经营周期内转换为现金或被企业用尽的资产。它可以分为现金、应收款(欠公司的钱)、预付款、库存(持有待售商品)、短期投资等。

流动资产就像企业的血液一样,如果没有流动资产的流入和流出形成正常的商业活动,就不可能对企业的所有经济活动(如购买、销售等)进行计量。

土地、厂房和设备,也称为固定资产,是指公司拥有的长期或相对永久性资产。它们通常具有相对较长的使用期限,包括土地、建筑物、机械、家具和设备等。它们也被视为重要的有形资产。

无形资产是指公司拥有的那些例如专利、版权、商标或商誉等资产。它们没有物理形态。但是在很多情况下,它们对公司来说非常有价值。

◆负债

根据国际会计准则委员会(IASC)的规定,当履行现时义务很可能导致表明经济利益的资源外流时,应当在资产负债表中确认负债。一个更简单的理解是负债是欠外人(债权人)的债务。负债通常很容易识别,因为其中大多数带有标题为"应付"的标题。例如,应付账款、应付票据等。负债分为两类:流动负债和长期负债。

流动负债是指必须在一年内或超过一年的会计期间内偿还的债务。流动负债的常见形式是应付账款、应付票据、应付利息、应交税金等。借入流动负债的目的是满足业务运营的短期需求。

长期负债的投资回收期超过一年。与流动负债相比,长期负债通常数额都很大。

◆所有者权益

所有者权益是指所有者投资于业务或在运营过程中积累的资源。如果是股份有限公司,则称为股东权益(请参阅第2单元的企业形式)。根据会计等式,企业的所有者权益是资产与负债之间的差额。

它代表所有者对商业资产的索赔,主要包括两部分:实收资本(所有者的投资)和留存收益(在业务运营过程中累积的收益)。

◆收入

收入是企业活动的正常运营中的现金流入或实体资产的其他增值,负债的清偿或两者的组合。收入引起所有者权益增加。

◆费用

费用是在业务活动的正常运营中的资金流出、其他资产消耗、负债产生或几者兼而有之。费用导致所有者权益减少。

2. 会计等式

资产、负债和所有者权益以及它们之间的关系描绘了企业财务的平衡状况。这种平衡称为会计等式,其中资产位于左侧,负债与所有者权益位于右侧。会计等式为会计实践奠定了理论基础,对于复式记账法和财务报表的编制都极为重要。

交易①在该业务中投资了3 000美元现金。

        资产 = 负债 + 所有者权益
①现金 + $3 000   资本 + $3 000
 余额 $3 000 $3 000

交易②以2 000美元的信用额购买办公设备。

        资产 = 负债 + 所有者权益
①现金 + $3 000   资本 + $3 000
②会计办公记录:
设备 + $2 000   支付 + $2 000
 余额 $5 000 $2 000 $3 000

1.5 记录业务交易:复式记账法

交易是影响企业实体财务状况的经济事件。公司每天可能有数百甚至数千笔交易。但是无论如何,会计等式仍然保持平衡。

我们已经看到资产如何等于负债和所有者权益的总和。这是因为双重性原则,这意味着所有经济事件都会产生双重影响,或者增加或者减少,或者两者都有,这将相互抵消也就是平衡。这个概念称为复式记账法。为了进一步了解这一点,我们需要从基本概念——会计账户入手。

1. 账户设置

我们介绍了基本的会计要素,其中包括属于资产、负债和所有者权益,收入和支出等类别的账户。因为企业的经济交易很复杂,所以每个账户都包含不同的特定内容。例如,现金和库存都是资产,但是它们具有不同的性质。这就是为什么我们将会计要素进一步分类为不同的账户,这是会计的基础元素。账户是进行会计分录和准备财务报表的基础。它是公司账户的列表,称为会计科目表。列出的账户已编号,以便于进行会计的识别和交易录入。

2. T形账户

<table>
<tr><td colspan="2" align="center">会计账户</td></tr>
<tr><td align="center">借方</td><td align="center">贷方</td></tr>
<tr><td align="center">借方余额</td><td align="center">贷方余额</td></tr>
</table>

实际上,最简单和最常见的账户形式是T形账户。之所以这样称呼它是因为它看起来像英文字母T。

T形账户由三部分组成:账户名称、借方和贷方。T形账户的左侧称为借方,右侧称为贷方。注意以下事实:借方和贷方仅表示"左"和"右",而不是"增加"或"减少"。通常,这两个术语缩写为Dr.和Cr.。

在账户左侧输入金额时,无论账户名称如何,都称为该账户的借方或该账户已借记;当金额位于账户右侧时,称为该账户的贷方或该账户已贷记。账户的借方和贷方之间的差额称为账户余额。

3. 借方和贷方规则

通过以上讨论,我们知道为了保持会计等式平衡,所以借方金额必须等于贷方金额。这些规则可以用图形方式说明如下:

	资产		=	负债		+	所有者权益	
	借方	贷方		借方	贷方		借方	贷方
①定理								
②增加	+				+			+
③减少		−		−			−	
④一般余额	×				×			×

	收入		支出	
	借方	贷方	借方	贷方
①定理				
②增加		+	+	
③减少	−			−
④一般余额		×	×	

第二单元　企业组织形式

企业所有权结构基本上有三种类型或形式:个人独资企业、合伙企业和公司。

2.1　个人独资企业

绝大多数的小企业起初都是个人独资企业。这种企业是个人所有的,他们日常经营业务。所有者拥有企业的所有资产以及企业产生的利润。他们还对其中的任何责任或债务承担全部责任。在法律和公众眼中,企业所有者与企业是同一个人。

(1)独资企业的优势
①最简单最方便的所有权形式。
②独资企业拥有完全的控制权,可以在法律允许的范围内做出自己认为合适的决定。
③独资经营者会获得企业产生的全部收入,以维持或进行再投资。
④从业务流量直接计入所有者的个人纳税申报表。
⑤在有必要解散企业时,企业很容易解散。

(2)独资企业的劣势
①独资经营者承担无限责任,并对企业的所有债务承担法律责任。所有者的业务和个人资产面临风险。
②在筹集资金方面可能处于不利地位,通常仅限于使用个人储蓄或消费者贷款中的资金。
③可能很难吸引高素质的员工或那些有机会拥有一部分业务的动机。
④一些所有者权益,例如所有者的医疗保险费,不能直接从营业收入中扣除(只能部分扣除,作为对收入的调整)。

2.2　合伙企业

合伙企业是两个或两个以上经营者为营利而经营的非法人协会。许多小型企业,包括零售、服务和专业从业者,都是以合伙形式组织的。

合伙人应该有一项合伙协议,规定如何做出决定,利润分配,纠纷解决,如何将未来的合伙人纳入企业,如何买断合伙人以及将采取哪些步骤来解决解散事宜。

(1)合伙制企业的优点

①合伙关系相对容易建立,但是应该花时间来制订合伙协议。

②拥有合伙人较多时,企业募集资金的能力可能会增强。

③业务利润直接流入企业的合伙人的个人纳税申报表。

④如果以成为合伙人为动力,可能会吸引公司的员工加入合伙。

⑤企业通常会从具有互补技能的合作伙伴中受益。

(2)合伙制企业的劣势

①合作伙伴应对其他合作伙伴的行为承担连带责任。

②利润必须与他人分享。

③由于决策是共享的,因此可能会出现分歧。

④有些雇员的福利不能从纳税申报表的业务收入中扣除。

⑤合伙关系的寿命可能有限;它可能在合伙人退出或死亡后终止。

2.3 公　　司

公司是法人实体,这意味着它是与称为股东的所有者不同的实体。公司被视为一个"人"并拥有"人"的大部分权利和义务。公司不得担任公职或投票,但必须缴纳所得税。它可以建立为营利性组织或非营利性组织,并且可以是公开或私有形式。上市公司的股票在证券交易所进行交易。上市公司中可能有成千上万的股东。私人公司的股票不在交易所交易,通常只有少数股东。

(1)公司的优势

①股东对公司的债务或对公司的判决承担有限责任。

②一般而言,股东只能对其在公司股票中的投资负责。(但是请注意,管理者可能对其行为承担个人责任,例如未预扣和缴纳就业税。)

③公司可以通过出售股票筹集更多资金。

④公司可以扣除向管理者和员工提供的福利成本。

(2)公司的劣势

①公司成立过程比其他形式的组织需要更多的时间和金钱。

②公司注册可能会导致更高的总体税收。支付给股东的股息不能从营业收入中扣除;因此会被征税两次。

2.4 独资企业和合伙企业的会计

在很多方面,合伙制企业的会计与独资制企业的会计相似,只是前者拥有更多的所有者。因此,合伙企业的会计子账户为每个合作伙伴维护一个单独的资本账户和提款账户。合伙企业不承认其为合伙人提供给组织的服务的薪金费用。支付给合作伙伴的账户通过对合作伙伴的账户进行借记来记录。

1. 初始投资核算

由于合伙企业的所有权在两个或多个合伙人之间分配,因此为每个合伙人维护单独的资本和提款账户。

如果合伙人将现金投资于合伙企业,则该合伙企业的现金账户会记入借方,而合伙人的资本账户则会计入投资额。

如果合作伙伴投资了除现金以外的其他资产,则会从资产账户中扣除借项,并以该资产的市场价值贷记该合作伙伴的资本账户。如果资产欠下一定金额,合伙企业可能承担责任。在这种情况下,资产账户记入借方,而合伙人的资本账户记入所投资资产的市场价值与承担的负债之间的差额。

2. 净损益分配

净损益根据合伙协议分配给合伙人。在合作伙伴之间没有达成任何协议的情况下,无论合作伙伴的投资比例如何,损益必须平均分配。如果合伙协议规定了应如何分配利润,则损失必须与利润分配的基准相同。净收入不包括合伙企业投资的收益或损失。

2.5 会计交易和股息

1. 以现金发行的股票

公司可以发行股票换现金。当像 Big City Dwellers 这样的公司以面值现金发行 5 000 股面值 1 美元的普通股换取现金时,这意味着该公司将获得 5 000 美元(5 000 股 × 每股 1 美元)。通过出售(借记)现金和增加(贷记)普通股 $ 5 000 来记录该股票的销售。分录如下:

借:现金　　　　　　　　5 000
　　贷:股本——普通股　　　5 000

2. 为换取资产或服务而发行的股票

如果公司发行股票以换取资产或作为购买的服务的付款,则必须使用成本原则。为换取公司股票而收取的资产成本为已发行股票的市场价值。如果尚未确定股票的市场价值(当公司刚成立时会发生），则将收到的资产或服务的市场公允价值用于交易的估值。如果总值超过已发行股票的面值或标明值，则超出面值或标明值的部分将添加到附加的实收资本（或实收资本的实值）账户中。

例如，一家初创公司 J Trio,Inc. 向其律师发行 10 000 股其面值为 0.50 美元的普通股，以支付该律师事务所支付的 $ 50 000 发票，这是作为律师事务所帮助建立公司的服务报酬。因为尚未确定公司股票的市场价值，所以记录此交换的分录将基于发票价值。记录交易的条目增加（借方）组织成本 5 万美元，增加（贷方）普通股 5 000 美元(10 000 股×0.50 美元面值)，并增加（贷方）额外的实收资本，即 $ 45 000（差额）。组织成本是一种无形资产，包含在资产负债表中，并在不超过 40 年的一段时间内摊销。

3. 股息

董事会必须批准所有股息。股利分配可以将现金、资产或公司的自有股票分配给其股东。资产分配，也称为财产股息，将不在此处讨论。在批准股息之前，公司必须拥有足够的未分配利润和现金（现金股息）或足够的授权股票（股票股息）。考虑股息时，三个日期是相关的：

(1) 宣布日期

宣布日期是董事会正式授权支付现金股利或发行股票的日期。该日期确定了公司的责任。在该日期，将从留存收益中扣除要支付或分配的股利的价值。

(2) 记录日期

记录日期不需要正式的会计分录。它确定谁将获得股息。

(3) 付款或分配日期

支付或分配的日期是将股利分配给在册股东的日期。

例如，5 月 1 日，Triple Play 董事会授权 6 月 30 日向 5 月 25 日在册的股东支付 5 万美元的现金股利。在 5 月 1 日宣布之日，该股利的价值为从留存收益中扣除并在单独的应付股利账户中将其设置为负债。

借：利润分配　　　　　　　　　　50 000

　　贷：应付股息　　　　　　50 000

应该注意的是，有些公司使用称为"普通股股息"和"优先股股息"的单独账户，而不是用留存收益来记录宣布的股息。如果使用这些账户，则在期末进行结账时，以减少（借方）留存收益并减少（贷方）"股息,普通股"和"股息,优先股"，以将股息余额清零。账户更新保留的收入余额。

在付款当日，将现金发送给股东时，应付股利账户减少（借方），现金账户减少（贷方）。

借：应付股息　　　　　　　　　　50 000

　　贷：现金　　　　　　　　50 000

一旦股利公告并支付股息后,现金股利将减少总股东权益,同时减少总资产。股息不在利润表中报告。会在留存收益表或股东权益表中找到,而在支付时会在现金流量表中找到。

第三单元　财务报表

日常会计信息通常是详细、具体、庞大、分散的。为了清晰地了解企业的财务状况、经营业绩和财务状况的变化,需要对日常会计数据进行记录、分类、汇总和解释。最后将结果传达给决策者。

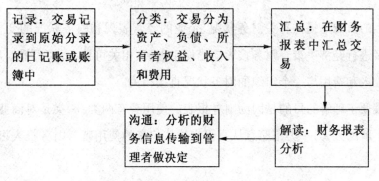

图 3.1　数据的方法

在沟通阶段,企业准备文件和表格以反映公司的财务状况,这些被称为财务报表。财务报表是会计过程的最终产物,因为用户需要知道企业是如何做经济决策的。为此,编制的财务报表需要符合大多数用户的共同需要。然而,财务报表并没有提供使用者在做出经济决策时可能需要的所有信息,因为它们主要反映过去事件的财务影响,并不一定提供非财务信息。

财务报表的目的是提供有关企业财务状况、经营表现和现金流量的信息。有关财务状况的信息主要在资产负债表中提供。有关公司经营表现的资料主要在利润表中提供。现金流量表提供有关现金流量的信息。资产负债表和利润表是最常用的两种基本财务报表。

3.1　定　义

财务报表是关于一个组织的财务结果和状况的报告的集合。它们之所以有用,原因如下：

①确定企业产生现金的能力,以及现金的来源和用途。

②确定企业是否有能力偿还债务。

③跟踪趋势线上的财务结果,发现任何潜在的盈利问题。

④从能够表明企业状况的报表中得出财务比率。

⑤调查某些细节商业交易,随附报表的披露所述。

3.2　企业主体使用财务报表的目的

财务报表的目的是提供有关财务状况、企业的经营表现和财务状况的变化的信息,有助于广大使用者进行经济决策。财务报表应当便于理解、相关可比、真实可靠。所报告的资产、负债、权益、收入和费用与一个组织的财务状况直接相关。

财务报表便于理解的目的是因为财务报表的使用者有两类,一类是对商业和经济活动及会计有合理了解的人,另一类是愿意认真研究这些信息的使用者。财务报表可供使用者用于不同目的：

①所有者和管理者需要财务报表做出影响其持续经营的重要经营决策。然后对这些报表进行财务分析,以便管理层更详细地了解这些数字。这些报表也被用作管理层向股东提交的年度报告的一部分。

②员工在与管理层签订劳资协议条款(CBA)时,也需要这些报告,特别是工会或个人在对薪水、升职、公司排名等方面谈判时,也需要这些财务报告信息。

③潜在投资者利用财务报表评估投资企业的可行性。财务分析通常由投资者使用,由专业人士(财务分析师)准备,从而为他们提供做出投资决策的依据。

④金融机构(银行和其他贷款公司)利用它们来决定是否向公司提供新的营运资本或延长债务证券(如长期银行贷款或债券)以资助扩张和其他重大支出。

⑤政府实体(税务机关)需要财务报表来确定公司申报和支付的税收和其他关税的适当性和准确性。

⑥向企业提供信贷的供应商需要财务报表来评估企业的信誉。

⑦媒体和公众也出于各种原因对财务报表感兴趣。

3.3 资产负债表

资产负债表显示企业在特定时间的财务状况。它报告资产(企业拥有的资源)和对这些资产的索赔。这些债权分为两类:债权人的债权(公司的债务)称为负债。所有者的债权(所有者在公司中的权益)称为所有者权益。

表 3.1 资产负债表
2007 年 12 月 31 日   单位:美元

资产		
现金		21 000
应收账款		4 500
设备		40 000
减:累计折旧	5 500	34 500
总资产		60 000
负债		
应付账款		4 000
应付薪酬		2 000
应付利息		1 700
应付票据		19 500
预收账款		1 500
负债总额		28 700
所有者权益		
资本		29 700
留存收益		1 600
所有者权益合计		31 300
负债和所有者合计		60 000

资产负债表显示企业在特定时间的财务状况。它报告资产(企业拥有的资源)和对这些

资产的索赔。这些债权分为两类:债权人的债权(公司的债务)称为负债。所有者的债权(所有者在公司中的权益)称为所有者权益。

3.4 利润表

利润表显示一个企业在一定时期内的经营表现和盈利能力。这也被称为损益报表。从利润表中,财务报表的使用者可以清楚地了解到某一特定时期(即会计期间)的经营成果或经营业绩。因此,用户能够分析业务利润增加或减少的趋势和原因。

收入是指会计期间经济利益的增加,其形式是资产流入或增加,或导致权益增加的负债减少,但与权益参与方出资有关的除外。收入的定义包括收入和收益,收入是在企业的日常活动中产生的,用不同的名称来称呼,如销售、费用、利息、股息、版税和租金

利润表列出了公司的收入和费用。然后计算它们之间的差异。如果收入大于支出,则结果显示为净收入。相反,如果费用超过收入,则结果显示为净损失。利润表报告一段时间(如一年)经营业务的结果。

表3.2 损益表
截至2007年12月31日年度　　　　　　　　　　　　单位:美元

收入:	
销售收入	708 255
租金收入	600
总收入	708 855
费用:	
销售商品成本	525 305
销售费用	7 082
管理费用	34 890
利息支出	2 440
总费用	633 455
净收入	75 400

3.5 留存收益表

留存收益是指公司留存的净收益。留存收益表是资产负债表和损益表之间的一个联系,因为它显示了所有者在一个会计期间对公司权益的变化以及如何通过净收益和股利来反映

变化的。这是一个有用的商业支持声明。

表 3.3 留存收益表
截至 2007 年 12 月 31 日年度   单位:美元

期初余额	76 000
加:净收入	3 700
	79 700
减:利润分配	1 000
期末余额	78 700

3.6 现金流量表

现金流量表显示了一个会计期间现金来源和流向。它报告企业现金在三个领域的流动情况:经营活动、投资活动和筹资活动。

表 3.4 现金流量表
截至 2007 年 12 月 31 日年度   单位:美元

经营活动	
收到客户现金	71 800
收到利息的现金	17 000
支付工资的现金	230 000
支付租金的现金	125 000
支付其他项目的现金	300 000
经营活动提供的现金	80 000
投资活动	
购买土地	250 000
融资活动	
股息支出	35 000
现金减少	205 000
1 月 1 日现金	400 000
12 月 31 日现金	195 000

3.7 财务报表关系图

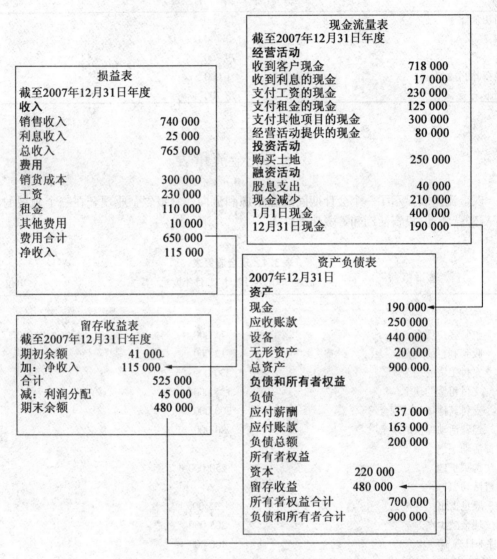

图3.2 财务报表关系

现金余额转入资产负债表,利润表余额转入留存收益表,留存收益表转入资产负债表。

第四单元 会计循环

会计循环是指企业为了记录和汇总会计数据而重复使用的步骤或程序。会计循环的步骤包括:

①分析源文档中的业务交易。
②在日记账中记录业务交易的影响。
③从日记账过账到总(和子)分类账账户。
④进行试算平衡。
⑤调整一些账户余额。
⑥编制财务报表。
⑦关闭临时账户。
⑧调整一些分录。

4.1 日记账和分类账

用于记录、分类和汇总会计信息的会计程序列通常称为会计循环。会计循环从最初记录商业交易开始,到正式财务报告的编制结束。总结这些交易对企业资产、负债和所有者权益的影响。

1. 日记账

企业业务发生的交易可以直接记入账户。但每个账户只显示该账户的变化,由于每笔交易的借方和贷方转到不同的账户,很难跟踪个别交易。例如,现金账户只包含现金变动的数据,不显示同一笔交易的相应分录。现金是如何产生或如何使用的,没有清楚说明。当一个企业的日常事务中涉及大量的事务时,记录交易中的错误很难追踪。这导致在分析业务评估时出现进一步的错误。解决这个问题的方法是采用按时间顺序记录业务交易。这叫作日记账。日记本也称为原始分录簿。

摘要是对每笔交易提供解释。然后将交易转移到适当的账户,以便更清楚地了解会计要素发生的变化。每笔交易都是一个单独的日记账分录,记录交易的过程称为记录日记账。日记账中的分录将过账到分类账,稍后将讨论。

日记账记录每笔交易的下列信息:
①交易日期。
②借记和贷记账户的名称。

③交易摘要。

④借记和贷记到每个账户。

表 4.1　资产负债表

2007 年 12 月 31 日　　　　　　　　　　　　　　　　　　　　　　　　　　第 1 页

日期	账户和交易摘要	过账标记	借方	贷方
3月2号	现金 应收账款——拉里 赊销给拉里		50 000	50 000

◆ 记账程序

①填写日期,日期为月在前日在后。

②在"账户和说明"标题下填写贷记和借记账户的准确名称。借记账户的名称写在该列左边的开头。贷记账户的名称写在下一行,缩进大约 1 英寸(1 英寸 =2.54 厘米)。交易摘要应该简短,但足以解释交易并将其与其他交易区分开来。

③将借方金额记入借方账户对应的相应列,贷方金额相应地记入贷方金额。

④在每个日记账分录后空一行。

⑤在将特定分录过账到总账之前,也就是说当金额不在"过账参考"列中记录任何内容。

2. 分类账

分类账提供了一种将具体资产、负债或所有者权益变动的所有信息汇总在一起的方法。它是会计系统的"参考书",用于对交易进行分类和汇总,并为财务报表编制数据。它对于管理提供了宝贵的信息来源。例如,资产现金的分类科目可以清楚地记录现金收入、现金支付和当前现金余额。

账户标题和编号出现在表格的顶部。"日期"列显示交易记录的日期,与在日记账上显示的日期相同。很少使用项目列,因为日记账中已经出现了交易摘要。过账标记列用于列出记录事务的日记账的页码。在账户的"余额"列中,每次借记或贷记账户时都会输入新的余额。它类似于 T 字账户。分类账比 T 字账户的优点是账户的当前余额总是可以显示的。但是,由于 T 型账户的易用性,它通常用于指示分类账的变化。

◆ 过账

交易记入日记账后需要过账,它们必须转移到分类账。将日记账中的数据传输到分类账的过程称为过账。其目的是总结交易对每个单独的资产、负债、所有者权益、收入和费用的影响。在过账过程中,日记账借方栏中列出的每个金额通过将其输入到分类账中相应账户的借方来过账,日记账贷方列中列出的每个金额都过账到分类科目的贷方。日记账分录的过账过程如表 4.2 所示,并采取以下步骤:

①将交易日期从日记账转移到分类账。
②将页码从日记账转移到分类账的日记账过账标记列。
③将日记账的借方金额过账为借方在分类科目中输入数字,贷方金额同上。
④一旦数字过账到分类科目,请在日记账的过账参考列中输入编码。

表4.2 会计科目表

资产负债表	损益表
1.资产	3.所有者权益
101 现金	301 实收资本
102 应收账款	302 留存收益
103 应收票据	303 备用金
104 办公用品	4.收入
105 设备	401 销售收入
106 库存商品	402 利息收入
107 预付保险费	5.费用
108 土地	501 工资支出
109 累计折旧	502 电话支出
110 无形资产	503 物资费
2.负债	504 广告费
201 应付账款	505 租金
202 应付票据	506 煤气费
203 应付工资	507 保险费
204 预收收入	508 折旧费

4.2　试算平衡表

　　试算平衡的目的是确保每个借方分录都有相应的贷方分录。由于每笔交易在账户中输入的借方和贷方金额相等,因此借方余额账户的总额应等于贷方余额账户的总额。
　　试算表是分类账中的科目列表,其中列出了各自的借方和贷方余额。
　　它是在一个会计期间结束时,在所有的交易都被记录下来后,为查看借方总额是否等于贷方总额而准备的,准备试算表的步骤如下:
①按资产、负债、所有者权益、费用和收入的顺序列出试算表中的所有账户名称。
②将借方余额从分类账账户转移到试算表的左栏,贷方余额转移到右栏。

③记录借方和贷方记录总数。
④比较总数,看它们是否相等。

表4.3 ABC服务公司试算平衡表
2011年11月30日   单位:美元

账户标题	借方	贷方
现金	3 800	
办公设备	2 000	
应付账款		2 000
资金		3 000
服务收入		1 000
薪资费用	200	
合计	6 000	6 000

4.3 调整分录

调整分录分为预付款或应计项目的日记账分录。每一个类别都有两个子类别。
◆预付款项
预付费用:在使用或消费之前以现金支付并记录为资产的费用。
预收收入:在获得收入之前作为负债收到的现金。
◆应计
应计收入:已获得但尚未收到现金或记录的收入。
应计费用:已发生但尚未支付现金或入账的费用。

表4.4 会计期末调整

调整类型	调整以前的账户	调整分录
预付费用	高估资产 低估费用	借方:费用 贷方:资产

续表4.4

调整类型	调整以前的账户	调整分录
预收账款	高估负债 低估收入	借方:负债 贷方:收入
应计收入	低估资产 高估收入	借方:资产 贷方:收入
应计费用	低估费用 低估负债	借方:费用 贷方:负债

为了正确地计量一个期间的收入和费用,需要调整分录,因为它们将实际发生的收入分配给收入的期间,将实际发生的费用分配给支出的期间。通过调整分录,相关资产和负债账户余额按照权责发生制的概念进行了更正。在编制财务报表之前,有必要调整分录。

编制试算表之后,由于要进行调整以与实际发生的费用和收入相匹配,借贷经常不平衡。

1. 预付费用

企业已支付但尚未受益的费用称为预付费用。常见的预付费用包括保险、税收、租金和折旧等。当费用预付时,资产账户会增加,以显示未来将收到的收益。在每个会计期末,需要进行分摊,记录本期发生的费用,在调整前,资产过多估计,费用过少估计(预付费用一般包括3个月、6个月等几个会计期间),因此,预付费用的调整分录会导致费用账户的增加(借方)和资产账户的减少(贷方)。

例4.1 预付保险

假设目标公司为3个月的保险支付了1 200美元。付款记录为一项资产的增加——预付保险和另一项资产现金的减少。因此,分录如下:

借方:预付保险费   1 200
　贷方:现金   1 200

在这个月的月末,三分之一的保险费用已经使用。就是400美元的预付费用已经用光了。因此在本月底调整分录为:

借方:保险费用   400
　贷方:预付保险   400

会计等式受到如下影响:

$$资产 = 负债 + 所有者权益$$
$$-400 \qquad -400$$

例4.2 物资

假设它购买了价值为5 000美元的物资。这是通过增加资产供应和减少资产现金来记录的。

借方:物资　　　　　　　　　　　5 000
　贷方:现金　　　　　　　　　　5 000

到月底,盘点存货显示,2 500 美元的供应品已经用完。因此,调整分录如下:

借方:物资费用　　　　　　　　　2 500
　贷方:物资　　　　　　　　　　2 500

会计等式受以下影响:

　　　资产　　＝　　负债　　＋　　所有者权益
　　　-2 500　　　　　　　　　　　-2 500

例 4.3　折旧

折旧是一种特殊的预付账款。指建筑物、设备、机动车辆等寿命长、在企业中使用年限长的固定资产的损耗。服务期称为资产的使用寿命或物资的使用寿命。由于固定资产预计提供服务年限较长,故按历史成本或实际成本作为资产而非费用入账。

按照配比原则,在资产使用寿命的每一期间,将该成本的一部分作为费用列报。折旧是将资产的成本在其使用寿命内分摊到费用中的过程(折旧见第 8 单元)。长期资产的购置实质上是对服务的长期预付款。因此,有必要对已使用的成本(费用)进行确认,并在会计期末报告未使用的成本(资产)。为了做到这一点,我们建立了一个称为累计折旧的账户,它是对它所抵消的资产账户的扣除。例如,如果一家公司以 100 万美元购买一台设备,并期望其使用寿命为 10 年,那么它将在 10 年内折旧。每一会计年度,公司将花费 10 万美元。

借方:折旧费用　　　　　　　　　100 000
　贷方:累计折旧　　　　　　　　100 000

会计等式的影响

　　　资产　　＝　　负债　　＋　　所有者权益
　　　-100 000　　　　　　　　　　-100 000

2. 预收账款

在收到对未来提供的服务的付款时,增加(贷记)一个称为未满期收入的负债账户,以确认产生的债务。诸如预付客户租金、客户未来服务的存款等项目可能会导致预收收入。预收收入随后通过向客户提供服务获得,因此需要调整。预收收入的调整分录导致负债账户的减少(借记)和收入账户的增加(贷记)。

例 4.4

西尔斯公司收到 4 000 美元的服务预付款,预计将在 4 个月内完成。这笔款项记作预收收入。月底,通过评估,本期收入 1 000 美元。以下是调整分录:

借方:预收账款　　　　　　　　　1 000
　贷方:服务收入　　　　　　　　1 000

这将影响会计等式如下：

$$资产 = 负债 + 所有者权益$$
$$-1\,000 \qquad\qquad +1\,000$$

3. 应计收入

在报表日已赚取但尚未记录的收入称为应计收入。应计收入可随着时间的推移而累积（应计），如利息收入。因此，需要调整分录来显示存在的应收账款。在调整之前，资产和收入都被低估了。应计收入的调整分录导致资产增加（借记）和收入账户增加（贷记）。

例 4.5

西尔斯公司以 300 美元的收入费用提供服务，直到稍后才能收到。在收到现金之前，资产和所有者权益将受到以下影响：

$$资产 = 负债 + 所有者权益$$
$$+300 \qquad\qquad +300$$

如果不作调整分录，资产和所有者权益将被低估。收到现金时：

借方：应收账款　　　　　　　　300
　贷方：服务收入　　　　　　　　300

如果没有调整分录，资产和所有者权益将被低估。

4. 应计费用

已发生但尚未支付或记录的应计费用称为应计费用。利息、税金和工资是应计费用的常见例子。应计费用产生的因素与应计收入相同。应计费用的调整对于记录已经存在的债务是必要的。在调整之前，负债和费用都被低估。因此，应计费用的调整分录导致费用账户增加（借方），负债账户增加（贷方）。

例 4.6 应计利息

西尔斯公司在 10 月 1 日签署了一份金额为 10 000 美元的三个月应付票据。该票据要求年利率为 12%。利息积累的数额由三个因素决定：票据面值、利率和期限。利息按以下方式确定：利息 = 票据面值 × 年利率 × 年数。

计算的时间一个月的利息成本为：$10\,000 \times 12\% \times 1/12 = 100$（美元）

会计等式影响如下：

$$资产 = 负债 + 所有者权益$$
$$+100 \qquad\qquad -100$$

月底将进行以下调整分录：

借方：利息支出　　　　　　　　100
　贷方：应付利息　　　　　　　　100

例 4.7

在服务完成后支付应计工资项目,如工资和佣金。仍以西尔斯公司为例,应付工资代表应计费用和相关负债。假设西尔斯已经累积了 2 000 美元的月底工资。该应计项目增加了负债、应付工资和费用账户,即工资费用,并对会计等式产生以下影响:

资产	=	负债	+	所有者权益
		+2 000		−2 000

调整分录为:

借方:工资支出　　　　　　2 000
　贷方:应付工资　　　　　　　　2 000

4.4　结账分录

结账分录包括结账临时账户和将数据转移到名为收入汇总的账户。它是一个非财务报表账户,仅用于促进结算过程。收入、费用和股息都是临时账户。与此相反,资产、负债和权益账户被称为真实账户,因为它们的余额在不同时期结转。关闭过程包括:①将收入和费用关闭到收入汇总表。②将收入汇总的账户余额转入留存收益。③股息从留存收益直接扣除。

例如,流动账户显示,国家城市公司有以下收入和费用信息:收入 35 000 美元,期间费用:工资 800 美元,广告费 5 000 美元,折旧费 5 000 美元,利息 200 美元;期间股息:200 美元。

①将收入和费用计入收入汇总表

借方:收入　　　　　　　　35 000
　贷方:收益汇总　　　　　　　35 000
借方:收益汇总　　　　　　11 000
　贷方:销售费用　　　　　　　　800
　　　广告费　　　　　　　　5 000
　　　折旧费　　　　　　　　5 000
　　　利息支出　　　　　　　　200

②现在收入汇总表有 24 000 美元的贷方余额,将结转到留存收益

借方:收益汇总　　　　　　24 000
　贷方:留存收益　　　　　　　24 000

③结清股利

借方:留存收益　　　　　　　　200
　贷方:股利　　　　　　　　　　200

4.5 调整后的试算平衡

调整及结清后,将重新编制试算平衡。这一次,它应该在财务报表编制的基础上保持完美的平衡。

第五单元 流动资产

在财务会计中,资产是经济资源,是某一主体控制的一种资源,它是过去事件的结果,未来的经济利益预计将由此流向该主体。

任何有形的或无形的,能够被拥有或控制以产生价值,并具有正经济价值的东西都被认为是资产。资产包括现金、应收账款、存货、供应品、设备、建筑物、土地等。会计资产通常具有以下三个特征:①预期未来将为公司带来经济利益;②由公司拥有或控制;③该公司是由于过去的交易或事件而获得的。资产被进一步分为流动资产和非流动资产,非流动资产将在下一个单元中讨论。

流动资产是指现金和其他预期能合理变现的资产,或在一年内或在超过一年的企业正常经营周期内出售或消耗的资产。除了现金和现金等价物外,流动资产通常还包括对短期有价证券投资、应收票据、应收账款、存货和预付费用。在流动资产类别中,项目按照流动性的顺序排列,流动性最强的在前,流动性最差的在后。现金显然是所有资产中流动性最强的。

5.1 现金与现金等价物

现金是指以纸币或硬币形式存在的货币,它还包括支票、汇票等现金等价物,以及从银行和其他金融机构可自由支取的存款。通常情况下,你可以认为现金是任何银行可接受的存入你账户的存款。现金是公司非常重要的组成部分,通过对现金流量的预测,用户可以确定现金的可用性以清偿到期债务,可以确定现金的可用性来支付股息,以及确定可用于未来安全投资的闲置现金的金额。

现金等价物是指满足以下两个条件的短期、流动性高的投入:第一,可随时转化为已知金额的现金;第二,快到期限时,市场价值受利率变化的影响不大。许多企业在资产负债表中将现金和现金等价物合并为一个项目列表。

现金是企业最具流动性的资产,企业的大部分交易都涉及现金的收支。所谓流动性是指企业的短期偿债能力。现金和现金等价物属于流动资产,这是因为它们可以随时被用于偿债,流动资产是企业保持高效率经营的必备条件。在资产负债表中,现金通常被列为流动资产中第一个项目。

由于现金比任何其他资产更容易被盗窃,为了安全起见,需要一个对现金适当进行内部控制的系统。一个有效的会计系统有助于对现金的管理和控制。对现金的有效管理包括以下措施:

①对现金收入、现金支出及其余额进行准确的核算;
②防止发生舞弊或盗窃事件而使现金遭受损失;
③始终保持足够的现金应对必要的支出,再加上一定的数额应付不测;
④避免持有过多的不能创造任何收入的闲置现金。

这里将探讨一下对现金交易和现金余额的一些主要内部控制。

首先,也是最重要的控制,现金的处理应该与现金的记录分开。也就是说,处理现金的员工不应该接触到会计记录,会计人员不应该接触到现金。这是因为当涉及两个人或两个人以上时,偷窃或出错更难发生。现金可能被偷,如果现金记录是由那些本身收支现金的人保管的话,这些员工可能通过伪造会计记录来掩盖现金短缺。

其次,所有的现金必须每天存入银行。这意味着处理现金是个人的责任,它主要针对那些被指定进行定期存款的个人。此外,这可以防止积累大量的现金,即使是最信任的员工也会受到大量现金的诱惑。

再次,除了由零用现金资金支付小额款项外,其他所有的付款最好都用支票。我们都知道,用现金支付的款项很容易就会被遗忘,也很容易被隐藏。相比之下,当用支票付款时,无论是我们个人支票登记册还是我们的银行支票册,都有详细的付款记录。付款不应该用收入的现金支付。

最后,在付款时要求每笔支出的有效性和金额都要经过核对,并将核准支出的功能与开支票的功能分开。

5.2 应收账款

应收账款也叫应收款项,是客户(顾客)欠企业的钱,作为资产反映在资产负债表上。它还意味着买方口头承诺为买到的货物和服务付款,通常可在 30 天至 60 天内收回,它是由于短期信贷延长而形成的未结账款。因此,在资产负债表上应收账款紧随现金和现金等价物之后出现。

与应收账款会计处理有关的两个问题:一是应收账款的确认;二是应收账款的计量。

第一,应收账款的初次确认比较简单。服务性企业在以赊销方式提供了服务之后,即记录应收账款,商业企业在以赊账的方式卖出商品后,即记录应收账款。商业企业在实现销售时,其应收账款和主营业务收入账户同时增加。销售折扣将减少应收账款。为了鼓励客户尽早付款,卖方可向客户提供销售折扣,例如,2/10、n/30(n 是净额,指发票价格)的销售条款。也就是说,如果客户在 10 天之内付款,将获得发票价格 2% 的折扣。如果客户选择在 10 天之内付款,卖方的应收账款将减少。销售退回也将减少应收账款。有时买方可能认为收到的商品无法接受并予以退货,卖方在收到退回的商品后,也将减少记录在应收账款的金额。

　　第二,应收账款入账后,接下来的问题是,企业应如何在财务报表中报告。应收账款无疑应在资产负债表中列为资产,由于坏账的原因,有时列报应收账款的金额就会很困难。

　　有时,公司采用长期分期付款的方式销售产品,需要 12 个月、24 个月甚至 48 个月才能从客户那里收回全部应收账款。从概念上讲,应收账款的正常收付周期是公司经营周期的一部分。因此,正常销售交易产生的应收账款,即使信用期限超过一年,通常也归入流动资产。

　　如果一个公司有应收账款,这意味着该公司已经进行了销售,但它必须从买家那里收取款项。向客户提供信贷的公司很少有不受信贷损失影响的。有时,可能会有一些买家无法支付他们的债务;因此,这些应收账款将无法收回。既然如此,什么时候应收账款会变成无法收回的?实际上,没有一般的规则来确定何时应收账款变成坏账。事实上,债务人的破产是应收账款一部分或全部无法收回的最重要迹象之一。其他迹象包括终止与客户的业务和多次尝试收款而失败。

　　如果这些信用损失发生,它们将被记入到一个适当科目账户,如坏账费用(或呆账费用)或坏账损失(或呆账损失)。

　　坏账准备是指无法收回的应收账款的预估金额。它是对可能收不回来的应收账款的坏账准备,或者我们可以说,坏账准备是一种资产的备抵账户。

　　未设置坏账准备的应当在坏账准备中冲销,或者计入当期损益。当一笔应收账款被核销为坏账时,顾客仍然有支付的义务。

　　有两种方法可以记录这些无法收回的东西。一种是直接核销法。在这种方法下,坏账费用是在一个账户被确定为无法收回时记录的,在期末没有记录调整分录来估计无法收回的款项。冲销坏账的分录如下:

借:资产减值损失——坏账损失　　××××
　　贷:应收账款　　　　　　　　　××××

该方法的优点是应用简单方便,缺点是收入与费用不匹配,除非销账与相关销售同期发生。

　　由于无法事先得知哪些应收账款将被证实是无法收回的,所以不可能将预估的无法收回应收账款的贷记到特定客户的账户上。

　　因此,另一个可行的选择是贷记一个单独的账户,称为坏账准备,贷记的金额为估计的坏账金额。该方法对当期销售预计产生的坏账总额进行估计,并记录当期与相关销售发生的费用。例如,一个公司估计有 1 000 元应收账款将无法收回。因此,借记 1 000 元作为资产减值损失——坏账损失(或坏账费用),贷记 1 000 元作为坏账准备。这样的分录为:

借：资产减值损失——坏账损失　××××
　　贷：坏账准备　　　　　　　　　××××

这是理论上正确的方法。这种方法的优点是它遵循保守原则,即低估资产和收入,高估负债和费用。这些估计是根据下列三种方法做出的。

首先是销售百分比法,也叫损益表法。这种方法由于简单易行,在实践中被广泛应用于估计坏账损失。企业经常使用这种方法在年度内定期估计坏账,然后在年终根据应收账款余额调整备抵账户。当使用这一基本原则时,在过去几年中不可收回的账款相对于总销售额的比例提供了不可收回账款的预计百分比。

根据目前的经验,这个百分比可以根据预期加以修正。由于呆账只发生在赊销时,所以将一定比例的呆账计入以往各期的赊销似乎是合理的。这个百分比将应用于当期的赊销。举例来说,如果当期的100 000元销售额收回的情况,有2%被认为是呆账,那么坏账准备的费用就是当期销售额的2%,即2 000元。资产减值损失——坏账损失的费用为当期销售额的2%,即2 000元。

这时期的分录很简单：

借：资产减值损失——坏账损失　2 000
　　贷：坏账准备　　　　　　　　　2 000

其次,它是应收账款的百分比。公司可以根据未偿付的应收账款总额百分比来估计坏账,而不是用销售额的百分比来估计坏账。这种方法强调应收账款余额与坏账准备之间的关系。

例如,如果应收账款总额为50 000元,估计其中3%将无法收回,那么备抵账户的余额应为1 500(50 000×3%)。如果备抵账户以前各期有600元的贷方余额,那么本期调整分录将是：

借：资产减值损失——坏账损失　900
　　贷：坏账损失　　　　　　　　　900

最后一种是账龄分析法(或账龄法)。这个方法将未偿还的应收账款按未偿还时间进行分类。应收账款的账龄法对每一类应收账款都按一定的比例进行估计,以确定应收账款总额中无法收回的部分。这种方法是最常用的方法,而且更可靠,因为它关注到实际逾期的特定账目上。对个人账户进行分析,以确定哪些是未到期的,哪些是逾期的。逾期账是按逾期时间长短分类的。根据以往的经验,对应收账款进行分析,每组可能发生的坏账损失如下：

账龄期	坏账比例
0~30天	2%
31~60天	4%
61~90天	10%
超过90天	30%

在2010年12月31日,以下是应收账款的账龄信息:

账龄期	坏账金额	比例	坏账准备
0~30天(过期未付)	25 000	2%	500
31~60天	15 000	4%	600
61~90天	5 000	10%	500
超过90天	3 000	30%	900
总计	48 000		2 500

假设坏账准备中现有的未调整余额为1 000元(贷方余额)。和之前的方法一样,根据应收账款余额的一定比例,借记资产减值损失——坏账损失,贷记坏账准备,使坏账准备账户达到所需余额。

调整分录为:

借:资产减值损失——坏账损失　1 500

　贷:坏账准备　　　　　　　　　1 500

这种方法提供了最令人满意的方法来评估应收账款的可变现净额。此外,通过应收账款账龄得到的数据可能对管理信用分析和控制非常有用。另一方面,老化方法的应用可能需要相当长的时间和成本。

应收账款百分比法和账龄法也称为资产负债表法。它们都关注估计的坏账总额,即坏账准备账户的余额。

销售百分率法和资产负债表法的区别在于,上一个会计期间的坏账准备余额是否需要计入当期。损益表的方法下,会计人员不需要考虑上一个会计期间准备账户的余额,而在资产负债表的方法下,会计人员必须计算坏账准备账户当前余额,当前账户余额应该与准备账户发生在当前会计期间与上一会计期间之间增加或减少后的差额相等。

5.3 存 货

存货是指企业在正常经营过程中为销售而持有的商品、产成品、半成品、在制品和各种物料等,对生产企业来说,是指在生产中的或将投入生产的商品。换句话说,它是由为了出售而购买的物品组成的。例如,在超市里,牛奶是库存,而购物车不是。在一家制造公司,有三种不同类型的库存:原材料、在制品和产成品。

原材料是生产或制造产品的基本材料。对于刀具公司来说,钢材是原材料之一。原料可以直接从天然来源获得,然而,它们大多数是从其他公司购买的,代表供应商的产成品。对于一家造纸厂来说,高质量、无酸的纸张是它的产成品,而对于一家图书出版公司来说,它却是原材料。

在产品包括生产过程中大量未完成的产品。这产品尚未生产完成,但要么正在生产,要么正在等待进一步加工。该术语用于生产和供应链管理。

作为"原材料"购买的东西被用来制造产品。在制造过程中没有生产完的东西称为"在制品"。当一件东西的生产已经完成,但还没有出售或分配给最终用户时,它就被称为"制成品",如汽车、电脑,这些都是待出售的制成品。

存货成本包括购买存货和准备出售存货的所有成本。正确计算库存成本对于生产、定价和战略决策至关重要。在生产和准备出售存货时发生的所有成本都应计入存货成本。与销售工作本身相关的成本是该期间的费用。公司按原始成本记录存货。存货项目的成本包括货物在现有条件和地点发生的所有支出。这些成本包括发票价格、运费、运输途中的保险以及货物运抵营业地的其他费用。

存货数额同时出现在资产负债表和损益表中。在资产负债表中,存货通常是最大的流动资产。在损益表中,期末存货从可供销售的商品成本中减去,以确定本期的销售商品成本。企业如何确定年末、月末或其他会计期间的存货数量和成本?

管理人员如何确定本期销售商品的成本?这些数额必须在编制资产负债表或损益表之前确定。事实上,存货价值和销售成本的确定可能是衡量企业盈利能力的最重要的一步。确定存货数量和销货成本的方法有两种,这两种可确定存货和销货成本的方法分别称为永续盘存制和定期盘存制。

想想你最近一次购物的情景。你买东西的那家公司有没有把他们卖给你的东西记录下来,还是只记录售价?在传统的收款机系统中,卖家只记录销售价格;卖方没有记录有多少数量的特定库存项目已售出。会计人员将这种类型的系统称为定期盘存系统,因为核实存货销售情况和存货余额的唯一方法是进行定期盘点。

在定期盘存制下,企业不需要对存货进行连续记录,在会计期末,企业对存货进行实物盘点,采用单位成本法确定期末存货成本。也就是说,正如其名称所暗示的那样,公司只是定期确定库存数量。使用这种方法时,存货购进按发生时记账,但存货账户和销货成本的期末余额,在清点存货后,于期末确定。这种方法通常用于相对便宜的商品。没有收银机的便利店不会记录每天出售的每一块面包和每一个钥匙链。相反,企业每隔一段时间清点存货,以确定手头的数量。餐馆和小型零售商店也使用定期盘存制,这种系统越来越不受欢迎,因为越来越多的企业通过计算机来保存库存记录。

例5.1 ABC公司在6月4日采购了价值4 000美元的库存商品,随后在6月16日该公司赊销库存商品价值5 000美元。在6月底时,该公司做实地盘点发现期末存货余额为900美元(假设期初存货余额为300美元)。

在6月4日,分录为:

借:库存商品   4 000
    贷:应付账款   4 000

在6月16日,分录将为:
借:应收账款　　　　　　　　5 000
　　贷:主营业务收入　　　　　5 000
在这个月底时,毛利为1 600美元,即:
$$[5\,000-(4\,000+300-900)]=1\,600$$
除定期盘存制外,另一种是永续盘存制。在永续盘存制下,企业在存货账户上保持连续的记录,销售时记录存货,每笔销售都记录销售价格和销售品种。该系统实现了对库存的控制。条形码扫描系统就是永续盘存制的一个例子。当企业选择这个系统时,销售人员知道所销售的每一件商品的数量和仍在库存中的数量。即使在永续经营的系统中,企业每年至少清点一次存货。实地盘点为财务报表确定了正确的期末盘存金额,同时也作为对永续记录的核对。例如,它在显示库存缩减量(库存丢失、被盗或损坏)方面很有用。

例5.2　正如上述例5.1中,在永续盘存制下,6月4日的分录同样。在6月16日,分录如下:
借:应收账款　　　　　　　　5 000
　　贷:主营业务收入　　　　　5 000
借:销售成本　　　　　　　　3 000
　　贷:库存商品　　　　　　　3 000
下面是定期盘存制与永续盘存制的比较。
◆ 定期盘存制:
① 不保存所有货物买卖的流水账。
② 每年至少清点一次存货。
◆ 永续盘存制:
① 保存所有货物买卖的流水账。
② 每年至少清点一次存货。

在计算机广泛应用于会计之前,只有销售数量有限、价值相对较高的产品的公司才使用实地盘存制。然而,由于计算机使记录工作变得容易得多,越来越多的公司正在从定期记录系统转向永久记录系统。

实地盘存制下需要企业每年进行一次实际库存盘点。然而,大多数企业需要更多关于其库存水平的最新信息,以防止缺货或过度采购,并帮助准备月度或季度财务数据。因此,许多企业利用改良的永续盘存制。该系统仅按美元数额(货币金额)提供详细的存货数量增减记录。它只是复式记账法之外的一个备忘录装置,有助于在任何时候确定库存水平。

无论一个企业是保存存货数量和美元金额(货币金额),还是只保持对数量记录的永续盘存制,或者根本没有永续盘存记录,它都可能每年进行一次实物盘点。无论企业使用何种类型的库存记录方式,它们都面临着丢失库存和错误的危险,以及浪费、破损、盗窃、不正确的记录,没有准备或记录申请和其他类似的可能导致库存记录与实际库存不同的情况。因此,所有企业都需要根据实际数量、重量或尺寸对库存记录进行定期核实,并将这些计数与详细的库存记录进行比较。公司会根据实际的数量更正记录。

在可能的情况下,企业应在接近其会计年度结束时进行实物盘点,以便在年度会计报告中正确报告存货数量。然而,由于这并不总是可能的,如果企业保持相当准确的详细库存记录,那么在一年内两三个月进行的实际盘点是符合要求的。

存货通常按成本原则所规定的历史成本入账。购买存货的历史成本包括购买价、运输、装卸、费用、保险、运输过程中发生的合理损坏或损失、入仓前发生的准备费用和应付税款。公司可以采用四种普遍用到的方法来核算存货:个别认定法;先入先出(FIFO);后进先出(LIFO);加权平均法。

个别认定法也称个别计价法,通常用于公司购买易于识别的商品时。假设艾尔蒙音乐公司购置了3台64寸电视机,成本分别为700美元、750美元和800美元。一年中,有两台卖出,每台卖价都是1 200美元。12月31日,手头上还剩一台750美元的电视机。期末存货余额为750美元,销售成本为1 500美元(700美元+800美元)。

这种方法最自然地适用于涉及相对较高单位价值的、稍微差异化的产品的操作。这类物品可以是船舶、飞机、设备、汽车、珠宝和房地产等。当我们使用这种方法时,总是因为某种特定的成本是决定销售价格的一个重要因素,因为商品是独一无二的。也就是说,在销售量低,单个成本高的情况下,运用个别认定几乎最灵活。这种方法可能看起来是合理的,它可能被用于购买和销售高价物品,如汽车和艺术品,但它不被许多公司使用,因为有两个明显的缺点。首先,跟踪单个项目的购买和销售通常是困难和不切实际的。第二,当一个公司经营相同的商品,但它以不同的成本购买,决定哪些商品被出售变得武断,因此,公司可以通过选择成本较低或较高的商品来提高或降低收入。

先进先出法假设购进的第一件商品是卖出的第一件商品,因此期末存货以最新购进的价格计价。在这些情况下,FIFO最接近于将成本流与可能的货物流匹配起来。例如,ABC公司销售电脑,同时手头有4台相同的MAC电脑——两款售价6 000美元的MAC(首次购买)和两款售价8 000美元的同款MAC(在首次购买后被公司购买)。顾客并不关心买哪一台,因为这四台电脑的价格完全一样。如果公司想增加销售成本,它将使用8 000美元作为销售成本。

这种方法的显著特点是购买最早的商品其成本先转移到销售出去的商品成本,而最近采购的商品成本留在库存。在过去的几年里,我们生活在一个通货膨胀的经济中,这意味着大多数价格会随着时间的推移而上涨。当购买成本上升时,先进先出法将较低的成本分配给售出的商品成本,将较高的(较近期的)成本分配给库存商品。有些公司喜欢采用先进先出法,这是出于财务报告的目的,因为他们的目标是报告尽可能最高的净收入。然而,就所得税而言,如果申报的收入多于必要收入,将导致缴纳的所得税多于必要的所得税。

后进先出法是指最后购买的存货的成本要记在卖出的货物成本上。这个方法是基于这样的假设:售出的是最后企业获得的物品。在价格上涨期间,采用后进先出的方法会比其他方法产生更少的净利润,被认为是价格上涨期间存货法中最保守的方法。原因是最近购买的商品的成本最接近它们的重置成本。因此,可以认为这种方法的使用使当期成本与当期收入相匹配。此外,还有一个实际的好处,就是节省所得税。在通货紧缩或价格水平下降的时期,上述效应被逆转,后进先出法产生最高的净利润。

在上面的例子中,销售商品的成本为8 000美元。这种做法与一般的商业流通方式不相适应,目前在我国已被取消。

加权平均法有时也称为平均成本法。这种方法意味着平均单位成本包括在商品销售成本中,它是基于这样一种假设,即所销售的商品应按平均成本计价,平均成本应按每一价格所购货物的数量加权。换句话说,要确定加权平均成本,你需要将现有库存的所有成本相加,并将结果除以库存数量。这种方法最适合用于常见地区大量无差异化商品的操作。在上面的例子中,计算如下:

$$(6\ 000 \times 2 + 8\ 000 \times 2)/4 = 7\ 000$$

第六单元 非流动资产

与诸如现金、银行存款、存货和应收账款这些预计会在一年内变现的流动资产相比,非流动资产预计不会在一年内或多于一年的一个企业经营周期内完全变现或使用。相反,这些资产将在获得后超过一年的时间内被消耗掉,因此非流动资产也被称为长期资产。非流动资产具有经济价值高、会计期间多、形式多样等特点,它是指企业在经营活动中消耗的、不出售给顾客的长期资产。

非流动资产通常可以进一步分为以下三类:第一,长期投资;第二,固定资产(或财产、厂房、设备,也称PPE);第三,无形资产(没有实物形态)。

6.1 长期投资

一家公司可以将当前经营所不需要的多余现金投资于由另一家公司包括股票或债券在内的证券。持有一年以上而购买的投资在资产负债表上属于长期投资。与短期投资相比,长期投资有两个特点。首先,偿还期超过一年。其次,影响和控制被投资公司,以实现长期发展战略,积累配套资金以满足业务的特殊需要,这是长期投资的主要目标。

长期投资一般分为两个方面,即股权投资和债权投资。股权证券是代表所有权利益的证券,如普通股、优先股或其他股本。当购买权益性证券时,其成本包括证券的购买价以及与购买相关的其他费用,如经纪费用、转让费用和税费。

1. 股权投资

股权投资的会计核算包括成本法、权益法和合并法。采用成本法时,投资者持股比例应小于20%。在这种情况下,投资者对被投资者几乎没有影响。在这种方法下,股票投资按其历史成本入账,收入作为收到的股息入账和报告。成本法因为没有衡量当前的公允价值而受到批评。

举例来说,假设ABC公司在2009年1月20日购买了XYZ公司的5 000股股票作为长期投资,每股20美元。总金额为10万美元,占被投资方总资本的10%。2009年底,XYZ公司报告净利润20万美元,其中包括5万美元的股息,ABC公司获得了2万美元的股息。2011年,ABC公司以30美元的价格出售了这些股票。记录该笔交易的分录如下:

在2009年1月20日,购买股份:

借:长期股权投资——成本　　　100 000
　　贷:银行存款　　　　　　　　　　100 000

在2011年底,收到股利:

借:银行存款　　　　　　　　　20 000
　　贷:应收股利　　　　　　　　　　20 000

2011年,售出股票:

借:银行存款　　　　　　　　　150 000
　　贷:长期股权投资——成本　　　　100 000
　　　　投资收益　　　　　　　　　　50 000

当采用权益法时,投资者的持股比例应在20%至50%之间。在这种情况下,投资者对其投资的公司的经营和财务政策或决定有重大影响。行使重大影响力的能力可以通过多种方式来确定,包括董事会代表、参与决策过程、公司内部人员和管理人员的交流。考虑到这种影响,投资者将其股权投资的价值调整为其从已购买股票的公司所获得的股息和损益。由于股息是投资者投资的部分回报,所以收到的股息作为减少投资价值而入账。

举例来说,假设姐妹公司在2010年1月1日以7.2万美元的价格收购了ABC集团30%的股份。在这一年里,ABC集团支付了总计3万美元的股息,净收入15万美元。根据股权法,姐妹公司获得的9 000美元股息(30 000×30%)将减少对ABC集团账户的投资,而不是作为股息收入报告。由于姐妹公司将净收入的30%(15万美元的30%)视为收入,这个账户将增加4.5万美元。到年底,投资ABC集团账户的余额为10.8万美元。

姐妹公司为记录购买ABC集团股份、获得股息和净收入的份额所作的分录如下。

2010年1月1日,购入ABC集团30%的股票:

借:长期股权投资——投资成本　72 000
　　贷:银行存款　　　　　　　　　　72 000

2010年12月31日,从ABC集团收回股利:
借:银行存款　　　　　　　　9 000
　贷:长期股权投资——损益调整　9 000

2010年12月31日,调整在ABC集团净收益份额:
借:长期股权投资——损益调整　45 000
　贷:投资收益　　　　　　　　45 000

在使用合并报表法时,投资者的持股比例应在50%或50%以上。在这种情况下,投资者对被投资方拥有控制权益,两个实体视为一个实体出于会计目的编制合并财务报表。

拥有另一个实体50%以上股份的公司称为母公司,而被拥有股份的公司称为子公司。母公司用权益法来核算其在子公司的投资。在编制财务报表时,母公司和子公司的资产和负债(资产负债表)、收入和费用(损益表)、现金流量(现金流量表)合并在同一份报表中。

这些报表被称为综合资产负债表、综合利润表和综合现金流量表,它们一起被称为综合财务报表,反映母公司及其控制的其他公司的财务状况、经营成果和现金流量。

2. 债券投资

对债务性证券的长期投资是另一种形式的长期投资。所谓的债务证券通常是投资于政府或公司发行的债券,包括政府债券、市政债券、公司债券、可转换债券和所有证券化债务工具。

在购买债券时,购买成本因不同的购买形式而异:平价、溢价或折价。任何从债券投资中获得的利息都被归类为损益表中的其他收入,因为它们不代表从经营活动中获得的收入。

在购买长期债券投资时,我们借记了一个名为"长期债权投资"的资产账户,任何溢价或折价都会在记录债券利息时摊销。溢价的摊销需要贷记到持有至到期投资账户,折价的摊销需要借记到持有至到期投资账户,因此,在债券到期日,持有至到期投资账户的余额将等于债券的面值。

例如,如果ABC公司在2010年7月1日购买XYZ公司发行的5份年利率为10%,10年期,每份价值为1 000美元的债券,共计5 000美元,支付代理费用为50美元,记录这次购买的分录将包括购置价格和代理费用,计入到投资成本账户。

2010年7月1日,购入XYZ公司债券:
借:持有至到期投资——投资成本　5 050
　贷:银行存款　　　　　　　　5 050

债券每年12月31日和6月30日支付利息,当2010年12月31日收到半年期的利息时,将记录库存现金增加(也就是借记),利息收入(也就是贷记),金额为250元(5 000×10%×6/12)。

2010年12月31日,收到债券利息:
借:库存现金　　　　　　　　250
　贷:利息收入　　　　　　　　250

6.2 固定资产

固定资产又称不动产、厂房、设备资产(也称PPE),是指企业在正常经营活动中使用的长期或相对永久性的有形资产。它们由企业所有,在正常运营中不出售。房地产、建筑结构(办公室、工厂、仓库)、汽车和设备(机器、家具、工具)都是固定资产的典型例子。

固定资产是指公司在正常经营活动中使用的,分类为有形的、非流动的资产。其他术语还有固定资产和经营资产。资产要包含在这个类别中必须具有三个特征:

第一,资产必须是为了使用而不是为了投资而持有的。只应包括在正常业务过程中使用的资产。但是,资产不必一直处于使用中;因此,为备用而拥有的机器也包括在内。相反,闲置的土地或建筑物不应包括在内,应单独归类为投资。

其次,资产的预期使用年限必须超过一年。资产表示在资产的生命周期内公司未来将接收到的服务。如果属于固定资产,那么这些受益必须在一年以上或超过一年的一个企业经营周期内。

第三,资产必须是有形的。必须有一种看得见摸得着的有形物质。相比之下,商誉或专利等无形资产没有实物形态。一般而言,与原材料不同,固定资产不会改变其物理特性,也不会被纳入产品性质。也就是说,固定资产是有实际形态的主体。它们不同于无形资产、应收账款和其他应收款。

固定资产主要分为可折旧资产和不可折旧资产两类。应计折旧资产是具有实物形态的固定资产,预计使用年限超过一个会计期间,具有有限的使用年限。折旧的目的是将各项固定资产的成本以费用的形式,通过合理、系统的分配方法,按使用的经济年度进行分配。费用应当计入损益表,正确反映企业的损益。例如,建筑物、设备和机器都属于应计提折旧的资产。不计提折旧的资产包括已计提折旧并继续使用的固定资产、单独计价入账的土地和待售的固定资产。

1. 固定资产的购置成本

当以现金交易时,成本很容易确定。在这种情况下,资产是为其支付的现金加上运费、运输途中的保险和其他必要的相关费用。如果购买资产产生了债务,那么利息费用不是资产的成本,而是贷款购买资产的费用。因此,这属于期间费用。这一原则有一个例外,即在资产构建期间产生的利息成本会适当包括在资产成本中。

固定资产的购置成本包括为使固定资产就位并准备使用而发生的一切合理和必要的支出。运费、运输途中的保险费和安装费等支出都包括在资产成本中,因为这些支出是资产运作所必需的。那些不属于为资产投入使用而产生的必要成本并不会增加资产的有用性,也不应包括在其成本中。例如,安装和测试一台机器的成本是机器的合法成本;但是,如果机器在安装过程中损坏了,修理费用是操作费用,而不是机器本身的费用。

总而言之,获得固定资产的成本包括销售税费、运费、安装费用、修理费用(使用过的资产而产生的)、翻新费用(使用过的资产所产生的)、资产运输途中的保险费用、装配费用、改装费用、使用测试以及政府机构的许可费用。另一方面,固定资产的成本不包括故意破坏、安装错误、未投保的盗窃、开箱和安装过程中的损坏以及未从政府机构获得适当许可的罚款。

2. 折旧费

土地有无限的使用年限,因此可以提供无限的服务。另一方面,其他固定资产如设备、建筑物等,随着时间的推移,它们失去了提供服务的能力。因此,设备、建筑物的费用应在预期使用寿命内有系统地转入费用账户。这种周期性的成本到期称为折旧。换句话说,固定资产在未来可以为企业带来一定的经济效益,但其服务潜力是有限的。随着固定资产在经营中的使用,服务潜力将会下降甚至消失。折旧是衡量和反映这些服务潜力变化的一种方法。折旧不同于大多数费用,因为它在入账时不需要现金支付。也就是说,折旧不会影响现金流量,但会影响当期损益。

折旧的基本目标是实现配比原则,也就是说,将一个会计期间的收入与为了产生收入而消耗的商品和服务的成本进行抵消。

造成固定资产提供服务能力下降的主要原因有两个。一种是由于元件的使用作用而导致的损耗,降低了其有用性的物理性折旧。另一种是由于不适当使用和荒置过时而导致降低其有用性的功能性折旧。

每个会计期间的折旧的计量是该期间的资产成本或费用。记入折旧费用的分录包括借记折旧费用和贷记累计折旧。在确定折旧费用金额时,要考虑三个因素。这三个因素是固定资产的初始成本、预期使用年限和使用寿命末期的估计值。最后一个因素也叫残值、报废价值、残余值。对于计算折旧费用的方法,有许多不同的类型。在实践中,四种主要使用的折旧方法是直线法、工作量法、年数总和法(SYD法)和双倍余额递减法。这四种方法如下所示。

(1)直线法

直线法是计算折旧费用最广泛、最保守的方法。这种方法假设折旧只取决于时间的流逝,资产的经济收入每年都是一样的。此外,每个时间段的维修保养费用也是一样的。在直线法下,折旧费用平均分配到资产的每个使用年限。因此,每年的折旧额是相同的。这种方法的公式如下。

例6.1 假设一家公司的汽车价值1万美元,在预计使用年限为5年后,其预计残值为1 000美元。在这种情况下,年折旧将是可折旧成本的20%,或者也就是直线法下的1 800美元。计算方式为(10 000 − 1 000)/5 = 1 800(美元)。

直线法特别适用于建筑、机械、管道等。

(2)工作量法

这种工作量法根据资产的使用量来确定折旧费用。资产的使用年限以生产能力的形式表示。初始成本减去任一残值再除以生产能力,以确定每单位使用的生产资料的折旧率。使用单位可以表示为生产的货物数量、使用的小时数、切割的数量、行驶的英里数或拖运的吨数等。

一个会计期间的折旧费用是用固定的生产资料的使用率乘以使用量来确定的。这种折旧方法通常是在资产使用情况逐年变化时使用。

在这种方法下,使用以下公式计算折旧。

$$折旧金额 = (产量/总产量) \times (原值 - 成本值)$$

例 6.2 一家耗资 1.1 亿美元的工厂于 2010 年 4 月 1 日被收购。残值估计为 1 000 万美元。预计产量为 1.5 亿台。截至 2010 年 12 月 31 日,该厂的产量为 1 500 万辆。计算截至 2010 年 12 月 31 日的年度折旧。

解 $折旧金额 = (15/150) \times (110 - 10) = 10(百万)$

这种方法与直线法相似,只是资产的使用年限是根据操作次数或机器使用小时数等来估计的。

(3) 年数总和法(SYD 法)

年数总和折旧法是一种加速折旧法,它是基于这样一种假设:新资产的生产率通常较高,而旧资产的生产率则随着时间的推移而下降。采用 SYD 法计算折旧的公式如下。

$$SYD 折旧金额 = 折旧基数 \times \frac{尚可使用年限}{预计使用年限总和}$$

在上式中,计提折旧基数为资产的原值与残值之差,年数之和为数列之和:
$1, 2, 3, \cdots, n$;其中 n 为资产的使用年限,以年为单位。

用下面的公式可以更方便地计算年数的和:

$$年数总和 = \frac{n(n+1)}{2}$$

例 6.3 如果一项资产的原始成本为 1 000 美元,使用年限为 5 年,残值为 100 美元,计算其折旧。

解 首先,确定年份。由于该资产的使用年限为 5 年,因此其年数为:5,4,3,2 和 1。
接下来,计算年数的和:$5 + 4 + 3 + 2 + 1 = 15$
年数的和也可以用 $n(n+1)/2$ 这个公式来计算,其中 n 为资产的使用年限。这个例题中表示出来为 $5(5+1)/2 = 15$。
折旧率如下:
第一年为 5/15,第二年为 4/15,第三年为 3/15,第四年为 2/15,以及第五年为 1/15。

表6.1　年底折旧费用计算表　　　　　　　　　　　　　　　　单位：美元

期初账面价值	应折旧总值	折旧率	折旧费用	累计折旧	期末账面价值
1 000（原值）	900	5/15	300（900×5/15）	300	700
700	900	4/15	240（900×4/15）	540	460
460	900	3/15	180（900×5/15）	720	280
280	900	2/15	120（900×5/15）	840	160
160	900	1/15	60（900×5/15）	900	100

（4）双倍余额递减法

余额递减法采用的折旧率是直线法的若干倍。当折旧率是直线折旧率的两倍时，我们称之为双倍余额递减法。因此，当直线折旧率为8%时，双倍余额递减法下的折旧率为2×8%＝16%。换句话说，使用这种方法，每个时期开始时的账面价值（或账面值）乘以一个固定的折旧率，该折旧率是直线折旧率的200%，或2倍。

双倍余额递减法是一种常用的加速折旧法。该方法在确定折旧率或计算定期折旧时不考虑残值估计。但是，资产的折旧不能超过预计净残值。折旧费第一年最高，以后逐年递减。

余额递减折旧按下式计算：

折旧金额＝折旧率×资产的账面价值

折旧率用以下公式计算：

折旧率＝2×直线法折旧率

为了说明双倍余额递减法，这里有另一个例子：

假设企业拥有一项资产，其原始成本为1 000美元，残值为100美元，预计使用年限为5年。

首先，计算直线法折旧率。由于该资产预计使用年限为5年，直线法折旧率为每年20%（100%/5）。使用双倍余额递减法，正如其名，双倍于这一折旧率，或者使用40%的折旧率。表6.2为双倍余额递减法计算折旧。

表6.2　运用双倍余额递减法计算折旧费用　　　　　　　　　　　　　单位：美元

期初账面价值	折扣率	折旧费用	累计折旧	期末账面价值
1 000（原值）	40%	400	400	600
600	40%	240	640	360
360	40%	144	784	216
216	20%	58	842	158
158	20%	58	900	100（残值）

请注意，固定折旧率总是适用于前一年的账面价值。其次，第一年贬值幅度最大，之后逐

年下降。最后，上一年度的折旧仅限于使账面价值减少到残值的必要数额。对于最后一年的折旧，可能需要做一个减法，以防止账面价值低于预计的残值。

年数总和法和双倍余额递减法都属于加速折旧法，加速折旧法在资产使用年限的前期会产生较高的折旧费用，因此报告的净收入要低于直线折旧法。这些方法是建立在时间的基础上的，假设许多种类的固定资产在新时是最有效率的，因此它们在使用年限的早期提供更多更好的服务。如果在早期获得的好处或服务更多，则将更多的折旧分配给早期而不是后期，这符合配比规则。

6.3 无形资产

无形资产这一术语是指在企业经营活动中使用的没有实物形态的非流动资产。应收账款或预付租金等流动资产不属于无形资产，尽管它们缺乏实物形态。

无形资产可以通过企业合并获得，也可以通过内部开发获得。在企业合并中取得的资产，按公允价值入账；在企业内部产生的无形资产，按开发阶段发生的成本确认。关于自创无形资产的开发有两个阶段：研究阶段和开发阶段。研究阶段包括无形资产在商业上可行之前发生的所有活动和成本，而开发阶段包括资产在商业上可行之后发生的所有活动和成本。研究阶段的所有费用在发生期间内支出，而开发阶段的费用则资本化。

无形资产包括版权、专利、商标、专营权等。

1. 版权

版权由政府授予，赋予版权所有者复制和出售艺术作品或已出版作品的独家权利。版权的保护期为创作者的寿命加上50年或使用年限，以较短者为准。版权的成本包括获取和保护版权的成本。

2. 专利

专利是由政府颁发的专有权，使接受者能够在申请日起的20年内制造、销售或以其他方式控制其发明。专利的初始成本是获得专利时支付的现金或现金等价物。专利权的费用应当在其20年的法律年限或使用年限内摊销，两者以较短者为准。

3. 商标及商号

商标包括公司标识，以及已在政府注册的产品名称，用于标识特定的公司和产品。与保护和维护商标和商标名称有关的所有支出是可摊销的。

4. 特许权

特许经营在我们的日常生活中变得如此普遍，以至于我们常常没有意识到我们正在与之打交道。事实上，如今在一个典型的购物中心很难找到一家非特许经营企业。特许经营权的购买者有权出售某些产品或服务，并有权使用某些商标或商号。这些权利是有价值的，因为它们为购买者提供了立即得到客户认可的机会。许多快餐店、旅馆、加油站和汽车经销商都是由向公司支付特许经营许可证的个人拥有的。特许经营许可证的成本在其使用年限（通常是合同时效期）内摊销。

无形资产摊销是指无形资产在使用年限内的费用化的过程。它实际上是无形资产的折旧。有些无形资产的使用年限是无限的。这些资产不需要摊销。其他有确定使用年限的，在他们的使用年限进行摊销。无形资产大多采用直线法摊销。使用年限是法律年限和经济年限两者较短的那个。例如，假设创新小工具有限公司为他们的一个产品申请了专利，花费了10万美元。该专利的执行期限为10年，因此法律期限为10年。然而，该公司预计只生产5年的专利产品，并希望在5年后用一个先进的版本取代它。公司采用直线法摊销。该公司需要将专利在5年内摊销完，即法律年限和经济年限相比较短的这个期限，因此每年摊销将为2万美元（100 000/5）。虽然使用年限无限的无形资产不进行摊销，但要定期进行减值测试。

第七单元　流动负债

什么是负债并不是一个简单的问题。显而易见，负债不仅包括由于借款而产生的债务，由于赊购商品或服务也会产生负债，这跟借款就很像了。不太相似的是，它们可能来自缴税、从雇员工资和薪金中扣缴税款和宣告股利等。

负债是企业由于过去发生的交易或事项而引起的、在未来向其他企业提供资产或服务的一种现行义务，该义务的履行将导致企业经济利益的流出。因此，负债表示的是企业未来资源转移的现时义务。负债是企业的债务，企业因过去交易而欠债权人一笔金额，通常在会计科目里，都带有"应付"的字样，其本质是一种在某一期限内必须偿还的金融债务。

负债通常都有某些共同特点，应注意五点。首先，"可能"是指企业充满了不确定性，这种不确定性体现在可能发生或不发生。其次，未来流出的经济利益的金额能够可靠地计量。再次，现时义务是指企业在现行条件下已承担的义务。未来发生的交易或事项形成的义务，不属于现时义务，不应当确认为负债。第四，"资产的转移或提供服务"是指大多数负债涉及将来转移资产或提供服务的义务。最后，"过去的交易或事件"是指负债来源于已经发生的交易或事件。

大多数的负债在合同中有明确规定的具体金额。因与所有者权益一样，负债可以被认为是公司获取资产的一个来源，也可视为公司对资产的债权。例如，某公司的资产负债表上报告其资产为100 000美元，应付账款为40 000美元，所有者权益为60 000美元。该企业资产有40 000美元来自债权人或供应商，有60 000美元来自所有者投入。债权人或供应商对该公司的资产拥有债权，当公司债务清偿后，所有者对公司剩余资产拥有所有权。

在财务报表中，负债在资产负债表里报告，通常有贷方余额。根据公司持有负债的时间，通常分为两种：流动负债和非流动负债（长期负债）。对负债的恰当分类为投资人及其他财务报表使用者提供了有利信息。它是公司外部人士考虑公司财务运行真实情况的关键。

7.1 流动负债的定义

　　流动负债是自资产负债表日起12个月到期，或超过12个月的一个经营周期内到期的负债。也就是说，如果公司的正常经营周期是超过12个月的，那么在这样的经营周期内到期的，也视为流动负债。换言之，对大多数公司来说经营周期短于一年的，但也并不总是这样，流动负债是预计在第二年或下一个经营周期支付的短期债务。作为流动负债还有另一个要求，即预期负债将从流动资产（或通过提供服务）中支付。不满足这一要求的负债则为长期负债。流动负债是大多数公司经营周期中的一个重要环节。在日常经营中，企业承担对供应商、雇员和其他实体的短期债务。通过销售商品和向客户提供服务中获得的现金将用于支付这些到期的债务。

　　最常见的流动负债有应付账款、短期借款、应付票据、长期债务中的短期部分、应付股利、应计负债（例如应付利息费、应付所得税以及工资费用）和预收账款。由于流动负债在相对短时间内支付，因此它们一般以其表面价值在资产负债表中列示，也就是负债本金需要偿还的现金金额。流动负债通常在资产负债表中"负债与所有者权益"这部分的顶部或者第一类列出。在某些情况下，流动负债作为一类在流动资产之后列出，其总额从流动资产总额中扣除，以获得营运资本。在流动负债这部分，科目可以根据从大到小的金额，按负债到期先后列示，也可按负债清偿的优先级别列出。

7.2 应付账款

　　在当前经济环境下，大多数商品及服务都可赊购。应付账款是这样一个术语，即企业在一定期限内需要偿还给其债权人的那部分款项金额。它们是最常见的流动负债，通常也指购销应付账款。应付账款代表的是向其他企业赊购商品、物资及服务所欠下的金额。应付账款的发生是因为企业接受服务或获得资产的所有权的时刻和支付时刻之间存在时滞。在美国超过90%的主要公司将应付账款在其资产负债表中单独列示在流动负债项下。应付账款余额的多少是反映企业财务状况的一个重要指标，特别是在零售行业，供应商是提供货物的主要来源。

　　例7.1　8月12日，维拉餐馆从ROI家具商店赊购了50把餐椅，每把餐椅100美元，付款将在15天内支付。对维拉餐馆来说，这笔交易的分录如下：

　　8月12日，收到餐椅。

　　　借：固定资产——家具　　　　5 000

    贷：应付账款   5 000
  8月22日，支付餐椅货款。
    借：应付账款   5 000
      贷：库存现金   5 000

例7.2 如果吉姆公司从供应商处赊购了办公用品，发票总金额为20 000美元。这笔账款总额会在吉姆公司的资产负债表的流动负债中列出。分录如下：
    借：管理费用——办公用品   20 000
      贷：应付账款   20 000
  当吉姆公司付款后，该公司做如下分录：
    借：应付账款   20 000
      贷：库存现金   20 000

应付账款是由于赊购而发生，通常不产生利息，因为赊销是卖方使用的促销方法。有时卖方会为了鼓励顾客即时付款而提供现金折扣。现金折扣对交易双方都有利，买方可以省钱，卖方可以尽早收回款项用于周转。

例7.3 7月15日，科林高中从瑞贝商店赊购了900本笔记本，总价值为2 700美元，此次交易信用期限为10天内付款享受2%折扣，30天内付款没有折扣。对于科林高中来说，此笔交易的分录为：
  7月15日，收到笔记本。
    借：管理费用——办公用品   2 700
      贷：应付账款   2 700
  7月23日，支付笔记本货款。
    借：应付账款   2 700
      贷：财务费用——现金折扣   54
         库存现金   2 646

应付账款通常与采购存货有关。大多数会计制度的目的都是当收到货物或实际收到发票时就记录负债。

7.3 短期借款

短期借款通常是企业根据生产经营需要，从银行或其他贷款公司借的钱。其偿还期通常从30天到1年，属于现金流量表中的融资活动。到期日（借款到期的时候），借款公司偿还本金以及从属于本金的利息。

例7.4 假设2019年9月1日，凯利公司向商业银行借款100 000美元，到期时将偿还本金100 000美元和3个月期的利息总额3 000美元（也就是每个月利息1 000美元）。这笔交易的分录如下：

在 2019 年 9 月 1 日，凯利公司从银行收到现金。

借：银行存款　　　　　　　　　100 000
　贷：短期借款　　　　　　　　　　100 000

在每月底，该公司将计提当月利息费用。整个三个月，该公司每月月底计提利息的分录一样。

借：财务费用——利息费用　　　1 000
　贷：应付利息　　　　　　　　　　1 000

到期时，该公司偿还银行本金 100 000 美元和利息 3 000 美元。

借：短期借款　　　　　　　　　100 000
　　应付利息　　　　　　　　　　3 000
　贷：银行存款　　　　　　　　　　103 000

7.4　短期应付票据

短期应付票据是以书面本票形式体现的负债。应付票据是当企业获得银行贷款时签发的，企业购置不动产或昂贵设备、商品也可以签发应付票据，逾期应付账款也可以转为应付票据。借款人是票据的出票人，放款人是收款人（持票人）。票据的出票人承诺在到期日（又称期满之日）支付票据的票面价值。应付票据通常要求借款人支付利息费用。如果利率与票据的本金分开列示，计算利息费用是最容易的。应付票据要么记录在短期应付票据账户，要么记录在长期应付票据账户，这取决于其偿付期的长短。短期应付票据可以是附息的，也可以是不附息的。短期应付票据通常是应付商业票据，是对供应商的短期债务，他们持有这些书面本票。在中国，应付票据只代表应付商业票据。公司向银行或其他放款人借款，通常都签协议。这在中国实际业务中称之为短期借款而非应付票据。

一种常见的情况是，借款可以换取签发一份应付本票。本票看起来是这样的。

本票

如数收讫，出票人承诺付款给巴斯科德公司或凭其指示。

总金额为伍仟柒佰美元。

未付款项随票支付年率 7% 的利息。本票据将于 2012 年 6 月 30 日同应计利息一并支付。

2012 年 1 月 1 日贝希尔·凯恩
出票日出票人

例 7.5　上面的本票显示，贝希尔·凯恩同意在 2012 年 6 月 30 日向巴斯·科德支付

5 700美元以及199.5美元的利息。这笔利息是5 700美元以年7%利率计算的半年(从1月1日起息到6月30日止息)的利息费用。

1月1日,记录借入款项。

借:库存现金　　　　　　　　　5 700
　贷:应付票据　　　　　　　　　5 700

6月30日,偿付票据,将票据的账面价值和实际支付现金价值之间的差额计入利息费用。分录如下:

借:应付票据　　　　　　　　　5 700
　财务费用——利息费用　　　　199.5
　贷:银行存款　　　　　　　　　5 899.5

例7.6　约翰公司无法向西蒙公司支付已到期的15 000美元应付账款。4月1日,西蒙公司接受了约翰公司作为和解而开出的一张价值15 000美元,票面年利率为12%的三个月期票据,以此给予到期债务的延期。

约翰公司在4月1日签发票据记入账上的分录如下:

借:应付账款——西蒙公司　　　15 000
　贷:应付票据　　　　　　　　　15 000

4月、5月、6月这三个月每个月底约翰公司记录如下分录:

借:财务费用——利息费用　　　150
　贷:应付利息　　　　　　　　　150

要注意的是票据并不清偿了债务。相反,债务的形式只是从应付账款变成应付票据。西蒙公司更愿意持有票据,因为一旦违约,票据是债务存在及债务金额很好的书面证据。

当票据到期,约翰公司将给西蒙公司一张价值450美元的支票,将票据的偿还和支付利息费用的分录登记入账:

借:应付票据　　　　　　　　　15 000
　财务费用——利息费用　　　　450
　贷:库存现金　　　　　　　　　15 450

如果公司从银行或其他金融机构借款且签发票据,这在现金流量表里属于融资活动。

在上述例子中,假设4月1日,西蒙公司放款,收到约翰公司签发的三个月期,年利率12%,价值15 000美元的票据。

4月1日约翰公司签发票据时记录如下:

借:库存现金　　　　　　　　　15 000
　贷:应付票据　　　　　　　　　15 000

· 205 ·

7.5　预收账款

公司在给客户提供商品或服务之前收到现金,正因如此,该公司有义务提供商品或服务,收到的这笔现金是一种债务,这些从客户那里提前收到的款项在会计上就称之为预收账款。在中国,除了预收账款这一科目名称外,也经常会用到预收收入这一科目名称。由于赚取收入在企业正常经营周期内,因此预收账款通常都被划分为流动负债。否则,它们应归入非流动负债。例如,提前出售杂志订阅,出售礼品卡,在活动之前出售预定门票。尽管预收收入带有"收入"的字样,但它却是负债,在资产负债表上流动负债中列示。在现金流量表中,从客户那收到的预收账款,属于经营活动。同时对买方来说,预先支付给供应商的账款属于流动资产。

通常一笔交易,预收账款的金额实际就是之后将收到的收入。这是因为当产品及服务全部交付后,卖方对客户的义务就履行完了,根据收入确认原则,这时也是确认收入之刻。因此,随着全部产品或服务的提供,预收账款将转化成实际商品销售收入或服务收入。

例7.7　芙洛拉花店在7月20日从罗伯特先生那里提前收到600美元的付款。这笔付款是为了在7月26日罗伯特夫人生日派对上装饰鲜花而用。对花店来说,这笔交易的分录如下:

7月20日,收到付款。

借:库存现金　　　　　　　　600
　贷:预收账款　　　　　　　　600

7月26日,提供了鲜花装饰服务。

借:预收账款　　　　　　　　600
　贷:主营业务收入　　　　　　600

例7.8　假设3月1日某个客人为她的运载车辆支付6个月的保险单费用3 600美元,对于保险公司来说,这笔交易的分录为:

首先,保险公司以资产(库存现金)增加、负债(预收账款)也增加来记录这笔交易。

3月1日,收到款项。

借:库存现金　　　　　　　　3 600
　贷:预收账款　　　　　　　　3 600

一个月后,保险公司会以减少预收账款、增加主营业务收入来记录这笔交易,金额为初始收款金额的1/6,因为提供了1/6的保险服务,因此实现了1/6的主营业务收入。

3月31日,提供了1个月的保险服务。

借:预收账款　　　　　　　　600
　贷:主营业务收入　　　　　　600

从会计角度来看,预收账款是一把双刃剑。对公司来说,早期的现金流对任何活动都是有利的,比如为购买更多的存货而支付债务利息。但该公司一旦收到预收账款就承担了按照付款条件交货的法律义务。

7.6　应付股利

作为派发给股东现金的一种方式,企业会分配股利。当公司的董事会宣告要向股东派发股利的时候即产生了一种负债(应付股利)。由于股利通常在宣告后几周内即派发,因此应付股利在资产负债表上划分为流动负债。给股东派发股利包括两个分录。第一笔分录是在董事会宣告股利这天记录,这是借记利润分配贷记应付股利,借贷的金额为派发的股利金额。

例 7.9　4月1日海沃德公司董事会宣告将在4月25日向其股东派发季度股利,该公司发行的10万股总份额,按每股2美元派发。对海沃德公司来说,这次派发的分录为:

4月1日,在宣告日记录将派发季度性股利:

借:利润分配　　　　　　　　200 000
　　贷:应付股利　　　　　　　　200 000

4月25日,记录实际派发季度性股利:

借:应付股利　　　　　　　　200 000
　　贷:库存现金　　　　　　　　200 000

应付股利与其他流动负债不同,因为应付股利代表的是所有者的欠债。尽管如此,从作为经济主体的企业角度来说,应付股利像其他负债一样,确实代表了一种法定义务。在公司的资产负债表上,应付股利属于负债,但在公司实际签发股利支票之前,它并不影响现金流量表。支付现金股利会影响现金流量表的融资活动。

7.7　应计负债

当费用已发生但尚未支付(未来才支付)的时候,应计负债就产生了。实际上,在某些费用实际支付之前就已产生,这就是应计负债,因此也称之为应计费用。例如,应付税费、应付利息、应付职工薪酬等都是应计负债。由于应计费用是在记录费用时产生,因此这类负债的发生时间与金额都受配比原则支配。所有企业都有应计负债。但是大多数情况下,这类负债通常不会累积到很大数额。在资产负债表中,它通常与应付账款合并,而不是单独列出。

1. 应付利息

利息是借款的代价,会随着借款时间的推移而增加。它通常是由于接受存款、短期或长期贷款及应付债券而产生。当企业签订长期融资协议时,企业则承诺将在未来支付大笔利息。利息是由交易金额和合同利率而计量的。由于负债是过去交易而形成的,因此应付利息是已经发生的未付利息。然而在任何资产负债表日,所有利息义务中仅仅有一小部分属于负债。在会计期末,应计应付利息以借记利息费用贷记应付利息而入账。

例7.10 假设约翰从银行借款500 000美元,期限为5年,年利率为12%。尽管借款本金在5年后才到期,但是利息仍然要从第一个月开始每个月都要支付。每年的借款利息为60 000美元(500 000×12%)。这5年里,约翰只承担一个月的利息债务,即自最后一次利息支付日起的应计利息。因此,约翰的资产负债表通常会体现仅仅5 000美元的应计未付利息(60 000×1/12)。

在每个月底,记录应计利息费用:

借:财务费用——利息费用　　5 000
　贷:应付利息　　　　　　　　5 000

如果每月底,约翰支付月利息:

借:应付利息　　　　　　　　5 000
　贷:库存现金　　　　　　　　5 000

如果这笔债务要求在每个月的最后一天支付应计利息,那么约翰的资产负债表上就不会有应计未付利息。借款人在未来期间支付利息的合同义务还不是债务,也不会在借款人的资产负债表上体现。然而,这类信息对投资者和债权人评估某公司的偿债能力和为其未来发展而融资的能力具有非常重要的意义。正因如此,会计原则要求公司在财务报表附注中披露主要借款安排的条款。

要确定某个公司当年的利息支出,财务报表的阅读者应该看损益表,而不是资产负债表。因为有关公司未来几年的利息债务,读者必须研究财务报表的附注。

2. 应付税费

企业必须按照国家规定履行纳税义务,对其经营所得依法缴纳的各种税。应付税费表明的即是企业应向政府部门缴纳的税费金额。这里的税包括增值税、所得税、消费税、资源税、土地增值税、房产税、车船税、土地使用税等。这些应缴税费应按照权责发生制原则进行确认、计提。盈利的企业需要缴纳相当于其应税收入一部分的所得税。每个会计期末,预估所得税费用且做如下调整分录:

借:所得税费用
　贷:应付所得税

7.8　或有负债

或有事项是指未来可能发生并影响公司财务状况,但无法准确预测或保证的财务事项。为了公平地比较不同公司的财务账目,会计准则将对处理诸如或有事项等具体问题制定了规则。

或有负债是依赖于一个或多个未来可能发生或不发生事件的一种负债,以便确认应付金额、收款人、应付日期,甚至来确定是否存在这一债务;也就是说,这些因素中的一个或多个取决于偶然性。或有负债并不能覆盖企业可能面临的所有成本。或有负债是由现存状况引起的一项潜在的负债,该现存状况的最终结果取决于未来的某个事项是否发生。一般来说,或有事项的金额都需要预计,因为只有在未来事项将或有负债确认为实际负债的时候才能确定金额,在此之前,负债的支付对象也往往不能明确。或有负债必须与公司的业务活动相关,而不是更广泛的风险,如极端天气事件或军事行动造成的损害。或有负债的例子不胜枚举。法律纠纷导致或有负债,环境污染事件导致或有负债,产品保修导致或有负债等。出售汽车所做的保证和其他产品保证,企业一般都需要入账,过去售出产品发生质量问题的比例可作为估计未来产品保证支出的依据。配比原则需求企业在销售发生的期间估计未来可能发生的保证费用并且入账,而不能在费用实际发生时再入账。或有事项不会在资产负债表上报告,而是在附注里报告。

公司在符合下列条件的情况下,将与或有事项有关的义务确认为负债:
(1)该义务是公司当前的义务;
(2)很可能需要公司经济利益的流出来清偿债务;
(3)可以对债务的数额做出可靠的估计。

如果债务的金额不确定,那么该金额应该是清偿债务所需支出的最佳估计值。如果偿还这笔债务的支出有一个范围,应确定该范围内最佳估计值平均数的下限和上限的范围。如果没有需要支付负债的支出金额范围,应按下列方法确定最佳的估计值:
(1)在涉及一个事项的情况下,应根据最可能的结果确定最佳估计值;
(2)当偶发事件涉及多个项目时,最好的估计应该是通过将所有可能的结果的相关概率加权来确定。

企业应当在财务报表的附注中披露下列或有负债:
(1)贴现商业承兑汇票引起的或有负债;
(2)未决诉讼或仲裁引起的或有负债;
(3)为其他企业债务提供担保而产生的或有负债;
(4)其他或有负债,不包括经济利益可能流出的或有负债。

对于应披露的或有负债,企业应披露以下内容:
(1)或有负债产生的原因;
(2)或有负债预期财务影响的估计(如无法估计,应说明理由);
(3)任何偿付的可能性。

第八单元 非流动负债

8.1 非流动负债的定义

非流动负债,也称为长期债务,是指偿还期超过一年或者一个营业周期的债务,包括长期应付票据、应付债券、应付抵押账款以及融资租赁条件下的债务的记账情况。非流动负债的核算十分复杂,因为利息的支付,或在一些情况下本息的支付是在不同的期间里定期地做出。

8.2 货币的时间价值

货币的时间价值是指在一定时间内赚取一定数量的利息的货币价值。货币时间价值是金融理论的核心概念,它影响着企业金融、消费金融和政府金融。

货币的时间价值源于利息的概念,这意味着现在可用的货币由于其潜在的收益能力,在未来会比同等数额的货币更有价值。因为这个普遍的事实,我们宁愿今天收到钱,而不是将来收到同样的数额。

例如,假设利率为5%,今天投资的100美元在一年内等于105美元(即100美元乘以1.05)。相反,假设利率为5%,一年后收到的100美元现在只值95.24美元(即100美元除以1.05)。

1. 单利和复利

利息的计算包括三个要素:本金、利率和时间。本金是借款或投资的起始金额;利率是未偿还本金的百分比;时间是未偿还本金的期限。让我们来看看不同利率类型的计算。

◆单利

单利是指仅在初始本金上支付的利息。是指计算利息的本金基数不随时间增加,而且每个期间的利息支付额保持不变。

例8.1 如果某人以100美元的起始价值收取5%的利息,第一年的利息将是:
$$100 \times 0.05 = 5(美元)$$

继续收取原来100美元的5%的利息,五年内原始投资的增长趋势如下:

第1年:100 的 5% = 5;5 + 100 = 105

第2年:100 的 5% = 5;5 + 105 = 110

第3年:100 的 5% = 5;5 + 110 = 115

第 4 年:100 的 5% = 5;5 + 115 = 120
第 5 年:100 的 5% = 5;5 + 120 = 125

因此,通过对 100 美元的初始价值应用单利计算,每年可获得 5 美元,最终 5 年可获得 25 美元的利息。

◆复利

复利是期初本金和任何额外累积本金所支付的利息。收到复利固然好,但付复利就不那么好了。在复利情况下,利息不仅计算在期初利息上,而且计算在期间累积的任何利息上。

例 8.2　如果某人以 100 美元的起始价值收取 5% 的复利,那么第一年的利息就相当于 100 美元的单利,即 5 美元。然而,第二年的利息将按第二年的开始金额计算,即 105 美元。所以利息是:

$$105 \times 0.05 = 5.25(美元)$$

在第二年年底,余额为 110.25 美元。如果这种情况持续 5 年,投资的增长将会是:

第 1 年:100 的 5% = 5.00;5.00 + 100.00 = 105.00
第 2 年:105.00 的 5% = 5.25;5.25 + 105.00 = 110.25
第 3 年:115.25 的 5% = 5.51;5.51 + 110.25 = 115.76
第 4 年 115.76 的;5% = 5.79;5.79 + 115.76 = 121.55
第 5 年:121.55 的 5% = 6.08;6.08 + 121.55 = 127.63

如果比较单利和复利的增长曲线,单利投资以线性方式增长,复利投资以几何增长。所以在复利的情况下,投资持有的时间越长,增长就越显著。

与其逐年计算利息,不如用复利公式简单地看出一项投资的未来价值。复利的公式是:

$$P_n = P_0(1 + i)^n$$

其中,P_n 代表本利和;
　　　P_0 代表初始本金;
　　　i 代表利率;
　　　n 代表时间。

以例 8.2 为例,如果某人以 100 美元的起始价值在 5 年内收取 5% 的复利,利用这个公式,只需插入适当的值并计算即可

$$P_n = 100 \times (1 + 0.05)^5 = 127.63$$

在大多数会计实务中,票据、借款和投资的利息都是按复利计算的。

2. 终值与现值

◆终值

终值(FV)是指货币在未来某一特定日期的价值。更准确地说,它衡量的是假设某一利率,某一特定金额在未来某一特定时间"价值"的未来名义金额,一般来说,是回报率;它是以当前价值乘以累积函数计算的。该价值不包括对通货膨胀或其他影响未来货币真实价值的

因素的修正。对于单一数额,其未来复利价值可以使用前面的公式计算:

$$FV = P_0(1+i)^n$$

例8.3 假设你今天投资5 000美元,每年将获得8%的利息。4年后你会有多少钱?

$$FV = 5\ 000 \times (1+8\%)^4 = 6\ 802$$

在公式中,$(1+i)^n$部分是复利终值系数,在复利终值系数表中包含有与各种利率和时间相对应的该系数的值。找出当前金额的终值,找出适当的年数和适当的利率,取得结果系数,乘以期初值。

◆现值

现值(PV),也称为现期贴现值,与终值是互逆的。它是复利终值的逆运算。另一种考虑现值的方法是在未来的时间线上采取一种立场,然后往前回顾,看看起始金额是多少。

复利现值可以用下面的公式计算出来:

$$PV = FV/(1+i)^n \text{ 或者 } PV = FV(1+i)^{-n}$$

例8.4 如果你认为你可以在5年内以25 000美元的价格出售一项资产,并且你认为合适的折现率是5%,那么你今天会为这项资产支付多少钱?

$$PV = 25\ 000/(1+5\%)^5 = 19\ 588.15$$

在公式中,$1/(1+i)^n$或$(1+i)^{-n}$部分是用来乘以终值的复利现值系数。注意现值系数都小于1。因此,当将终值乘以这些系数时,终值折现为现值。现值表的使用方法与前面讨论过的终值表大致相同,确定适当的年数和适当的利率,取得结果系数并将其乘以终值。

3. 年金的终值和现值

年金是时间间隔相同的一系列现金流。年金可以是相等的年度存款,相等的年度取款,相等的年度付款,或相等的年度收入。关键在于年度现金流。

当现金流出现在年底时,这使得它们成为普通年金(年终现金流),如果现金流出现在年初,它们就是到期年金(年初现金流)。在这一部分我们只讨论普通年金。

年金有三个基本特征:

①期限相等(通常为一年);
②每个期限的年金金额相等;
③每个利率期限的复利或折现相等。

◆年金的终值

普通年金的终值是指一系列预期或承诺的未来付款在特定复利期限结束后增长到的价值。假设每年存款100美元,在年底存入,三年内获得5%的利息。

第1年:年底存入100(美元)=100.00(美元)
第2年:$100 \times 0.05 = 5.00$　$5.00 + 100 + 100 = 205.00$
第3年:$205 \times 0.05 = 10.25$　$10.25 + 205 + 100 = 315.25$

普通年金的终值可以通过使用终值公式计算该系列中每个终值,然后对结果进行加和来求解。更直接的公式是：

$$FA = A[(1+i)^n - 1]/i$$

还有年金的表格。在公式中，$[(1+i)^n - 1]/i$ 部分是年金终值系数。年金终值系数表的使用方法与前面的表相同。查找合适的期限数目，找到合适的利率，取得系数，乘以年金的金额。

例8.5 国家储蓄基金承诺每月0.75%的回报，如果你连续15年每月存入100美元。15年后会累积多少钱？

$$FV = 100 \times [(1+0.75\%)^{180} - 1]/0.75\% = 37\,840.58$$

例8.6 威利刚刚买了一栋房子。她估计20年后屋顶需要花费25 000美元更新。为了支付这些费用，她打算在每年年底存下等额的钱，年利率为6%。这样一年的年金要多少钱？

$$25\,000 = A \times [(1+6\%)^{20} - 1]/6\%$$
$$A = 679.61$$

◆ **年金的现值**

普通年金的现值是指一系列预期或承诺的未来付款在今天已经折现为一个等值的价值。在某种程度上比较两个不同的现金流是非常有用的。PA也可以被认为是你今天必须在一个特定利率下投资的金额，这样当你在每个期间提取等量的本金时，在年金结束时，原始本金和所有累积的利息都将完全耗尽。

普通年金的现值可以用现值公式计算每笔付款的现值，然后对结果进行加和。更直接的公式是：

$$PA = A[1-(1+i)^{-n}]/i$$

例8.7 以6%的利率计算4年期、每年3 000美元的年金的现值。

$$PA = 3\,000 \times [1-(1+6\%)^{-4}]/6\% = 10\,395.32$$

在公式中，$[1-(1+i)^{-n}]/i$ 部分是年金现值系数。在年金现值系数表中查找合适的期限，找到合适的利率，找到系数，乘以年金的金额。

例8.8 皮特考虑买房子。目前，他以每月1 000美元的价格租了一个房子。现时按揭贷款的每月利率为0.5厘。他的计划期限是20年。如果他不想增加住房成本，他能得到多少抵押贷款？

$$PA = 1\,000 \times [1-(1+0.5\%)^{-240}]/0.5\% = 139\,580.8$$

8.3 应付债券

债券有很多种，且各有其自身特点。有些债券的持有者可以选择将其转换成普通股，称为可转换债券。另外那些发行者可选择在到期前以一定金额赎回的债券，被称为可提前（可通知）赎回债券。此外，有明确作为担保的抵押资产的债券是担保债券，无担保债券是不具有明确作为担保的抵押资产的债券;定期债券在固定的到期日到期分期还本债券在不同到期日分期偿还;还有根据是否以持有者名字签发来分的记名债券和不记名债券。无论哪种债券都是一种附息应付票据。

如果息票利率(即名义利率)与市场利率(实际利率)恰巧一致时,债券以票面价值销售。但是这种情况很少发生,因为市场利率经常变化,公司在印制债券时很难预测出售债券时的市场利率。所以债券经常不以票面价销售。如果息票利率低于市场利率则折价销售,如果市场利率低于息票利率则溢价销售。债券折价和溢价的摊销应在每个会计期间以直线摊销法或实际利率法单独记录和报告。因而债券折价销售并不代表发行者财务状况令人担忧,债券溢价销售也不能说就意味着其财务实力雄厚。长期债权人总是对公司偿息能力和到期偿付票面价值的能力特别关心。下面两个比值对投资方来说具有一定的参考价值:

(1)资产负债比

总负债额(包括流动负债和长期负债)除以总资产额得出资产负债比。资产负债比越高,公司无法按期偿债的可能性就越大。

(2)已获利息倍数

已获利息倍数代表公司支付到期利息的能力或用所得支付利息的程度,其计算公式是:息税前利润/利息费用。已获利息倍数越低,意味着能用来支付利息的收益越少,那么公司提高利息率的可能性就越小。

应付债券是指为了筹集(长期)使用资金而发行的一种书面凭证,并承诺在一定时间内偿还。应付债券包含的主要要素包括以下几种:

①债券的票面金额;

②债券的发行价格;

③债券的偿还期;

④利息的支付日;

⑤债券票面利率。

债券的面值和票面利率是固定的。如果发行价低于面值,债券为折价发行;如果债券发行价高于面值,为溢价发行;如果发行价等于面值,为平价发行。

例8.9 B公司于2019年7月发行3年期、到期一次还本付息、年利率为8%、面值总额为40 000 000元的长期债券,筹集的资金用于固定资产的生产经营。

(1)当收到资金时:

借:银行存款   40 000 000

  贷:应付债券——面值   40 000 000

(2)2019年年底计提利息时:

借:在建工程   1 600 000 (40 000 000×8%×1/12×6)

  贷:应付债券——应计利息   1 600 000

(3) 到期还本付息:
借:应付债券——面值   40 000 000
      ——应计利息   9 600 000(4 000 000×8%×3)
  贷:银行存款   49 600 000

第九单元　所有者权益

9.1　股东的权利和特权

1. 普通股

普通股在股份公司中代表所有权。一股就是一份所有权。如果一个公司发行 10 股,那么每一股就代表公司的 10% 的所有权;如果该公司发行 100 股,每一股则代表公司 1% 的所有权。这种股票使所有者除有权获得公司的一份利润外,还有权对公司的决策进行表决。当然,大多数的公司发行数以百万计的股票,使得每一股所含的权益只是公司股本总额极其微小的一份。这些股票是可以转让的,你每次进行的交易也就是股票的转让。

普通股的股利分为现金股利、股票股利和资产股利。最常见的分配方式是现金股利。公司董事会决定是否给普通股股东分配股利。股利的增加或减少取决于公司的经营状况。经营状况不良的公司甚至会推迟分配股利,直到它的资产负债表所显示的财政状况好转。

如果发行股票的公司破产且不得不卖掉它的资产,那么只有在其他所有的债权人、债券持有者和优先股的股东获得清算资产后,才轮到普通股的股东。

普通股股东享有的主要权利:
①在年度会议上对董事会的选举进行投票。
②通过获取股息分享公司的收益。
③发行新股时,保留同等份额的所有权。
④根据所持股份的比例分享资产清算的利益。

2. 优先股

优先股在股份公司里也代表所有权。优先股的持有者相对于普通股的持有者来说,享有某些优先权利。优先股经常享有如下权利:
①股利分配的优先权。
②破产时享有优先清偿权。
③可以转换为普通股。

享有上述优先权利的交换条件是优先股股东不能在股东大会上表决或享有其他特定的权利。

股利的优先分配权并不保证公司一定会支付股利。它仅仅是保证公司在支付普通股股利之前,必须以一定股息率或适当金额先支付优先股的股利。

优先股可以是有面值股,也可以是无面值股。

有面值股是指在公司章程中分配了每股价值的股份资本。票面价值可以由公司决定为任何数额。通常,有面值股的票面价值数额很小,但与它的市场价无关。例如,某公司有面值股的票面价值为每股1.25美元,但它股票最近的市场价可能已经上涨到每股80美元。

其股利为面值的固定比率。例如,如果股票的面值为100元,年利息为6%,那么年股利为每股6元。近年来,一些公司也开始发行股息率随银行利率变化的优先股。

9.2 股票发行的核算

创建股份公司时,公司章程将说明普通股及优先股的核定股数。经常是核定的股数多于计划发行的股数。这是为了在将来扩大再生产时不必再申请更多的核定股数。当通过发行股票筹得现金时,通常借记库存现金账户,贷记特定的股东权益账户,例如,如果发行有面值的普通股,普通股被贷记;如果普通股按溢价发行,则要贷记"资本公积——普通股"。

例9.1 为了说明这一问题,我们假设B公司获准组建股份公司。因此3月1日B公司按每股$25的价格发行80 000股面值为$10的普通股。记录股票发行的分录如下:

借:库存现金(80 000×25)　　　　2 000 000
　贷:普通股(80 000×10)　　　　　　　800 000
　　　资本公积——普通股(80 000×15)　1 200 000

如果有面值的股票为优先股,分录如下:

借:库存现金(80 000×25)　　　　2 000 000
　贷:优先股(80 000×10)　　　　　　　800 000
　　　资本公积——优先股(80 000×15)　1 200 000

如果所发行的股票是无面值股票,但有设定价值,分录同理。请见下例:

例9.2　假如B公司的核定股票为无面值股票,但设定价值为每股1美元,再假如B公司按每股5美元的价格发行了400 000股。分录如下:

借:库存现金(400 000×5)　　　　2 000 000
　贷:普通股(400 000×1)　　　　　　　400 000
　　　资本公积——普通股(400 000×4)　1 600 000

9.3 库存股

当股份公司想从投资者手中收回其股票时,它可以买回一部分流通在外的股票。股份公司买回股票有若干原因:首先,管理部门想把该股票作为对员工的补贴或购股选择权。第二,管理部门可能觉得股票交易价格异乎寻常地低。第三,公司需要这些股票来购买另一家公司。第四,公司想通过减少在外股数提高每股收益。

注意:库存股不能被认定为资产,因为股份公司不可以拥有自己的一部分。库存股通常按照成本核算,即借记购买日里的该股票(按市值),而不按其面值或设定价值入账。

例9.3 假设 B 公司按照每股 60 美元回购 10 美元面值的普通股 1 000 股。记录回购的分录如下:

借:库存股——普通股　　　　60 000
　贷:库存现金　　　　　　　　　60 000
(购买 1 000 库存股,每股 60 美元。)

9.4 留存收益

由盈利的经营带来的股东权益的增加,即为留存收益。年末,收入账户的余额结入留存收益账户。如果公司有足够的现金,则可向股东分配收益。这种性质的分配被称为分红,同时总资产和股东权益减少。因此,在任一资产负债表日的留存收益都代表了公司自建立之日起的累积收益减去损失和股利的余额。

在公司里,提款必须经过正规的程序。股东选出的董事会必须在向股东进行分配之前开会"宣布股利"。股利是作为投资的回报支付给股东的收益。在分红过程中,以下三个时间非常重要:

①公布日:董事会宣布分红的日期。
②记录日:从该日起拥有股份的股东有权获得分红的日期。
③支付日:股利支票寄送给股东之日。

公布分红减少了公司所有者权益的留存收益部分,并产生负债——应付股利。支付股利清偿了负债,减少了资产(通常为现金)。

与留存收益有关的主要交易包括以下几种。

(1)现金股利

现金股利被公布时即减少了留存收益,成为流动负债。支付现金股利的三个要求是:留存收益、充足的现金和由董事会进行分红行为。股利只能通过董事会分配。交易过程如下:

宣告日:

借:留存收益   × × ×
　　贷:应付股利——现金股利   × × ×
支付日:
借:应付股利   × × ×
　　贷:库存现金   × × ×

(2)股份股利

股份股利是根据股东现持有股份比例与额外股份的分配,是留存收益向相应股份的转换。现金股利和股份股利有很大的区别。现金股利同时减少资产和股东权益,而股份股利对资产和总的股东权益没有影响。每个股东都获得额外的股份,所有权的比例与以前并无变化。

宣告日:
借:留存收益   × × ×
　　贷:应付股利——股份股利   × × ×
支付日:
借:应付股利——股份股利   × × ×
　　贷:股本   × × ×

第十单元　财务报表分析

10.1　水平分析

财务报表分析属于管理会计,它涉及数据转换成有用的信息以及使用分析工具帮助报表使用者做出更好的经营决策。报表使用者包括公司内外部的决策者。会计信息的内部使用者是公司的管理者、经营者。对这些主管人员来说,财务报表分析的目的是为他们提供科学决策及改善公司效率的信息。这有助于减少猜测和直觉。外部使用者是那些不直接参与公司经营的人,包括股东、银行工作人员、客户、供应商、监管人员、律师等。外部使用者依据财务报表分析做出更好、更全面的决策,以达到自己的目标。让我们举例说明。董事会使用财务报表分析之信息来监控管理部门的决策;雇员及工会使用该信息进行劳动谈判;股东及债权人使用这些信息对公司的前景进行投资和放款决策;供应商使用该信息确定其信用条件;客户对财务报表进行分析,以决定是否建立采购关系;公用事业部门通过财务报表分析制订客户的费率;而审计师用财务报表分析来评估客户的财务报表数据的"公允表达"。

水平分析是对两个或更多的连续的会计期间进行比较。当我们审阅比较财务报表时,水平分析涉及一种自左至右的眼部运动。水平分析着手于变化的计算,计算从前一年到本期的金额变化以及百分比变化。

1. 计算金额变化及百分比变化

我们可以这样计算财务报表某项的金额变化:

$$金额变化 = 报告期金额 - 基期金额$$

在公式中,报告期是分析时的时间点,基期是用来比较的时间点,前一个年度常被用作基期。

计算百分比变化时,我们用金额变化除以基期金额,然后乘以100%:

$$百分比变化 = \frac{报告期金额 - 基期金额}{基期金额} \times 100\%$$

2. 金额及百分比变化实例

通过比较财务报表的形式我们提供一个有关洛特律师事务所的金额及百分比变化的实例。现在我们向您提供一份计算金额及百分比变化的比较财务报表,其中2月份为报告期,1月份为基期。

例10.1

表10.1 洛特律师事务所比较资产负债表

2019年2月28日,2月和1月   单位:美元

	2月	1月	金额变化	百分比变化
资产				
流动资产				
现金及现金等价物	42 657	7 307	35 350	483.78%
应收票据	550		550	
材料	120	500	380	
流动资产合计	43 327	7 807	35 520	454.98%
非流动资产,净值	47 000	2 000	45 000	2 250.00
总资产	90 327	9 807	80 520	821.05%
负债及资本				
负债				
流动负债				
应付账款	25 400	400	25 000	6 250%
应付银行服务费	400		400	

续表 10.1

	2月	1月	金额变化	百分比变化
应付公用事业费	80		80	
应交税费	16 512		16 512	
流动负债合计	42 392	400	41 992	10 498.00%
非流动负债				
应付债券				
应付抵押账款				
非流动负债合计				
负债合计	42 392	400	41 992	10 498.00%
资本				
期初资本－泰德.洛特	9 407	8 000	1 407	17.59%
资本增加额	38 528	1 407	37 121	2 638.3%
期末资本－泰德,洛特	47 935	9 407	38 528	409.57%
负债及资本合计	90 327	9 807	80 520	821.00%
规费收入	60 000	3 500	56 500	1 614.3%
费用				
销售费用	460	200	260	130.00%
管理费用	4 100	1 400	2 700	192.86%
财务费用	400	23	377	1 639.14%
费用合计	4 960	1 623	3 337	205.61%
税前利润	55 040	1 877	53 163	2 832.33%
减:所得税(30%)	16 512		16 512	
净利润	38 528	1 877	36 651	1 952.64%

注意:当基期出现负值,报告期出现正值(或者相反)时,我们不能计算其百分比变化。另外,当基期无数据时,百分比变化也无法计算。最后,当基期有数据,而报告期为零时,减少的数值为100%。

对金额变化和百分比变化进行计算之后,我们就要确定这些变化的原因,尽管洛特律师事务所有些增长数据令人难以置信。

10.2 垂直分析

当我们在查看百分比财务报表时,垂直分析涉及一种自上而下的眼部运动。垂直分析也使用百分率。百分率用来表明财务报表中的某个部分(财务报表的单一项目或一组项目)与总额(基数)之比。在资产负债表上,总额(基数)为总资产,或负债与所有者权益合计。在利润表上,总额为销售收入净额或销售净额。总额为100%,而每一部分的百分比根据这个总额进行计算。列示百分比的最终报表被称为百分比报表。这种百分比被称为common-size,而这种分析被称为百分比分析。

1. 百分比报表

既然百分比报表显示部分与总额之间的比率,这个百分比是一个关键点。百分比用分析中的每一个单独的财务报表数值除以基数计算得出。

$$百分比 = \frac{分析值}{基数} \times 100\%$$

2. 百分比财务报表实例

百分比资产负债表和百分比利润表构成百分比财务报表。

百分比资产负债表实例在百分比资产负债表中,每一项资产、负债、所有者权益的百分比是用总资产作为基数进行计算的。当公司的连续的资产负债表用这种方法展示时,资产、负债、所有者权益的变化便一目了然。例10.2展示了一个洛特律师事务所的百分比比较资产负债表。

例10.2

表10.2 洛特律师事务所百分比比较资产负债表

20019年2月28日,2月和1月   单位:美元

			百分比	
	2月	1月	2月	1月
资产				
流动资产				
现金及现金等价物	42 657	7 307	47.23%	74.5%
应收票据	550		0.6%	
材料	120	500	0.13%	5.1%
流动资金合计	43 327	7 807	47.97%	79.61%
非流动资产,净值	47 000	2 000	52.03%	20.39%
总资产	90 327	9 807	100.00%	100.00%

续表 10.2

			百分比	
负债及资本				
负债				
流动负债				
应付账款	25 400	400	28.12%	4.07%
应付银行服务费	400		0.44%	
应付公用事业费	80		0.09%	
应交税费	16 512		18.28%	
流动负债合计	42 392	400	46.93%	4.07%
非流动负债				
应付债券				
应付抵押账款				
非流动负债合计				
负债合计	42 392	400	46.93%	4.07%
资本				
期初资本——泰德·洛特	9 407	8 000	10.41%	81.57%
资本增加额	38 528	1 407	42.65%	14.35%
期末资本——泰德·洛特	47 935	9 407	53.07%	95.92%
负债及资本合计	90 327	9 807	100.00%	100.00%

重要的信息包括：(1)现金及现金等价物的减少(从 74.5% 减少到 47.23%)，因此流动资产受到了影响(从 79.61% 降到 47.97%)；(2)非流动资产增加(从 20.39% 增加到 52.03%)，应付账款增加(从 4.07% 增加到 28.12%)；(3)期末资本减少(从 95.92% 减少到 53.07%)。造成这些数字增加和减少的原因必须认真予以审查和解释。

◆ 百分比利润表实例

通过对百分比利润表的审查，我们的分析也会从中受益。收入通常为基数，如 100%。每一个百分比利润表的项口都是收入的一个百分比。例 10.3 显示了洛特律师事务所的百分比比较利润表。

例 10.3

表 10.3 洛特律师事务所百分比比较利润表

2019 年 2 月,2 月和 1 月　　　　　　　　　　　　　　　　单位:美元

	2 月	1 月	百分比 2 月	百分比 1 月
费用收入	60 000	3 500	100%	100%
费用				
销售费用	460	200	0.77%	5.71%
管理费用	4 100	1 400	6.83%	40%
财务费用	400	23	0.67%	0.66%
费用合计	4 960	1 623	8.27%	46.37%
税前利润	55 040		91.73%	
减:所得税(30%)	16 512		27.52%	
净利润	38 528	1 877	64.21%	53.63%

这个例子表明与其他行业相比,作为收入的一个百分比,洛特的费用是相当低的(8.27%)。这是因为 2 月份的利润表不能显示洛特律师事务所的全部情况。总之销售费用急剧下降(从 5.71% 下降到 0.77%),管理费用也大幅减少(40% 减少到 6.83%)。2 月份所披露的财务费用是估计数值,因为银行对账单尚未到达。最重要的是发生了所得税费用(从零到 27.52%),但净利润稳步上升(从 53.63% 上升到 64.21%)。

10.3　比率分析

比率是财务报表分析中普遍而广泛使用的分析工具。通过比率分析,财务报表各项目之间的关系显而易见,需进一步关注的方面也露出端倪,比率有助于我们审视现状和未来趋势。因此比率分析和其他分析工具一样通常都是面向未来的。

比率的有用性取决于准确的解释,这是比率分析中最具挑战性的一个方面。本节将介绍一系列财务上的比率以及如何使用这些比率。这里所选择的比率分为流动性比率和效率比率、偿债能力比率、盈利比率。

1. 流动比率和效率比率

流动性是指公司满足短期或非预期现金需求的能力。效率是指公司在使用资产时的生产力的大小。流动性和效率在我们的分析中是十分重要的。如果公司不能偿还本期债务,那么它能否持续经营则令人怀疑。例如,如果企业所有者拥有无限责任(如独资企业和合伙企业),缺乏流动性将危及其个人财产。如果一家公司缺乏流动性,其债权人对利息和本金的收回就会被延误。另外,公司的客户和供应商关系将会因短期流动性方面的问题而受到影响。

◆ 营运资本比率及流动比率

营运资本等于流动资产减流动负债。公司需要足够的营运资本来满足流动负债,采购存货,给于现金折扣。

在评估公司的营运资本的时候,我们要考虑流动资产与流动负债之间的流动比率,如下所示:

流动比率 = 流动资产/流动负债

采用例10.1的数据,洛特律师事务所的流动比率如下:

2019 年 2 月份 43 327/42 392 = 1.02∶1

2019 年 1 月份 7 807/400 = 19.5∶1

洛特律师事务所 1 月份的流动比率较高,说明流动状况很好。高流动比率意味着企业有能力偿还本期债务,但是过高的流动比率意味着公司流动资产投资过多,这并不被认为是资金的有效利用,因为流动资产并不创造额外的收入。低流动比率被认为是迫在眉睫的偿债危险。广为接受的流动比率是 2∶1,但是对于像洛特律师事务所这样的服务企业来说,1∶1 的流动比率也是可以接受的,因为除办公用品之外,它需要的存货很少或无存货。另一方面,销售高价商品的公司需要一个更高的比率,这是因为公司难以判断客户需求。

◆ 速动比率

速动比率是用来测算短期偿债能力的。速动比率计算如下:

速动比率 = 速动资产/流动负债

速动资产是现金、短期投资、应收账款、应收票据。这些是流动资产中流动性最强的资产。使用例10.1中的数据,洛特律师事务所的速动比率如下:

	2019 年 2 月	2019 年 1 月
现金及现金等价物	42 657	7 307
应收票据	550	
速动资产合计	43 207	7 307
流动负债合计	42 392	400
速动资产	43 207 = 1.02:1	7 307 = 18.3:1

◆ 应收账款周转率

应收账款周转率衡量公司将应收账款转化为现金的频率。其计算公式如下：

$$应收账款周转率 = 销售净额/应收账款平均值$$

由于 B 公司只有一个会计期间，所以我们无从计算其应收账款平均值。洛特律师事务所也没有应收账款。因此我们使用 MK 公司 2018 年和 2019 年的财务数据来说明该问题。见表 10.4、表 10.5。

表 10.4　MK 比较资产负债表

5 月 31 日，2019 和 2018　　　　　　　　　　　　　　　　　　　　单位：美元

	2019	2018	金额变化	百分比变化
资产				
流动资产				
现金及现金等价物	445 421	262 117	183 304	69.9%
应收账款-减坏账准备 57 233 和 43 372	1 754 137	1 346 125	408 012	30.3%
存货	1 338 640	931 151	407 489	43.8%
递延所得税	135 663	93 120	42 543	45.7%
预付费用	157 058	94 427	62 631	66.3%
流动负债合计	3 830 919	2 726 940	1 103 979	40.5%
不动产、厂房和设备净值	922 369	643 459	278 910	43.3%
可辨认无形资产和商誉	464 191	474 812	10 621	2.2%
递延所得税及营业外资产	143 728	106 417	37 311	35.1%
总资产	5 361 207	3 951 628	1 409 579	35.7%

续表 10.4

	2019	2018	金额变化	百分比变化
负债及股东权益				
流动负债				
一年内到期的非流动负债	2 216	7 301	5 085	69.6%
应付票据	553 153	445 064	108 089	24.3%
应收账款	687 121	455 034	232 087	51.0%
应计负债	570 504	480 407	90 097	18.8%
应交税费	53 923	79 253	25 330	32%
流动负债合计	1 866 917	1 467 059	399 858	27.3%
非流动负债	296 020	9 584	286 436	2 988.7%
递延所得税及其他负债	42 132	43 285	1 153	2.7%
承付款项及或有事项				
可赎回优先股	300	300	0	0.0%
股东权益				
设定价值普通股:				
A 类可转换的:在外股 101 711 和 102 240 股	152	153	1	0.7%
B 类:在外股 187 559 和 185 018 股	2 706	2 702	4	0.1%
设定价值资本公积	210 650	154 833	55 817	36.0%
外币换算调整	31 333	16 501	14 832	89.9%
留存收益	2 973 663	2 290 213	683 450	29.8%
股东权益合计	3 155 838	2 431 400	724 438	29.8%
负债及股东权益总额	5 361 207	3 951 628	1 409 579	35.7%

表 10.5 MK 比较利润表

截至 5 月 31 日的各年度,2019 和 2018   单位:美元

	2019	2018	金额变化	百分比变化
收入	9 186 539	6 470 625	2 715 914	42.0%
成本及费用				
销货成本	5 502 993	3 906 746	1 596 247	40.9%
销售及行政费用	2 303 704	1 588 612	715 092	45.0%

续表 10.5

	2019	2018	金额变化	百分比变化
利息费用	52 343	39 498	12 845	32.5%
其他收入/费用,净值	32 277	36 679	4 402	12.0%
成本及费用合计	7 891 317	5 571 535	2 319 782	41.6%
税前利润	1 295 222	899 090	396 132	44.1%
所得税	499 400	345 900	153 500	44.4%
净利润	795 822	553 190	242 632	43.9%
普通股每股净收益	2.68	1.88	0.8	42.6%
普通股和普通股等价物平均股数	297 000	293 608		

根据这些数据,MK 2019 年的应收账款周转率计算如下:

$$\frac{9\ 186\ 539}{(1\ 754\ 137 + 1\ 346\ 125)/2} = 5.93\ 次$$

MK 的应收账款周转率为 5.9 次;与同类企业是类似的。如果应收账款被迅速收回,应收账款周转率肯定会高。高周转率是非常有利的因为这意味着公司不必将巨额资本用于应收账款上。但如果信用条件非常苛刻的话,应收账款周转率也会非常高,这会给销售造成负面影响。

◆应收账款平均回收天数

这个比率测算应收款项回收的平均时间,计算如下(使用表 10.4、表 10.5 的信息):

应收账款平均回收天数 = 每年天数/应收账款周转率

= 365 天/5.93 次

= 61.55 天

◆存货周转率

如果公司想知道在出售之前对商品的持有时间有多长,存货周转率将回答这个问题。用下列公式计算:

存货周转率 = 销货成本/平均存货

让我们再次用表 10.4、表 10.5 的数据来说明:

$$存货周转率 = \frac{5\ 502\ 993}{(931\ 151 + 1\ 338\ 640)/2} = 4.8\ 次$$

存货周转率高的公司只需对存货进行较小的投入。

◆存货平均周转天数

该比率测算销售库存货物的平均天数。以上面的存货周转率为例，MK 的存货平均周转天数计算如下：

$$存货平均周转天数 = 每年天数/存货周转率$$
$$= 365 \text{ 天}/4.8 \text{ 次}$$
$$= 76 \text{ 天}$$

这个公式计算出 MK 公司需要 76 天的时间将存货转化为应收款项（或现金），这并不是一个很快的速度。

◆总资产周转率

总资产周转率描述公司使用资产创造销售的能力，用下列公式计算：

$$总资产周转率 = 收入/总资产平均值$$

计算总资产平均值的通常方法是将会计期间的期初资产和期末资产加总，然后除以2。

使用表 10.4、表 10.5 的信息，该比率计算如下：

$$总资产周转率 = \frac{9\,186\,539}{(5\,361\,207 + 3\,951\,628)/2} = 1.97 \text{ 次}$$

2. 偿债能力比率

偿债能力是指公司偿付长期债务的长期财务能力。分析资本结构是评估偿债能力的关键。在此，我们将介绍各种偿债能力分析工具。我们的分析涉及公司长期的偿债和保护债权人的能力。

◆负债比率

该比率评估所有者投入的资产和债权人投入的资产之间的比例，它表达出总负债占总资产的百分比。其计算公式如下：

$$负债比率 = 总负债/总资产 \times 100\%$$

◆股东权益比率

股东权益比率表达股东权益总值占资产的百分比。其计算公式如下：

$$股东权益比率 = 股东权益总值/资产总值 \times 100\%$$

3. 盈利比率

盈利能力指的是公司创造利润的能力。盈利能力也与偿债能力有关。盈利能力能引发我们大家的兴趣。那么让我们来讨论盈利能力在财务报表分析中的重要性吧。

◆净利率

净利率反映公司从销售中赚取净利润的能力。用下列公式计算：

$$净利率 = 净利润/收入 \times 100\%$$

◆总资产收益率

该比率测算公司的综合盈利能力，用下列公式计算：

$$总资产收益率 = 净利润/总资产平均值$$

采用表10.4、表10.5的信息，MK公司2019年的总资产收益率如下：

$$\frac{795\ 822}{(5\ 361\ 207 + 3\ 951\ 628)/2} \times 100\% = 17.1\%$$

和大多数企业相比，17.1%的总资产收益率是相当不错的。

◆净资产收益率

该比率计量所有者权益的报酬率，测算企业每美元净资产利润产出的效益，也表明公司运用投资时创造收益的情况。净资产收益率用下列公式计算：

$$净资产收益率 = 税后净利/所有者权益 \times 100\%$$

使用表10.4、表10.5的信息，MK公司2019年的净资产收益率为：

$$净资产收益率 = 795\ 822/3\ 155\ 838 \times 100\% = 25.2\%$$

4. 杜邦分析法

杜邦分析是净资产收益率的一种综合分析法。它将净资产收益率分解为三个组成部分：净利率、总资产周转率、财务杠杆。分解为截然不同的部分可使经理人员或投资者审查企业净资产的使用效益，因为绩效不好的组成部分会拖垮综合数据。净资产收益率使用下列公式计算：

$$净资产收益率 = 总资产报酬率 \times 权益乘数$$
$$总资产报酬率 = 净利率 \times 总资产周转率$$
$$权益乘数 = 总资产 \times 所有者权益$$

基于上述内容，计算公式为：

净资产收益率 = (税后净利/销售收入) × (销售收入/总资产) × (总资产/所有者权益)

= 净利率 × 总资产周转率 × 权益乘数

使用表10.4、表10.5的数据，MK公司2019年的净资产收益率计算如下：

净资产收益率 = (795 822/9 186 539) × (9 186 539/5 361 207) ×

(5 361 207/3 155 838)

= 8.66% × 171.3% × 1.698

= 25.19%

运用杜邦分析法，我们获得结果相同的净资产收益率，但是这种方法有助于我们融入其他比率进行更好的财务分析。

除了上面介绍的比率外，还有其他一些比率可用于财务报表分析。

Part III Key to Exercises

Unit One

Exercises 1.1

1. C   2. D   3. D   4. A   5. A   6. C   7. C

Exercises 1.2

1. T   2. F   3. T   4. T   5. T   6. F

Exercises 1.3

(1) Increase in one asset, decrease in another asset. 3. 8

(2) Increase in an asset, increase in a liability.

(3) Increase in an asset, increase in capital. 1. 4. 5

(4) Decrease in an asset, decrease in a liability. 6

(5) Decrease in an asset, decrease in capital. 2. 7. 9. 10

Unit Two

Exercises 2.1

1. A   2. D   3. C   4. B   5. C   6. D   7. D   8. A   9. B   10. B

Exercises 2.2

1. Dr: Cash	15 000	
Cr: Common stock		15 000
Dr: Cash	25 000	
Cr: Common stock		25 000
2. Dr. Cash	600 000	
Cr: Common Stock, par 5		500 000
Paid-in Capital in Excess of Par, common stock		100 000
3. Dr. Cash	10 000	
Land	60 000	

Building	100 000
Inventory	60 000
Cr: Mike, Capital	230 000
4. Dr: Cash	40 000
Cr: Mike. Capital	20 000
Brown, Capital	20 000

Exercises 2.3

1. 公司制企业即公司,是一个法律实体。另外,股东个人不对公司的负债负责。因此股东的损失最大不超过其对公司的投资额。
2. 一般地说,企业可以采用三种法律组织形式:独资企业、合伙企业和公司。
3. 支付给合伙人的款项借记合伙人提用账户。
4. 因此,应为每个合伙人保有一个单独的资本账户和提用账户。
5. 董事会会批准股息的发放。股息可以现金、资产或者公司自有股份的形式派发给股东。

Unit Three

Exercise 3.1

1. D 2. A 3. B 4. C 5. A 6. C 7. D 8. D 9. B 10. A

Exercise 3.2

1.

MAJESTIC LIMO
Balance Sheet
February 28, 2001

Assets		Liabilities & Owner's Equity	
Cash	69 000	Notes Payable	288 000
Accounts Receivable	78 000	Accounts Payable	26 000
Supplies	14 000	Total Liabilities	314 000
Automobiles	165 000	J. Snow, Capital	162 000
Building	80 000		
Land	70 000		
Total Assets	476 000	Total Liabilities & Owner's Equity	476 000

2.

FOWLER COMPANY	
Income Statement	
August 31 2001	
Revenues:	
Services provided to customers ··	10 000
Operating Expenses:	
Expenses required to provide Services to customers ················	7 500
Operating Income ··	2 500
Net income ··	2 500

Exercises 3.3

A. operating

B. financing

C. financing

D. investing

E. operating

F. financing

G. investing

H. operating

I. investing

Exercises 3.4

1. 如果有了正确编制的资产负债表,你就能知道你公司的每一个会计期末的价值是更多了还是更少了,你的债务是更高了还是更低了,你的实收资本是更高了还是更低了。

2. 就股东而言,税后净利润是一个关键数据,因为它揭示了可分配给股东或为未来增长进行再投资的企业最终受益。

3. 流动资产通常代表公司资金中的现金,或者未来一年之内可转化为现金的部分,如现金、应收账款、存货、有价证券、预付账款以及短期投资。

4. 资产负债表使企业在某一特定时日,通常是在会计年度末财务状况的反映。

5. 折旧是一项资产在使用年限内因磨损或因技术老化逐渐转移到产品或服务的成本中去的

那一部分价值。

Unit Four

Exercises 4.1

1. D 2. D 3. B 4. D 5. D 6. B 7. D 8. B 9. C 10. C

Exercises 4.2

Nov. 1	Cash	120 000	
	JG., Capital		120 000
	JG, the owner, deposit in business account		
Nov. 8	Land	70 000	
	Building	58 600	
	Notes Payable		95 000
	Cash		33 600
	Buy land and building, using cash and notes payable		
Nov. 15	Office Equipment	3 200	
	Accounts Payable		3 200
	Buy office equipment		
Nov. 21	Accounts Payable		
	Office Equipment		
	Return parts of office equipment bought on Nov. 15		
Nov. 25	Notes payable		
	Cash		
	Payment against notes payable		
Nov. 30	Vehicles	9 400	
	JG, Capital		9 400
	JG, the owner, invest vehicles		

2. Sept. 1   Dr: Cash   50 000
              Cr.: Louis Dixon, Capital   50 000
   Sept. 10   Dr: Land   106 000
              Building   76 400
              Cr: Cash   36 500
              Note payable   145 900
   Sept. 15   Dr: Computer System   4 680
              Cr: Cash   4 680
   Sept. 19   Dr: Office Furnishing   5 760
              Cr: Cash   960
              Accounts Payable   4 800

Exercises 4.3

(1) Dr: Cash   25 000
    Office Equipment   6 000
    Cr: Capital   31 000
    Dr: Prepaid Rent   1 800
    Cr: Cash   1 800
    Dr: Office Equipment   3 000
    Office Supplies   600
    Cr: Accounts Receivable   3 600
    Dr: Cash   500
    Cr: Service Revenue   500
    Dr: Accounts Receivable   2 000
    Cr: Service Revenue   2 000
    Dr: Prepaid Insurance   1 500
    Cr: Cash   1 500
    Dr: Cash   1 600
    Cr: Accounts Receivable   1 600
    Dr: Accounts Receivable   660
    Cr: Service Revenue   660
    Dr: Drawing   1 800

Cr: Cash	1 800
Dr. Office supplies	200
Cr: Accounts Payable	200
Dr: Utilities Expense	175
Cr: Cash	175

(2) Adjusting entries

Dr: Rent Expense	600
Cr: Prepaid Rent	600
Dr: Insurance Expense	125
Cr: Prepaid Insurance	125

(3) Closing entries

Dr: Service Revenue	3 160
Cr: Income Summary	3 160
Dr: Income Summary	900
Cr: Utilities Expense	175
Rent expense	600
Insurance expense	125
Dr: Income Summary	2 260
Cr: Capital	2 260
Dr: Capital	1 800
Cr: Drawing	1 800

Unit Five

Exercises 5.1

1. A 2. C 3. B 4. B 5. A 6. D 7. C 8. A 9. D 10. A

Exercise 5.2

1. (1) Dr. Inventory	2 000
Cr. Accounts Payable	2 000

(2) Dr. Cash　　　　　　　　　　　　　　　　　　1 500
　　　　Cr. Sales Revenues　　　　　　　　　　　　　　　1 500
　(no entry recorded to reflect outflow of inventory)

2. (1) Dr. Accounts Receivable　　　　　　　　　　　　4 000
　　　　Cr. Sales Revenues　　　　　　　　　　　　　　　4 000
　　(2) Dr. Cash　　　　　　　　　　　　　　　　　　2 000
　　　　Cr. Accounts Receivable　　　　　　　　　　　　2 000
　　(3) Dr. Bad Debts Expenses　　　　　　　　　　　　800
　　　　Cr. Allowance for Bad Debts　　　　　　　　　　　800

3. 2011：

　The bad debts expense is 600 000 × 0.3% = 1 800

　　Allowance for bad debts is 300

　应计提的坏账 = 1 800 − 300 = 1 500

　Dr. Bad Debts Expense　　　　　　　　　　　　　　1 500
　　Cr. Allowance for Doubtful Accounts　　　　　　　　1 500

　2012：

　The bad debts expense is 500 000 × 0.3% = 1 500

　Allowance for bad debts is 2 000　1 500 − 2 000 = −500(冲销)

　Dr. Allowance for Doubtful Accounts　　　　　　　　　500
　　Cr. Bad Debts Expense　　　　　　　　　　　　　　500

Exercises 5.3

1. 现金在资产负债表中位于流动资产之首,因为它流动性最强。
2. 待摊费用应当按受益期分摊,未摊销余额在会计报表中应当单独列示。
3. 会计人员将现金定义为银行的一种存款,以及银行接受作为即时存款的任何项目。这些物品不仅包括硬币和纸币,还包括支票和汇票。另一方面,应收票据、借据和远期支票不接受即时存款,也不包括在会计对现金的定义中。
4. Marketable securities shall be accounted for according to historical cost as obtained and be shown in book balance in accounting statement. Income received or receivable from marketable securities in current period and the difference between the receipt obtained from securities sold and book cost shall be all accounted for as current profit or loss.
5. In manufacturing business there are three major types of inventories: raw materials, goods in

process of manufacture, and finished goods. All three classes of inventories are included in the current asset section of the balance sheet.

Unit Six

Exercise 6.1
1. C 2. C 3. D 4. A 5. B 6. C 7. A 8. D 9. D 10. A

Exercise 6.2
1. (1) property; plant; equipment
   (2) three; long-term investments; fixed assets; intangible assets
   (3) straight-line method; units-of-production method; sum-of-the-years-digits method; double-declining balance method
   (4) accelerated depreciation method
   (5) patents; trademark
2. (1) 1 875
   (2) 2 500
   (3) 4 125
   (4) 3 438
   (5) 2 000
   (6) 4 000

Exercise 6.3

1. Dr. Fixed Assets—Machinery   51 500
      Cr. Cash   51 500

2. Dr. Cash   6 000
      Accumulated Depreciation   7 000
      Cr. Gains on Disposal of Plant Assets   3 000
          Fixed Assets—Pickup Truck   10 000

3. Computation Process:

   Total amount to be depreciated or depreciable cost is 24 000 − 3 000 = 21 000

Depreciation expenses each year：21 000/7 = 3 000

In this case, the entry to record the depreciation for the third year is as follow：

Dr. Depreciation Expenses—Delivery Truck　　　　　3 000

　　Cr. Accumulated Depreciation—Delivery Truck　　　3 000

Exercise 6.4

(1) 长期投资通常有两个方面,即权益性证券投资和债务性证券投资。

(2) 在中国会计实践中,单位价格超过2 000元以及使用年限超过一年的物品都应视为固定资产,即使这些物品不直接用于生产和经营活动。

(3) 无形资产是指应用于企业的经营活动,但没有实物形态的非短期资产。

(4) 无形资产属于长期资产,需要摊销。

(5) 无形资产的摊销是一个将无形资产在其使用年限内全部分摊到费用的过程。

Unit Seven

Exercise 7.1

1. C　2. A　3. A　4. D　5. C　6. A　7. C　8. D　9. C　10. B

Exercise 7.2

Transaction Number	Assets	=	Liabilities	+	Owners' Equity
Example	+600 000				+600 000
Subtotal	600 000				600 000
a.	+12 000		+12 000		
Subtotal	612 000		12 000		600 000
b.	+7 000				
	−7 000				
Subtotal	612 000		12 000		600 000
c.	+500 000				
	−500 000				
Subtotal	612 000		12 000		600 000
d.	+15 000				

Transaction Number	Assets	=	Liabilities	+	Owners' Equity
	−15 000				
Subtotal	612 000		12 000		600 000
e.	+115 000		+115 000		
Subtotal	727 000		127 000		600 000
f.	−65 000		−115 000		
			+50 000		
Subtotal	662 000		62 000		600 000
g.	+30 000				
	−30 000				
Subtotal	662 000		62 000		600 000
h.	+42 000				
	−42 000				
Subtotal	662 000		62 000		600 000
i.	+75 000		+75 000		
Subtotal	737 000		137 000		600 000
j.			−26 000		+26 000
Total	737 000		111 000		626 000

Transaction k. is not recorded until delivery of the trucks.

Exercise 7.3

a. Dr. Cash   9 000
    Cr. Notes Receivable   8 000
        Interest Receivable   1 000
b. Dr. Notes Payable   16 000
    Interest Payable   800
    Cr. Cash   16 800
c. Dr. Accounts Payable   20 000
    Cr. Cash   20 000
d. Dr. Cash   80 000
    Cr. Bonds Payable   80 000
    Dr. Fixed Assets—Building   80 000

Cr. Cash	80 000
e. Dr. Merchandise Inventory	30 000
Cr. Cash	16 000
Accounts Payable	14 000
f. Dr. Cash	15 000
Cr. Intangible Assets—Land Usage Right	15 000
g. Dr. Cash	50 000
Cr. Capital Stock—Common Stock	40 000
Additional Paid-in Capital	10 000

Unit Eight

Exercises 8.1
1. A 2. D 3. B 4. B

Exercises 8.2
Cash $100 000   Bonds payable $100 000

Unit Nine

Exercises 9.1
1. B 2. A 3. A

Exercises 9.2
¥500 000, increased, unchanged, decreased

Exercises 9.3

Cash	420 000
Common Stock	320 000
Preferred Stock	100 000

· 243 ·

Unit Ten

Exercises 10.1

1. better
2. guesses; ituition
3. informed
4. left-to-right
5. up-down
6. percentages; base
7. skillful interpretation
8. short-term; unexpected
9. productive

Exercises 10.2

Tallman Works, Inc.
Comparative Income Statement
For the Years Ended December 31, 2019 and 2018   unit: $

	2019	2018	Dollar changes	Percentage Changes
Net sales	180 000	145 000	35 000	24.1%
Cost of goods sold	112 000	88 000	24 000	27.3%
Gross margin	68 000	57 000	11 000	19.3%
Sales expenses	40 000	30 000	10 000	33.3%
Operating income	28 000	27 000	1 000	3.7%
Interest expenses	4 000	5 000	1 000	20.0%
Income before income taxes	24 000	22 000	2 000	9.1%
Income taxes 30%	7 200	6 600	600	9.1%
Net income	16 800	15 400	1 400	9.1%
Earnings per share (10 000 shares outstanding)	1.68	1.54	0.14	9.1%

Exercises 10.3

Longman Works, Inc.
Common-size Comparative Balance Sheet
December 31, 2019 and 2018   unit: $

	2019	2018	Common-size Percents 2019	Common-size Percents 2018
Assets				
Current assets	24 000	20 000	15.6%	16.7%
Property plants and equipment (net)	130 000	100 000	84.4%	83.3%
Total assets	154 000	120 000	100%	100%
Liabilities and Stockholders' Equity				
Current liabilities	18 000	22 000	11.7%	18.3%
Non-current liabilities	90 000	60 000	58.4%	50%
Stockholders' equity	46 000	38 000	29.9%	31.7%
Total liabilities and stockholders' equity	154 000	120 000	100%	100%

Exercises 10.4

1. Curent ratio $= \dfrac{\text{Current assets}}{\text{Current liabilities}} = \dfrac{24\,000}{18\,000} = 1.33:1$

2. Acid-test ratio $= \dfrac{\text{Quick assets}}{\text{Current liabilities}} = \dfrac{2\,199\,558}{1\,866\,917} = 1.18:1$

   (2017)

   Acid-test ratio $= \dfrac{\text{Quick assets}}{\text{Current liabilities}} = \dfrac{1\,608\,242}{1\,467\,059} = 1.1:1$

   (2018)

3. Debt ratio $= \dfrac{\text{Total liabilities}}{\text{Total assets}} \times 100\%$

   (2019) $= \dfrac{2\,205\,369}{5\,361\,207} \times 100\%$

   $= 41.1\%$

4. Profit margin $= \dfrac{\text{Net income}}{\text{Revenue}} \times 100\% = \dfrac{38\,528}{60\,000} \times 100\% = 64.2\%$

   (Feb.)

   Profit margin $= \dfrac{\text{Net income}}{\text{Revenue}} \times 100\% = \dfrac{1\,877}{3\,500} \times 100\% = 53.6\%$

   (Jan.)

Appendix

Causes of International Differences

Part One   Introduction

That there are major international differences in accounting practices is not obvious to all accountants, let alone to non-accountants. The latter may see accounting as synonymous with double entry, which is indeed fairly similar universally. It is not possible to be sure that the factors discussed below cause the accounting differences, but a relationship can be established and reasonable deductions made.

A large list of possible causes of international differences can be found in the writings of previous researchers. Some researchers have used their estimates of such causes as a means of classifying countries by their accounting systems. Other researchers have studied whether perceived differences in accounting practices correlate with perceived causal factors.

Before going further, it is also important to define "accounting". In this context, we mean published annual financial reporting by companies. To the extent that it is useful to use a term such as "accounting system", we mean the set of financial reporting practices used by a particular company for an annual report. Different companies in a country may use different accounting systems.

Several factors that seem linked to the differences in accounting systems are now examined. These are not necessarily causes, as will be discussed later.

Part Two External Environment and Culture

Clearly, accounting is affected by its environment, including the culture of the country in which it operates. Hofstede (1980) develops a model of culture as the collective programming of the mind that distinguishes the members of one human group from another. Hofstede argues that, much as a computer operating system contains a set of rules that acts as a reference point and a set of constraints to higher-level programs, so culture includes a set of societal values that drives institutional form and practice. As Gray notes:

Societal values are determined by ecological influences and modified by external factors... In turn, societal values have institutional consequences in the form of the legal system, political system, nature of capital markets, patterns of corporate ownership and so on.

Culture in any country contains the most basic values that an individual may hold. It affects the way that individuals would like their society to be structured and how they interact with its substructure. Accounting may be seen as one of those substructures. As Gray explains:

the value systems of attitudes of accountants may be expected to be related and derived from societal values with special reference to work related values. Accounting ' value' will in turn impact on accounting systems.

To get some idea of the basic cultural patterns of various countries, we turn again to Hofstede. Based on a study of over 100 000 IBM employees in 39 countries, Hofestede defined and scored the following four basic dimensions of culture, which can be summarized as follows:

1 *Individualism versus collectivism.* Individualism stands for a preference for a loosely knit social framework in society wherein individuals are supposed to take care of themselves and their immediate families only. The fundamental issue addressed by this

dimension is the degree of interdependence that a society maintains among individuals.

2 Large versus small power distance. Power distance is the extent to which the members of a society accept that power in institutions and organizations is distributed unequally. People in societies that have large power distance accept a hierarchical order in which everybody has a place which needs no further justification. The fundamental issue addressed by this dimension is how society handles inequalities among people when they occur.

3 *Strong versus weak uncertainty avoidance*. Uncertainty avoidance is the degree to which the members of a society feel uncomfortable with uncertainty and ambiguity. This feeling leads them to beliefs promising certainty and to maintain institutions protecting conformity. Strong uncertainty avoidance societies maintain rigid codes of belief and behaviour and are intolerant towards deviant persons and ideas. Weak uncertainty avoidance societies maintain a more relaxed atmosphere in which practice counts more than principles and deviance is more easily tolerated. A fundamental issue addressed by this dimension is how a society reacts to the fact that time runs only one way and that the future is unknown: whether it tries to control the future or lets it happen.

4 *Masculinity versus femininity*. Masculinity stands for a preference in society for achievement, heroism, assertiveness and material success. Its opposite, femininity, stands for a preference for relationships, modesty, caring for the weak, and the quality of life.

Gray (1988) applies these cultural differences to explain international differences in the behaviour of accountants and therefore in the nature of accounting practices. For example, Gray suggests that a country with high uncertainty avoidance and low individualism will be more likely to exhibit conservative measurement of income and a preference to limit disclosure to those closely involved in the business.

Gray developed the following pairs of contrasting 'accounting values':
- professionalism versus statutory control;
- uniformity versus flexibility;
- conservatism versus optimism;
- secrecy versus transparency.

The first two relate to authority and enforcement. Here Gray sees a clear contrast between the 'Anglo' culture area on the one hand and Asian areas on the other. The second two relate to measurement and disclosure. Gray contrasts the 'Anglo' and the Latin and Germanic cultures.

This approach may well be particularly useful for examining such issues as international differences in the behaviour of auditors (e. g. Soeters and Schreuder, 1988). However, for financial reporting, the measures of cultural attributes seem vague and indirect, compared with the measurement of certain elements of the external environment of accounting, such as legal systems or equity markets (see below). In order to use culture data in an accounting context, it is necessary to rely on the data collected from time to time by researchers in other fields and for other purposes; for example, Hofstede classifies West African countries together, but they have very different legal and accounting systems. Another problem arises from the fact that, for good reasons, Hofstede looked at employees in a large multinational company. When measuring cultural attributes, how does one cope with the fact that many employees of multinationals in Abu Dhabi, Singapore, etc. come from other countries or from particular minority populations? Baskerville (2003) suggests that it is dangerous to equate nation with culture and that there are difficulties in trying to understand a culture by means of numerical indices.

Salter and Niswander (1995) tried to test Gray's hypothesis for 29 countries but met considerable difficulty in measuring several of Gray's "accounting values" so that indirect measures were generally used. For example, the degree of uniformity was partly measured by whether a country has common law or code law, but this is not really a test of differences in accounting practices but of a possible cause of them. For a more direct measure of uniformity, Gary's hypothesis did not hold. For conservatism, some hypothesized relationships held and others did not. The most convincing support for an element of Gray's hypothesis was that transparency increased as uncertainty avoidance decreased, but the other predictions related to secrecy did not hold.

Another way of looking at the environment of accounting is to identity more direct potential influences such as legal systems, corporate financing, tax systems and so on. These interact with culture in a complex way, and they seem to affect the style of financial reporting and accountancy profession that a country has. We look at some of these external environmental factors in the rest of this chapter.

When studying possible causes of accounting differences, it will also be useful to note that the environment of accounting may include the effects of imperialism. Many countries are heavily influenced by others, particularly former colonial powers whose culture may be overwhelming. Consequently, when predicting or explaining the accounting practices of many African or Asian countries, it may be more efficient to look at the colonial history rather than at other possible causes. These issues are taken up again when classification is discussed in Chapter 4, and they are referred to in some of the chapters on particular countries.

Chanchani and MacGregor (1999) provide a summary of papers on accounting and culture.

Part Three Legal Systems

Some countries have a legal system that relies upon a limited amount of statute law, which is then interpreted by courts, which build up large amounts of case law to supplement the statutes. Such a 'common law' system was formed in England, primarily after the Norman Conquest, by judges acting on the king's behalf (van Caenegem, 1988). It is less abstract than codified law (see below); a common law rule seeks to provide an answer to a specific case rather than to formulate a general rule for the future. Although this common law system emanates from England, it may be found in similar forms in many countries influenced by England. Thus, the federal law of the United States, the laws of Ireland, India, Australia, and so on, are to a greater or lesser extent modelled on English common law. This naturally influences commercial law, which traditionally does not prescribe rules to cover the behaviour of companies and how they should prepare their financial statements. To a large extent (at least up until the UK's Companies Act 1981), accounting within such a context is not dependent upon law. Instead, accountants themselves establish rules for accounting practice, which may come to be written down as recommendations or standards.

Other countries have a system of law that is based on the Roman ius civile as compiled by Justinian in the sixth century and developed by European universities from the twelfth century. Here, rules are linked to ideas of justice and morality; they become doctrine. The word "codified" may be associated with such a system. This difference has the important effect that company law or commercial codes need to establish rules for accounting and financial reporting. For example, in Germany, company accounting is to a large extent a branch of company law.

Table 1 illustrates the way in which some developed countries' legal systems fall into these two categories. In some Roman law countries, dirigisme (centralization and a desire to control the economy) results in the existence of an "accounting plan". Classification of legal systems is discussed by David and Brierley (1985).

It is clear that the nature of accounting regulation in a country is affected by its general system of laws. There also seems to be some association of common law.

Table 1 Western Legal Systems

Common law	Codified Roman law
England and Wales	France
Ireland	Italy
United States	Germany
Canada	Spain
Australia	Netherlands
New Zealand	Portugal
	Japan (commercial)

Note: The laws of Scotland, Israel, South Africa, Quebec, Louisiana and the Philippines embody elements of both systems.

countries and large equity markets. Further, there seems to be an association of common law countries with particular types of accounting practices, but causation is unclear. Jaggi and Low (2000) find, for example, that companies in common law countries have higher levels of disclosures.

Part Four   Providers of Finance

The prevalent types of business organization and ownership also differ. In Germany, France and Italy, capital provided by banks is very significant, as are small family-owned businesses. By contrast, in the United States and the United Kingdom there are large numbers of companies that rely on millions of private shareholders for finance. Evidence that this characterization is reasonable may be found by looking at the number of listed companies in various countries. In the previous chapter shows the numbers of domestic listed companies on Stock Exchanges where there are over 250 such companies with a market capitalization of $350 billion or more in 2003. Table 2 takes those data for four countries and puts them into context by deflating them for the size of the economy or population.

The comparison between the United States or United Kingdom and Germany or France is instructive. A two-group categorization of these countries is almost as obvious as that for legal systems in Table 1. La Porta et al. (1997) find a statistical connection between common law countries and strong equity markets. La Porta et al. (1998) note that common law countries have stronger legal protection of investors than Roman law countries do. Incidentally, the country with the longest history of "public" companies is the Netherlands. Although it has a fairly small stock exchange, many multinationals (such as Unilever, Philips, Royal Dutch) are listed on it. It seems reasonable, then, to place the Netherlands with the English-speaking world in a "shareholder" group as opposed to a "bank/family" group. Also, Table 3 shows gearing ratios in Europe at a particular date. On the whole these fit the hypothesis, because less reliance on equity suggests more reliance on debt. The United States also has low gearing, like the United Kingdom.

A proposed grouping of countries into types by financial system has been formalized by Zysman (1983) as follows:

Table 2　The Strength of Equity Markets

Domestic listed companies/million of population		Equity market capitalization/GDP
Germany	8.6	0.35
France	12.4	0.72
United States	17.9	1.07
United Kingdom	40.3	1.15

Table 3　Gearing Ratios of European Companies

Rank	Country	Gearing ratios*
1	Switzerland	0.55
2	Belgium	0.51
3	Italy	0.45
4	Ireland	0.40
5	Denmark	0.34
6	France	0.34
7	Germany	0.30
8	Sweden	0.27
9	Netherlands	0.26
10	Spain	0.25
11	United Kingdom	0.20

Note: * Ratio of debt to plus equity.
Source: Based on Tucker (1994).

1 capital market systems (e.g. United Kingdom, United States);
2 credit based governmental systems (e.g. France, Japan);
3 credit based financial institution systems (e.g. Germany).

Parker (1994) applies this analysis to ten countries of the western Pacific and suggests its explanatory power for financial reporting practices. Some of these countries are also examined in Chapter 13 in this book.

A further point of comparison between "equity" and "credit" countries is that, in the latter countries, even the relatively few listed companies may be dominated by shareholders who are bankers, governments or founding families. For example, in Germany, the banks in particular are important owners of companies as well as providers of debt finance. A majority of shares in many public companies are owned or controlled as proxies by banks, particularly by the Deutsche, Dresdner and Commerz banks. In such countries as Germany, France or Italy, the banks or the state will, in many cases, nominate directors and thus be able to obtain information and affect decisions. If it is the case that even listed companies in continental countries are dominated by banks, governments or families, the need for published information is less clear. This also applies to audit, because this is designed to check up on the managers in cases where the owners are "outsiders".

Although it is increasingly the case that shares in countries such as the United Kingdom and the United States are held by institutional investors rather than by individual shareholders, this still contrasts with state, bank or family holdings. Indeed, the increased importance of institutional investors is perhaps a reinforcement for the following hypothesis: in countries with a widespread ownership of companies by shareholders who do not have access to internal information, there will be a pressure for disclosure, audit and "fair" information. Institutional investors hold larger blocks of shares and may be better organized than private shareholders. So, they should increase this pressure, although they may also be able successfully to press for more detailed information than is generally available to the public.

"Fair" needs to be defined. It is a concept related to that large number of outside owners who require unbiased information about the success of a business and its state of affairs (Flint, 1982; Parker and Nobes, 1994). Although reasonable prudence will be expected, these shareholders are interested in comparing one year with another and one company with another; thus the accruals concept and some degree of realism will be required. This entails judgement, which entails experts. This expertise is also required for the checking of the financial statements by auditors. In countries such as the United Kingdom, the United States and the Netherlands, this can, over many decades, result in a tendency for accountants to work out their own technical rules, as suggested earlier. This is acceptable to governments because of the influence and expertise of the accounting profession, which is usually running ahead of the interest of the government (in its capacity as shareholder, protector of the public interest or collector of taxation). Thus "generally accepted accounting principles" control accounting and these are set by committees dominated by accountants and in the private sector. To the extent that governments intervene, they impose disclosure, filing or measurement requirements and these tend to follow best practice rather than to create it.

In most continental European countries and in Japan, the traditional paucity of "outsider" shareholders has meant that external financial reporting has been largely invented for the purposes of protecting creditors and for governments, as tax collectors or controllers of the economy. This has not encouraged the development of flexibility, judgement, fairness or experimentation. However, it does lead to precision, uniformity and stability. It also seems likely that the greater importance of creditors in these countries leads to more careful (prudent, conservative) accounting. This is because creditors are interested in whether, in the worst case, they are likely to get their money back, whereas shareholders may be interested in an unbiased estimate of future prospects.

Nevertheless, even in such countries as Germany, France or Italy, where there are comparatively few listed companies, governments have recognized the responsibility to require public or listed companies to publish detailed, audited financial statements. There are laws to this effect in the majority of such countries, and in France and Italy the government also set up bodies specifically to control the securities markets: in France the Commission des Operations de Bourse (COB), and in Italy the Commissione Nazionale per le Societa e la Borsa (CONSOB). These bodies are to some extent modelled on the Securities and Exchange Commission (SEC) of the United States (see Chapter 8). They have been associated with important developments in financial reporting, generally in the direction of Anglo-American practice. This is not surprising, as these stock exchange bodies are taking the part otherwise played by private and institutional shareholders who have, over a much longer period, helped to shape Anglo-American accounting systems.

To some extent, this clear picture has been changing. For example, institutional and private investors have been increasing in importance in France and Germany. also, as explained in later chapters, private sector standard-setters were set up in those two countries in the late 1990s. Nevertheless, the two-way contrast seems intact.

In conclusion, we suggest that this differentiation between credit/insiders and equity/outsiders is the key cause of international differences in financial reporting. n initial classification of some countries on this basis is suggested in Table 4.

Table 4   Initial Classifications Based on Corporate Financing

A	B
Strong equity market	Weaker equity market
Many outside shareholders	Core, insider shareholders
Large auditing profession	Small auditing profession
Separate accounting and tax rules	Tax dominates accounting rules
Examples of countries	
Australia	France
United Kingdom	Germany
United States	Italy

Several important results flow from this two-way split. First, in credit/insider countries, there is no great market demand for audited and published financial reporting. The demand for annual accounting is therefore strongly associated with the government's need for a calculation of taxable income. Consequently, tax considerations will dominate accounting rules. By contrast, in equity/outsider countries, accounting performs a market function, and so the rules need to be separated from taxation. The result is two sets of accounting rules: one for financial reporting and one for the calculation of taxable income. This is examined in the next section.

A second effect of the split of countries based on financing systems is that credit/insider countries will need far fewer auditors than equity/outsider countries. This will affect the age, size and status of the accountancy profession.

Part Five Taxation

Although it is possible to make groupings of tax systems in a number of ways, only some of them are of relevance to financial reporting. For example, it is easy to divide EU countries into those using "classical" and those using "imputation" systems of corporation tax. However, this distinction does not have a major effect on financial reporting. What is much more relevant is the degree to which taxation regulations determine accounting measurements, for reasons discussed in the previous section. To some extent this is seen in a negative way by studying the problem of deferred taxation, which is caused by timing differences between tax and accounting treatments. In the United Kingdom, the Netherlands and the United States, for example, the problem of deferred tax has caused much controversy and a considerable amount of accounting standard documentation. Turning to conventional accounting rules in France or Germany, it is found that the problem is minor; for in these countries it is largely the case that the tax rules are the accounting rules. In Germany, the tax accounts (Steuerbilanz) should be the same as the commercial accounts (Handelsbilanz). There is even a word for this idea: the Massgeblichk eitsprin zip (Haller,1992).

One obvious example of the areas affected by this difference is depreciation. In the United Kingdom the amount of depreciation charged in the published financial statements is determined according to custom established over the last century and influenced by the accounting standard FRS 15, which requires (para. 77) that:

The depreciable amount of a tangible fixed asset should be allocated on a systematic basis over its useful economic life. The depreciation method used should reflects as fairly as possible the pattern in which the asset's economic benefits are consumed by the entity.

The injunctions contained in the standard are of a fairly general nature, and their spirit is quite frequently ignored. Convention and pragmatism, rather than exact rules or even the spirit of the standard, determine the method chosen (usually straight-line, because it is easier), the size of the scrap value (usually zero, because it is easier) and the expected length of life.

The amount of depreciation for tax purposes in the United Kingdom is quite independent of these accounting figures. It is determined by capital allowances, which are a formalized scheme of tax depreciation allowances designed to standardize the amounts allowed and act as investment incentives in fact. Because of the separation of the two schemes, there can be a complete lack of subjectivity in tax allowances, but full room for judgement in financial depreciation charges.

At the opposite extreme, in countries such as Germany, the tax regulations lay down maximum depreciation rates to be used for particular assets. These are generally based on the expected useful lives of assets. However, in some cases, accelerated depreciation allowances are available: for example, for industries producing energy-saving or anti-pollution products or for those operating in parts of eastern Germany and, in the past, West Berlin. If these allowances are to be claimed for tax purposes (which would normally be sensible), they must be charged in the financial accounts. Thus, the charge against profit would be said by a UK accountant not to be 'fair', even though it could certainly be 'correct' or 'legal'. This influence is felt even in the details of the choice of method of depreciation in Germany, as shown by BASF's explanation: Movable fixed assets are mostly depreciated by the declining balance method, with a change to straight-line depreciation if this results in higher depreciation rate.

A second example of the overriding effect of taxation on accounting measurement is the valuation of fixed assets in France. During the in flationary 1970s and before,

French companies were allowed to revalue assets. However, this would have entailed extra taxation due to the increase in the post-revaluation balance sheet total compared with the previous year's. Consequently, except in the special case of merger by "fusion", when tax-exempt revaluation is allowed, revaluation was not practised. However, the Finance Acts of 1978 and 1979 made revaluation obligatory for listed companies and for those that solicit funds from the public; it was optional for others. The purpose was to show balance sheets more realistically. The revalu-ation was performed by use of government indices relating to 31 December 1976. The credit went to an undistributable revaluation reserve. As a result of this, for depreciable assets an amount equal to the extra depreciation due to revaluations is credited each year to profit and loss and debited to the revaluation account. Thus the effect of revaluation on profit (and tax) is neutralized. This move from no revaluations to compulsory revaluations was due to the change tax rules. The effects of this revaluation can still be seen in many French companies which have old fixed asset amounts. In Spain, Italy and Greece, government-induced revaluations have occurred several times (e. g. In 2000 in Italy, and in 1996 in Spain).

Further examples are easy to find: bad debt provisions (determined by tax laws in Italy or Spain) or various provisions related to specific industries. The chapters on Germany and Japan contain more examples.

The effects of all this are to reduce the room for operation of the accruals convention (which is the driving force behind such practices as depreciation) and to reduce "fairness". With some variations, this Massgeblichkeitsprinzip operates in Germany, France, Belgium, Italy, Japan and many other countries. It is perhaps due partly to the pervasive influence of codification in law, and partly to the predominance of taxation authorities as users of accounting. A major exception to this point, concerning consolidated statements, became especially important in the 1990s. Since taxation generally relates to the taxable income of individual companies rather than that of groups, national tax authorities are able to take a relaxed view of consolidated statements. This has facilitated international harmonization of accounting at the group level, particularly for French and German companies.

The alternative approach, exemplified by the United Kingdom, the United States and the Netherlands, is found in countries where published financial statements are designed mainly as performance indicators for investment decisions, where commercial rules operate separately from tax rules in a number of accounting areas. The countries on the left in Table 1 are, in varying degrees, like this. In most cases, there is not the degree of separation between tax and financial reporting that is found in the United Kingdom in the shape of capital allowances. However, in all such countries the taxation authorities have to make many adjustments to the commercial accounts for their own purposes, after exerting only minor influence directly on them. There is a major exception to this in the use of LIFO inventory valuation in the United States, largely for tax reasons.

Attempts have been made to put countries into groups by the degree of connection between tax and accounting. For example, Hoogendoorn (1996) classifies 13 countries. However, there are problems with this because seven groups are necessary for the classification, and two matters are being considered at the same time: the tax/accounting connection, and the treatment of deferred tax. Lamb et al. (1988) try to separate out the first issue. They conclude that it is possible to distinguish between UK/US separation of tax and accounting and a German close connection.

Part Six The Profession

The strength, size and competence of the accountancy profession in a country may follow to a large extent from the various factors outlined above and from the type of financial reporting they have helped to produce. For example, the lack of a substantial body of private shareholders and public companies in some countries means that the need for auditors is much smaller it is in the United Kingdom or the United States. However, the nature of the profession also feeds back into the type of accounting that is practised and could be practised. For example, a 1975 Decree in Italy (not brought into effect until the 1980s), requiring listed companies to have extended audits similar to those operated in the United Kingdom and the United States, could only be brought into effect initially because of the substantial presence of international accounting firms. This factor constitutes a considerable obstacle to any attempts at significant and deep harmonization of accounting between some countries. The need for extra auditors was a controversial issue in Germany's implementation of the EU's fourth Directive.

The scale of the difference is illustrated, which lists some accountancy bodies whose members act as auditors of the financial statements of companies (although see below for an explanation of the difference between accounting and auditing bodies in France and Germany). These remarkable figures need some interpretation. For example, let us more carefully compare the German and the British figures in that Table. First, in Germany there is a separate, though overlapping, profession of tax experts (Steuerberater), which is larger than the accountancy body. By contrast, in the United Kingdom the accountants' figure is inflated by the inclusion of many who specialize in or occasionally practise in tax. Second, a German accountant may only be a member of the Institut if in practice, whereas at least half of the British figure represents members in commerce, industry, government, education, and so on. Third, the training period is much longer in Germany than it is in the United Kingdom. It normally involves a four-year relevant degree course, six years' practical experience (four in the profession) and a professional examination consisting of oral and written tests plus a thesis. This tends to last until the aspiring accountant is 30 to 35 years old. Thus, many of the German 'students' would be counted as part of the qualified figure if they were in the British system. Fourth, in the late 1980s, a second-tier auditing body (of vereidigte Buchprufer) was established in Germany for auditors who may only audit private companies.

These four factors help to explain the differences. However, there is still a very substantial residual difference which results from the much larger number of companies to be audited and different process of forming a judgement on the "fair" view. The differences are diminishing as auditing is extended to many private companied in EU countries.

It is interesting to note a further division along Anglo-American versus Francon-German lines. In the former countries, governments or government agencies require certain types of companies to be audited, and put certain limits on who shall be auditors, with government departments having the final say. However, in general, membership of the private professional accountancy bodies is the method of qualifying as an auditor. On the other hand, in France and Germany there is a dual set of accountancy bodies. Those in Table 2 are not the bodies to which one must belong to qualify as an auditor of companies, although to a large extent the membership of these professional bodies overlaps with that of the auditing bodies, and membership of the former permits membership of the latter. The auditing bodies for France and Germany are shown in Table5. The professional bodies set exams, consider ethical matters, belong to the international accounting bodies, and so on.

Table 5 Accountancy Bodies in France and Germany

	Private professional body	State auditing body
France	Ordre des Experts Comptables	Compagine Nationale des Commissaires aux Comptes
Germany	insutut der Wirtschaftsprüfer	Wirtschaftsprüferkammer

The auditing bodies are run by the state. The Compagine Nationale is responsible to the Ministry of Justice; the Wirtschaftspruferkammer to the Frderal Minister of Economics. With the implementation of eighth Directive on company law, this situation obtains in principle throughout the EU. However, in such countries as the United Kingdom and the Netherlands, the existing accountancy bodies have taken over a regulatory role for audit, under the supervision of the government.

Part Seven Inflation

Another factor which affects accounting practices is the level of inflation. Although accountants in the English-speaking world have proved remarkably immune to inflation when it comes to decisive action, there are some countries where inflation has been overwhelming. In several South American countries, the most obvious feature of accounting practices has been the use of methods of general price-level adjustment (Tweedie and Whittington, 1984). The use of this comparatively simple method is probably due to the reasonable correlation of inflation with any particular specific price changes when the former is in hundreds of per cent per year; to the objective nature of government-published indices; to the connection of accounting and tax; and to the paucity of well-trained accountants. Without reference to inflation, it would not be possible to explain accounting differences in several countries severely affected by it.

As has already been noted, the fact that it was governments that responded to inflation in France, Spain, Italy and Greece from the 1970s is symptomatic of the regulation of accounting in these countries. By contrast, in the United States, the United Kingdom and Australia, it was mainly committees of accountants that developed responses to inflation in the 1970s. One might conclude that, although any country will respond to massive inflation, the more interesting point is that the reaction of a country's accounting system to inflation is an illustration of the basic nature of the system.

Part Eight Theory

In a few cases, accounting theory has strongly influenced accounting practice, perhaps most obviously in the case of microeconomics in the Netherlands. Accounting theorists there (notably Theodore Limperg, Jr) had advanced the case that the users of financial statements would be given the fairest view of the performance and state of affairs of an individual company by allowing accountants to use judgement, in the context of that particular company, to select and present accounting figures. In particular, it was suggested that replacement cost information might give the best picture. The looseness of Dutch law and tax requirements, and the receptiveness of the profession to microeconomic ideas (partly due, no doubt, to their training by the academic theorists), have led to the present diversity of pracitce, the emphasis on "fairness" through judgement, and the experimentation with replacement cost accounting.

In other countries, theory is less noticeable. In most of continental Europe and Japan, accounting has been the servant of the state (e.g. for tax collection). In the Anglo-Saxon world, theory was traditionally of little importance in accounting practice, although the development of conceptual frameworks since the mid-1970s has changed this.

Part Nine Accidents and External Influences

Many other influences have been at work in shaping accounting practices. Some are indirect and subtle such as the type of ownership of companies, others are direct and external to accounting such as the framing of a law in response to economic or political events. For example, the economic crisis in the United States in the late 1920s and early 1930s produced the Securities Exchange Acts that diverted US accounting from its previous course by introducing extensive disclosure requirements and state control (usually by threat only) of accounting standards. Other examples include the introduction into Italy of Anglo-American accounting principles by choice of the government, and the introduction into Luxembourg of consolidation and detailed disclosure as a result of Eu Directives-both against all previous trends there. In Spain, the adoption of the accounting plan from France follows the latter country's adoption of it after influence by the occupying Germans in the early 1940s. Perhaps most obvious and least natural is the adaptation of various British Companies Acts or of international standards by developing countries with a negligible number of the sort of public companies or private shareholders that have given rise to the financial reporting practices contained in these laws or standards. In its turn, the United Kingdom in 1981 adopted uniform formats derived from the 1965 Aktiengesetz of Germany because of EU requirements. For their part, Roman law countries now have to grapple with the "true and fair view".

A major example of external influence is the adoption of, or convergence with, the standards of the International Accounting Standards Board (IASB). For example, the EU has made these standards compulsory for the consolidated statements of listed companies. This was done for political and economic reasons and it overrides the other factors in this chapter. More subtly, the remaining national standards of the EU and elsewhere are gradually converging with the international standards.

Part Ten Conclusion on the Causes of International Differences

International differences in financial reporting are many and various, as is examined in detail throughout this book. Cultural differences are clearly of relevance here, at least as causes of factors that influence financial reporting. Doupnik and Salter (1995) suggest a model in which accounting differences can be explained by Gray's four cultural variables plus six others. However, Nobes (1998) suggests that this is problematic because (a) the cultural variables might be better seen as influencing the second six independent variables rather than directly affecting accounting, and (b) several of the second six variables (e. g. the nature of the accountancy profession) seem to be largely dependent rather than independent.

Nobes (1998) proposes that, at least for the purposes of dividing developed countries into major groups, the most important direct cause of the financial reporting differences is a two-way split of countries into: (i) those with important equity markets and many outside shareholders; and (ii) those with a credit-based financing system and with relatively unimportant outside shareholders. The equity/outsider system leads to a separation between tax and accounting rules, and to large auditing professions. This is also generally associated with the common law system, although the Netherlands seems to be an exception: a country with Roman law but where many other features related to accounting are like those of the United States or the United Kingdom.

Ball et al. (2000) suggest connections between common law and certain aspects of accounting, such as the speed of reporting of losses. As noted earlier, La Porta et al. (1997 and 1998) examine some connections between common law and large equity markets.

Factors that might be relevant as causes but have not been addressed above include language, history, geography, religion, education, and many others. Some of these may be too vague to be useful; for example, it is the history of equity markets or the legal system that may be particular relevant, rather than history in general.

However; when looking at countries that are strongly culturally influenced from elsewhere (e.g. many former colonies), the best predictor of the accounting system may be that it will be like that of the former colonial power. This will usually overwhelm other factors, even the corporate financing system. For example, some former British colonies in Africa have an accounting system based on that of the United Kingdom, even though they have no equity market at all. In other cases (e.g. New Zealand), a former colony may inherit a legal system, an equity market and an accountancy profession, as well as an accounting system. For many Common-wealth countries, the British influence has now been replaced by that of the IASB.

References

[1] JOY B HOYLE, THOMAS F SCHAEFER, TIMOTHY S DOUPNIK. Advanced Accounting [M]. New York:Mc Graw-Hill Education, 2012.

[2] WILLIAM R SCOTT. Financial Accounting Theory[M]. New Jersey:Prentice-Hall, 2006.

[3] ARTHUR J KEOWN, JOHN D MMARTIN, J WILLIAM PETTY. Financial Management:Principles and Applications[M]. New Jersey:Pearson/Prentice-Hall, 2005.

[4] 孙坤. 会计英语[M]. 大连:大连出版社,2012.

[5] 张其秀. 会计英语:财务会计(双语版)[M]. 上海:上海财经大学出版社,2010.

[6] 叶建芳,孙红星. 会计英语[M]. 4版. 上海:上海财经大学出版社,2011.

[7] 黄东坡. 会计英语[M]. 北京:清华大学出版社,2009.

[8] 叶建芳,孙红星. 会计英语[M]. 上海:上海财经大学出版社,2003.

[9] 刘建华. 会计英语[M]. 北京:清华大学出版社,2009.

[10] 胡锦祥. 会计英语[M]. 南京:南开大学出版社,2008.

[11] 黄东坡. 会计英语[M]. 北京:清华大学出版社,2010.

[12] 葛军. 会计英语[M]. 北京:科学出版社,2007.

[13] 刘胜军. 现代会计与财务管理专业英语[M]. 哈尔滨:哈尔滨工程大学出版社,2010.

[14] 侯立新. 会计英语(高等学校教材)[M]. 北京:机械工业出版社,2006.

[15] 刘永泽. 中级财务会计[M]. 大连:东北财经大学出版社,2008.

[16] 刘建华,等. 会计英语[M]. 北京:清华大学出版社,2011.

[17] 刘胜军,等. 现代会计与财务管理专业英语[M]. 哈尔滨:哈尔滨工程大学出版社,2008.

[18] 刘永泽,等. 中级财务会计[M]. 大连:东北财经大学出版社,2009.

[19] 克里斯托弗·诺比斯,罗伯特·帕克. 比较国际会计[M]. 大连:东北财经大学出版社,2005.

[20] 常勋,萧华. 初级会计专业英语[M]. 上海:立信会计出版社,2002.